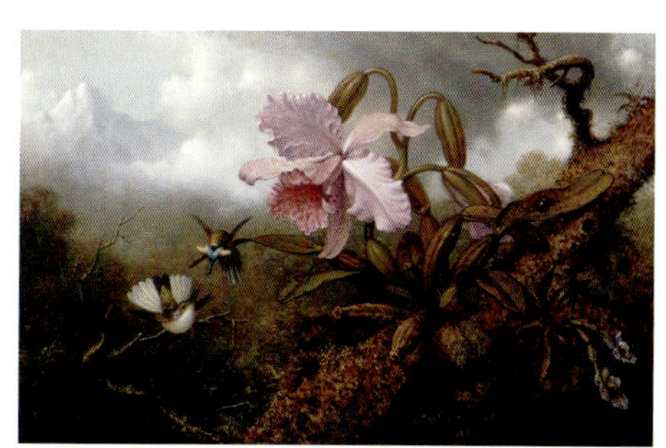

AF478536

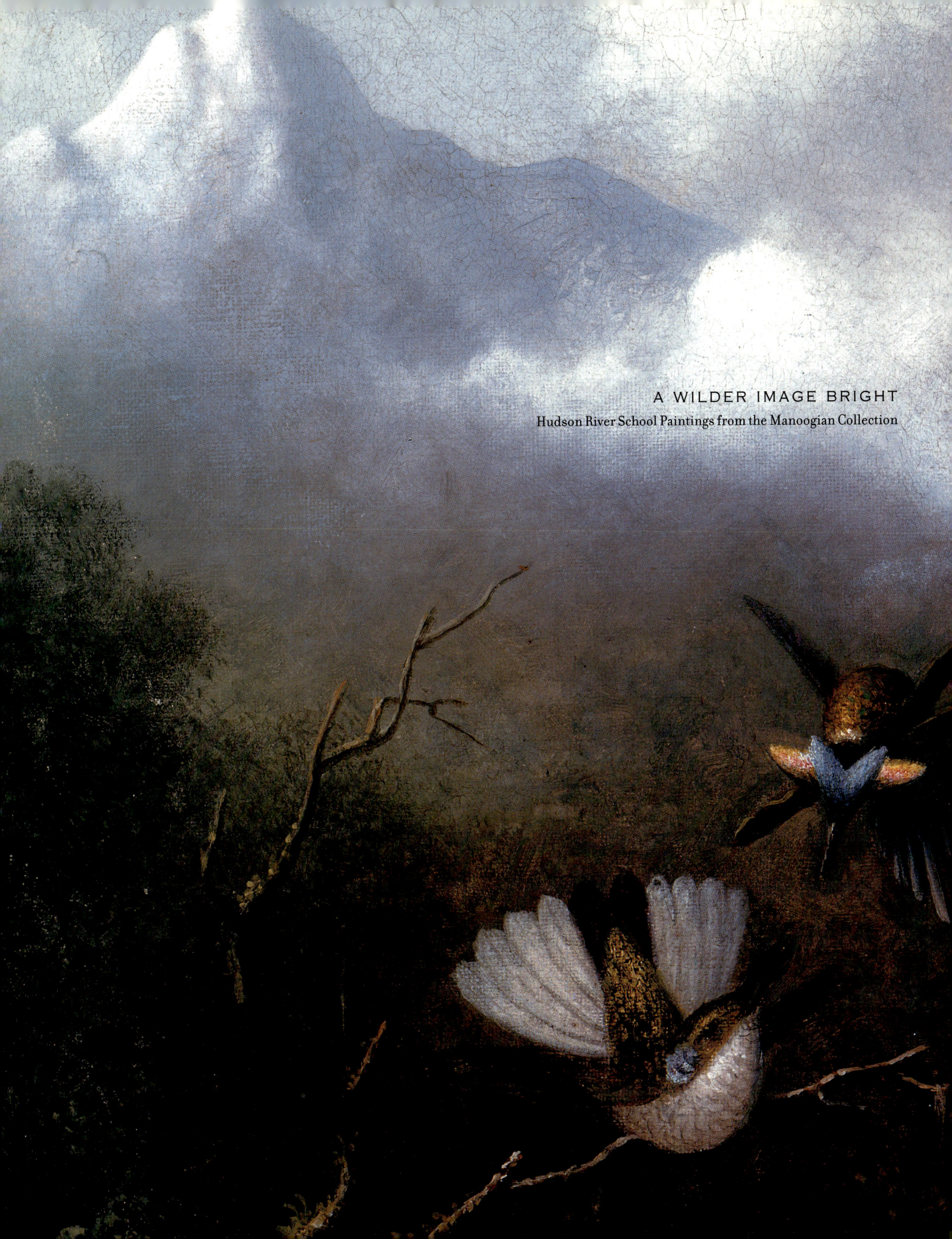

A WILDER IMAGE BRIGHT
Hudson River School Paintings from the Manoogian Collection

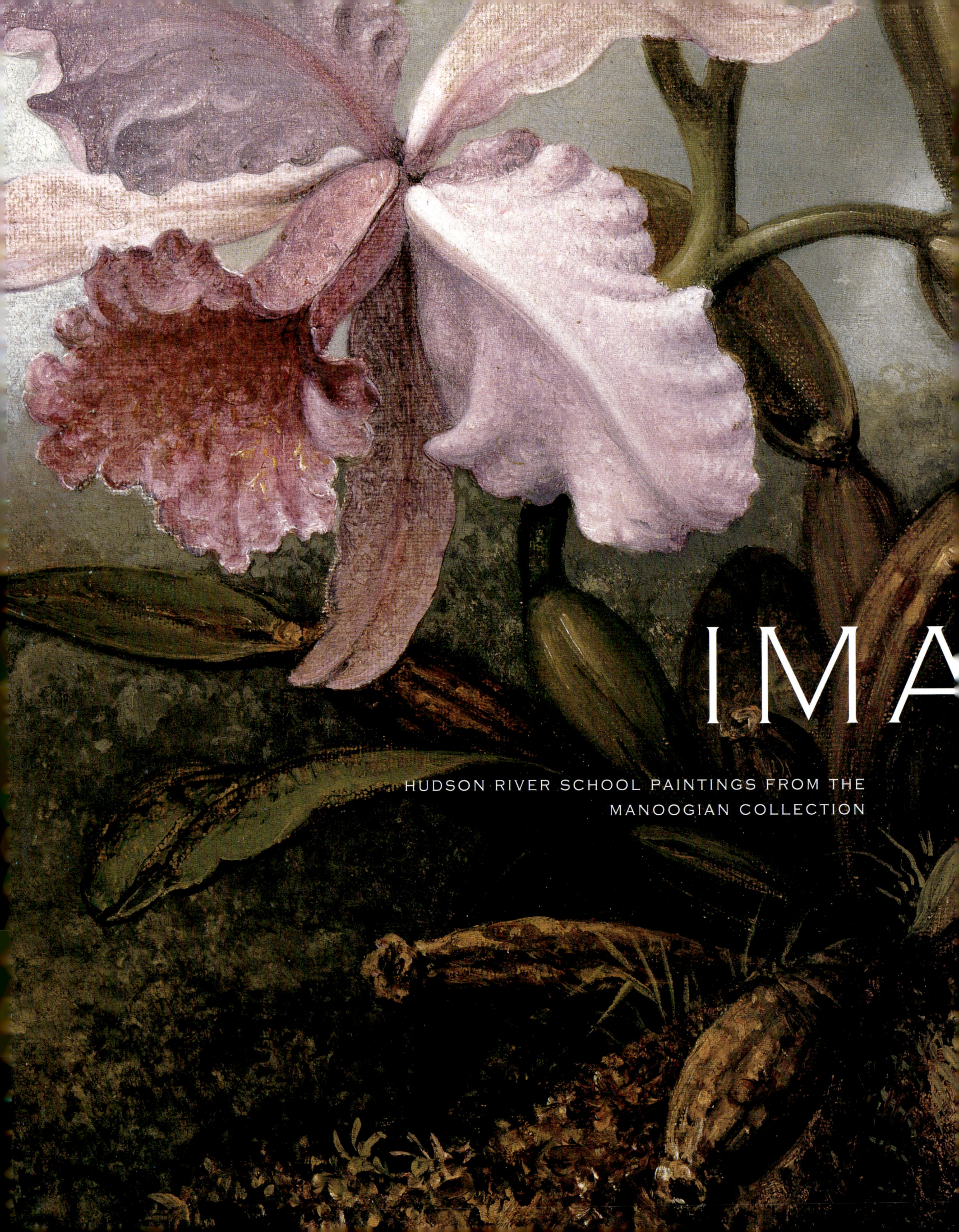

IMA
HUDSON RIVER SCHOOL PAINTINGS FROM THE
MANOOGIAN COLLECTION

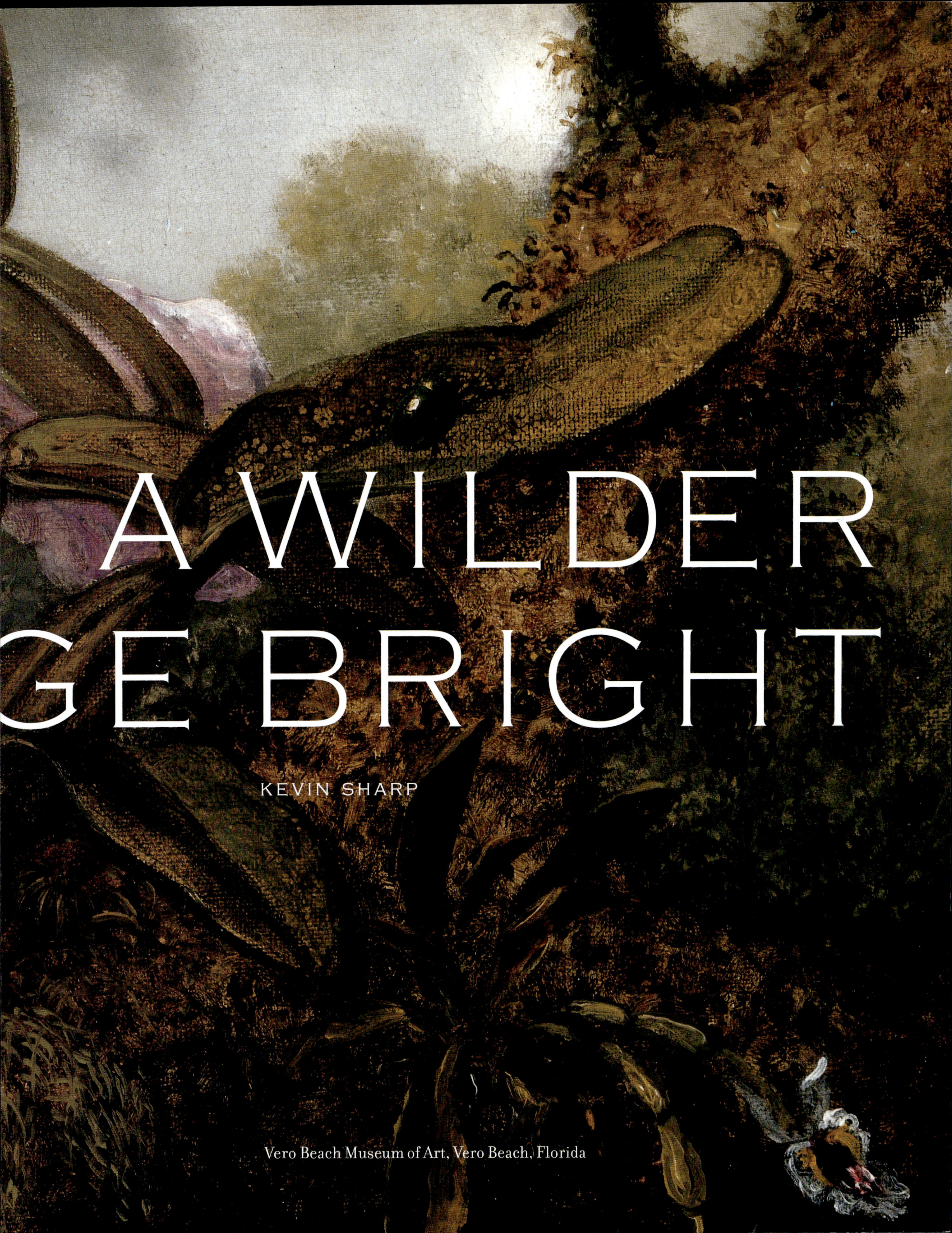

A WILDER GE BRIGHT

KEVIN SHARP

Vero Beach Museum of Art, Vero Beach, Florida

CONTENTS

This catalogue was published in conjunction with the exhibition *A Wilder Image Bright: Hudson River School Paintings from the Manoogian Collection*, which was organized by the Vero Beach Museum of Art.

January 31–March 28, 2004
Vero Beach Museum of Art
3001 Riverside Park Dr.
Vero Beach, FL 32963
www.vbmuseum.org

Distributed by the University of Washington Press
P.O. Box 50096
Seattle, WA 98145
www.washington.edu/uwpress

Library of Congress Control Number: 2003115529
ISBN: 0-295-98407-4

Designed and produced by studio blue, Chicago (www.studioblueinc.com)
Edited by Kari Dahlgren
Printed by Tien Wah Press, Singapore

cover: detail, plate 16; page 1: plate 30; pages 3-5: details, plate 30; page 8: detail, plate 1; page 12: plate 8; page 13 detail, plate 8; page 38: plate 23; page 39: detail, plate 23; page 138: detail, plate 32.

Printed in Singapore

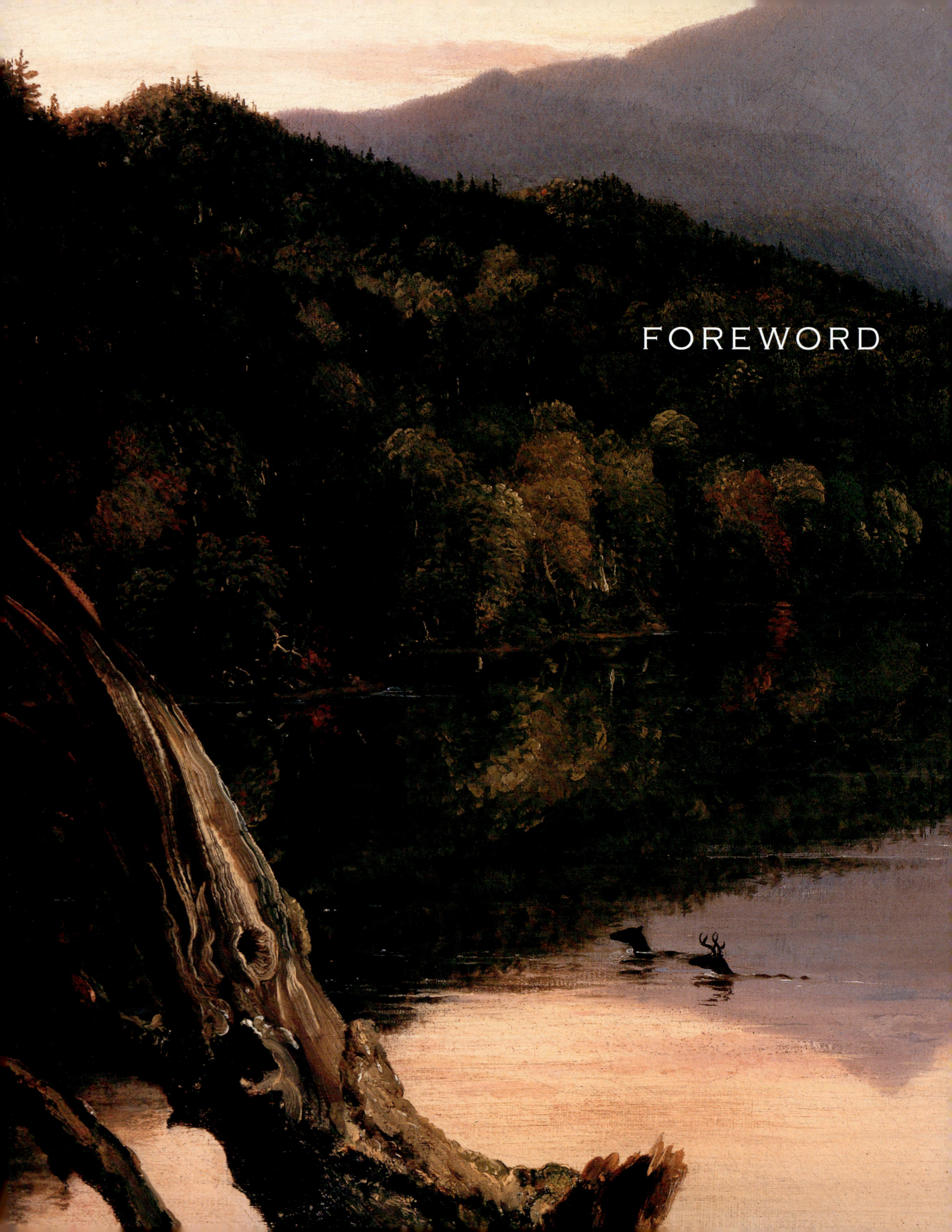
FOREWORD

A WILDER IMAGE BRIGHT *and*
THE THANKS OF A GRATEFUL MUSEUM

In 1829, as the young landscape painter Thomas Cole prepared for his first trip to Europe, the poet William Cullen Bryant penned a sonnet to commemorate his friend's departure. Cole had spent the last five years painting in the Catskills, the Adirondacks, and the White Mountains, and had almost single-handedly forged America's first native artistic tradition. Bryant was concerned that Cole might be seduced by the sophistication of English, French, and Italian cultures, and that the instinctive vigor of his American landscapes would be somehow lost or compromised. In the first lines of the sonnet, Bryant insisted that Cole would find European scenery not so very different than the American landscape:

Thine eyes shall see the light of distant skies:
Yet, Cole! Thy heart shall bear to Europe's strand
A living image of our own bright land,
Such as upon thy glorious canvas lies.

Bryant then offered an inventory of landscape motifs that he expected Cole to encounter, and that he would no doubt find familiar and justifiably appealing:

Lone lakes — savannahs where the bison roves —
Rocks rich with summer garlands — solemn streams —
Skies where the desert eagle wheels and screams —
Spring blooms and autumn blaze of boundless groves.

But Bryant knew there was one profound difference between European and American landscapes, and that was the inescapable influence of man. The English, French, and Italian cultivation of their native soil was admirable and centuries old, but it was also unavoidable:

Fair scenes shall greet thee where thou goest — fair
But different — everywhere the trace of men.
Paths, homes, graves, ruins, from the lowest glen
To where life shrinks from the fierce Alpine air.

To Bryant, European scenery was "fair but different." Any semblance of the pristine wilderness that America held in unexplored abundance had long ago been cleared, consumed, or raked into tidy gardens by generations of European culture. In the final couplet,

Bryant offered his blessing to Cole, but also an unexpectedly firm recommendation:

Gaze on them, till the tears shall dim thy sight,
But keep that earlier, wilder image bright.

Bryant's insistence that Cole keep a "wilder image bright" had everything to do with maintaining his personal vision in the face of Europe's myriad cultural influences. But it was also a reminder to Cole of America's rich potential and the possibility of every kind of greatness that lived within its borders. In the nineteenth century, the United States was yet considered a young and awkward behemoth of untold prospect and extraordinary resources. Bryant was determined that Cole would sail for Europe knowing that the greatest challenge he would ever face as a painter was describing the wonder of America's boundless possibility to its own people.

Cole was deeply affected by his three years in Europe, but the trip also confirmed the wisdom of Bryant's sonnet. Cole's landscape aesthetic grew more ambitious after his exposure to European art, but he always kept a "wilder image bright," and the light of his brilliant canvases became a beacon for eager followers. Asher B. Durand, although older than Cole, was the first to embrace his aesthetic ideals, followed by younger painters of such prodigious abilities as Frederick Kensett, Worthington Whittredge, Jasper Cropsey, George Inness, Frederic E. Church, Sanford Gifford, and later Martin Johnson Heade, Albert Bierstadt, William Stanley Haseltine, Thomas Moran, and James M. Hart, among others. Eventually dubbed the Hudson River School, most of these artists were enormously successful and became the popular celebrities of their age. But more importantly, they infused the American landscape with the dreams, ambitions, and desires of a young nation poised for greatness.

During the last decade, the Vero Beach Museum of Art has experienced impressive growth in its physical space, in the scope of its programs, and in the importance of its permanent collection. Like Thomas Cole, we have come a long way in a short time, and our exhibitions and education initiatives reverberate across the cultural landscape of this community and the entire region. With *A Wilder Image Bright: Hudson River School Paintings from the Manoogian Collection*, the Vero Beach Museum of Art has taken another monumental stride in organizing and presenting perhaps the most important exhibition of nineteenth-century American paintings ever held in south Florida.

Surprisingly, it was not so long ago that the paintings of the Hudson River School were considered old-fashioned relics of a bygone era. It has taken scholars, museums, dealers, and insightful collectors to restore these extraordinary artists to their rightful place in American history. Richard Manoogian recognized early that these important canvases were indeed rich artifacts of America's past, and that they were also timeless expressions of values and aspirations that live as vividly today as they did in the nineteenth century. Over the past thirty-five years, Mr. and Mrs. Manoogian have assembled an unparalleled group of Hudson River School paintings, which they have graciously allowed the Vero Beach Museum of Art to exhibit as an ensemble for the first time. We offer our heartfelt thanks to the Manoogians for their extraordinary generosity, for their ongoing support of the Museum, and for providing our visitors with a remarkable opportunity to examine, to enjoy, and to learn.

A project of this magnitude requires the efforts of many, as well as contributions of time and money from dedicated supporters of the Vero Beach Museum of Art. We are blessed with a group of committed donors, whose generosity enriches so many lives in this community, just as it touches our visitors from across the country and around the world. We have been deeply gratified by the financial support this project has attracted. We owe sincere appreciation to The Patten Endowment, a generous sponsor of the Museum's Anniversary Exhibition for the past sixteen years. We are grateful to our corporate sponsor, Windsor Properties, to the many kind members of The Armstrong Society for the Arts, and to The Anne F. Forbes Family Foundation. Their ongoing support has made this project and many others possible at the Vero Beach Museum of Art. We would also like to thank Mr. and Mrs. William O. Fleming, Mr. and Mrs. John B. Ford III, and Dr. and Mrs. Henry L. Newman for their additional support of this exhibition and catalogue.

This project has benefited greatly from the staff of the Masco Corporation, the company founded by Richard Manoogian's family. The unwavering support of Gene Gargaro has been instrumental not only in making this exhibition a reality, but in forging the satisfying relationship that now exists between the Masco Corporation and the Vero Beach Museum of Art. Curator Jonathon Boos has helped make the Manoogian Collection the finest private ensemble of American paintings in the world, and he has been an enthusiastic advocate of this endeavor from the start. Cheryl M. Robledo, Registrar and Exhibition Coordinator, has contributed in more ways than I can number, and Vera Novak has been a most pleasant contact. To them and to all the courteous staff at the Masco Corporate Headquarters, we extend our warmest thanks.

A significant voice in the study of American art, Kevin Sharp organized the exhibition and is the author of this exceptional catalogue. He has introduced his considerable expertise and professionalism to this project, and we are deeply grateful. Kevin Sharp has just been named Director of Visual Arts at the Cedarhurst Center for the Arts in Mount Vernon, Illinois, and we wish him all the best. The reliable staff of the Vero Beach Museum of Art has done outstanding work to bring this project to resolution. Curator Jennifer A. Bailey has managed the many details that go into an exhibition and publication with great skill and resourcefulness. Kelly Mahony, Registrar, Travis Childers, Preparator, Jim Liccione, Conservator, and our Director of Operations, Ron Brockway, and his staff also have contributed in meaningful ways. Thank you, and well done.

Many colleagues at museums, galleries, and libraries have contributed their knowledge and advice to this project. We wish there were space to express our gratitude more fully, but we offer our thanks to the following: Michael N. Altman, Michael N. Altman Fine Art, New York; Judith A. Barter, The Art Institute of Chicago; Susan Aprill, Brooklyn Public Library; Nancy Barr and Sylvia Inwood, Detroit Institute of Arts; Sylvia Yount and Melody Hanlon, High Museum of Art, Atlanta; Debbie Miller, Minnesota Historical Society, Saint Paul; Anne Cassidy, New York State Office of Parks, Recreation and Historic Preservation; Marcia Erickson and Natalia Lonchyna, North Carolina Museum of Art, Raleigh; Valerie A. Balint, Olana State

Historic Site, Hudson, N.Y.; and Christine Michelini, Peabody Essex
Museum, Salem, Mass. We would also like to thank Kathy Fredrickson,
Cheryl Towler Weese, Matt Simpson, Garrett Niksch, and Marty
Maxwell at studio blue in Chicago for their design and production of
this handsome book, and we gratefully acknowledge Kari Dahlgren
and Erin Riordan for their editorial contributions.

One hundred seventy-five years after Thomas Cole's voyage
to Europe, the United States is a much different nation. But just as
William Cullen Bryant suggested in 1829, our future depends upon our
willingness to grasp our own rich potential. With *A Wilder Image
Bright: Hudson River School Paintings from the Manoogian Collection*,
the Vero Beach Museum of Art has again expanded the boundaries
of possibility.

John Z. Lofgren, PhD
Executive Director/CEO

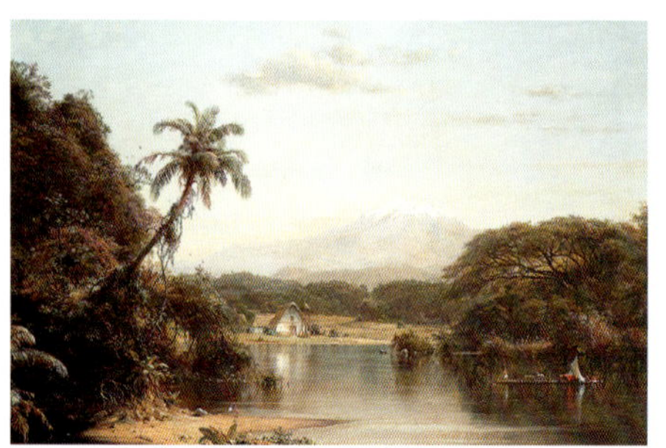

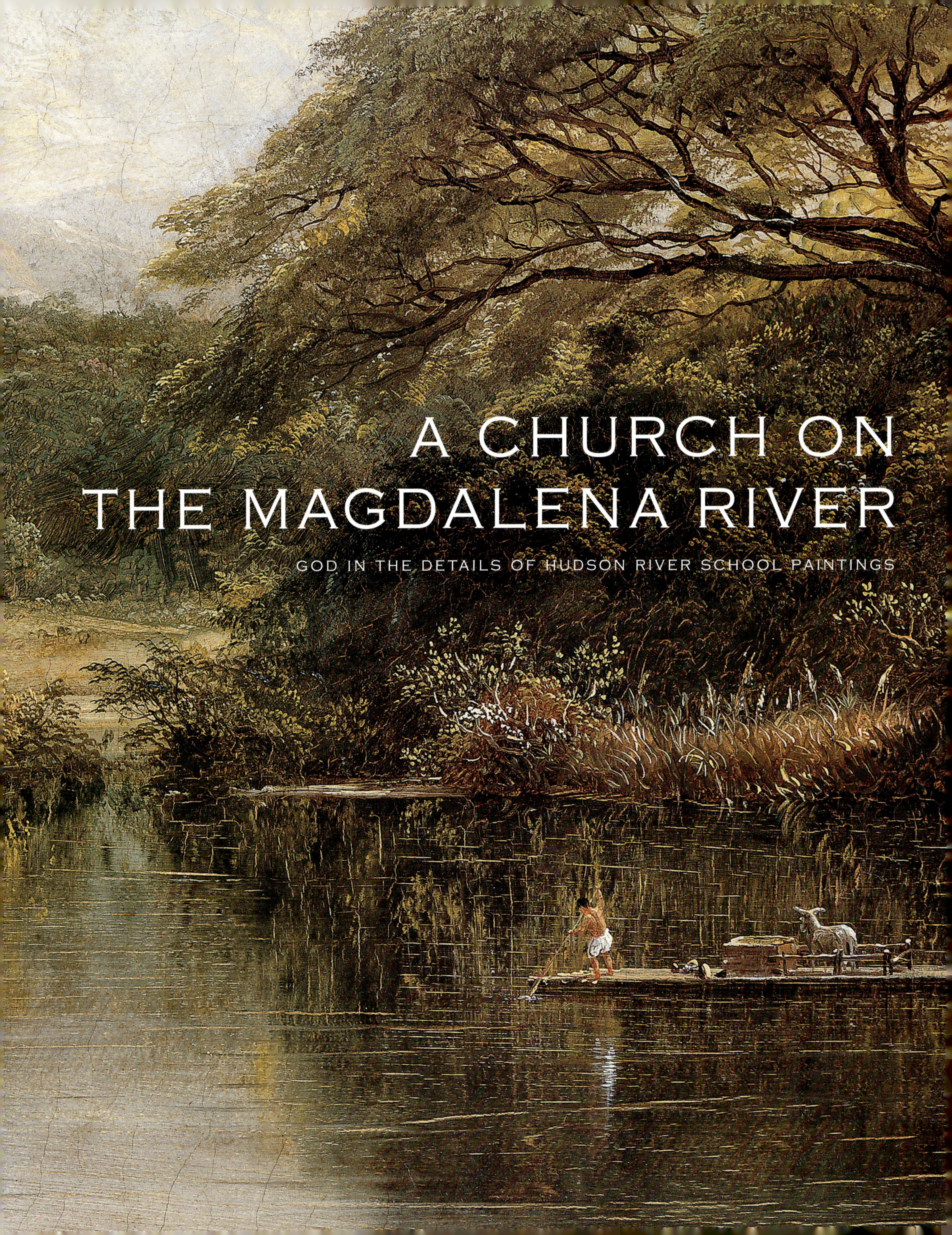

A CHURCH ON
THE MAGDALENA RIVER
GOD IN THE DETAILS OF HUDSON RIVER SCHOOL PAINTINGS

[AN ARTIST IS PERCHED ON THE EDGE of a wooden chair in front of an easel. He holds a palette and extra brushes in one hand, while the other rests on the supportive virtue of a mahlstick. At the fingertips of the supported hand, a brush with badger-hair bristles is loaded with a mixture of oil paint, mineral spirits, and a drop of varnish. As the hand slides along the mahlstick, narrowing the gap between the brush and the canvas, it also closes the distance between the memory of color and form and the one precise area on the surface of the canvas where color and form will soon be determined. The pigment lands, the brush travels, returns, pauses, then withdraws. The painter leans back in the chair for a few more inches of perspective, but there are still no generalities from this close distance, only details. From where the artist sits, the very essence of process is specificity.]

A rush of wide approval greeted young Thomas Cole, then a complete unknown, when his work was first displayed in 1825. He emerged from the Catskill wilderness with paintings unlike any New York had ever seen, and they proved a revelation to connoisseurs, writers, and especially to his fellow artists. Cole's views of rugged mountain scenery were beautiful, but they were also profound statements of native identity that brilliantly reconciled America's unformed youth with its ambitions of greatness. Only the land, the robust physicality of America itself, provided imagery sturdy enough to represent the desires, the expectations, the myths, and the contradictions of a young nation thoroughly absorbed in the satisfying uncertainty of its destiny. Cole's landscapes seemed to parallel perfectly America's vitality, its untapped potential, and its abundant unexplored frontier, but they also accounted for the country's moral foundation, its desire for cultural tradition, and its burgeoning sense of its own meaningful history. In that dialogue of disparate parts, Cole integrated near and far, new and old, tame and wild; his conceptual genius resided in that capacity to shepherd grand opposites into coherent wholes. Before him, American artists were considered able if they could hold up even one side of such complex conversation.[1]

The conceptual balance of Cole's canvases articulated the plurality of the American character and resonated with the very core of the American experience. But that future success would have scarcely occurred to him as he sketched along the banks of Catskill Creek or looked out over

Kaaterskill Clove. Cole was a painter of landscape subjects, and his first concern was to grapple with a problem directly relevant to his occupation: to glean compositional balance and pictorial order from the cacophony of choices that lived in the primitive wilderness. But Cole's solution was infinitely more sophisticated than the challenge posed to him. While his elders and his contemporaries painted tepid amalgams of overly differentiated details stitched together like quilts, Cole allowed the brilliant chaos of his frontier subjects to become the very basis for carefully planned compositional unity.

On a metaphysical level, Cole produced order by subtraction, allowing time and distance to erase irrelevant or pedestrian elements from his memory of vivid landscape settings. He wrote to Asher B. Durand:

> *I never succeed in painting scenes, however beautiful, immediately on returning from them. I must wait for time to draw a veil over the common details, the unessential parts, which shall leave the great features, whether the beautiful or the sublime dominant in the mind.*[2]

It may have been straightforward enough for an artist of Cole's brilliance to sieve the more banal aspects of a scenic view through the filter of his incontestable genius, leaving only radiant detail and a unifying blanket of beauty inscribed upon his memory and imagination. But not every painter could call upon such powers of transformative internal vision. It was probably no coincidence that Cole described this particular method to his close friend and colleague Durand, who was commonly plagued by charges of being overly literal. Although not precise equivalents, sacrificing unity for detail and painting too literally were decidedly related shortcomings. Artists who could not see the forest for the trees, critics argued, were more inclined to render the forest just as they stumbled upon it rather than in the ideal form it could take on canvas.

Whether brilliantly synthetic like Cole or borderline prosaic as Durand was unjustly accused of being, these artists still faced the problem of how to bring the engaging qualities of the specific and the grandeur of the general into harmony on the painted surface.[3] On a practical level, Cole manufactured pictorial unity through brushwork that was lively and even agitated in the foreground, but increasingly subtle in the receding spaces. Influenced by the various optical theories bandied about in the early nineteenth century, Cole did more than simply represent the landscape; he approximated the action of the human eye as it experienced the landscape.[4] In his most successful paintings, he directed the viewer to foreground elements rich with individual character, nuanced color, and physical texture, leaving background information to be absorbed more schematically by the otherwise occupied eye. But the background areas of Cole's paintings were of no lesser importance than his foregrounds, and did more than simply fall away. Indeed, they were essential to the persuasive sense of compositional unity Cole consistently achieved.

Cole's sketchbook drawings were nearly always accompanied by detailed written descriptions that estimated his distance in miles from mountains rising in the background. He made careful notes of weather conditions and indicated shades of color and value often in poetic terms, but always with an empirical accuracy borne of years assessing picturesque vistas. Cole had developed and mastered his own system of calculating and capturing the relative intelligibility of distant peaks in clear sunlight, cloudy skies, or gray shadow from five, ten, fifteen miles away. That stubborn realism imbued the generalized backgrounds of Cole's paintings with an attenuated authenticity that was not so different from his more keenly articulated foregrounds. The curious specificity of Cole's most generalized visual statements lent a compositional unity to his landscape subjects that was at once subliminal and of unexpectedly powerful integrity and verisimilitude.[5]

Durand followed Cole's strategy in his panoramic landscapes, and occasionally produced paintings of well-ordered perfection. But critics still complained that his work was too redundant, too literal, and at times overwrought. Durand did have a tendency to paint fingernails on the tiny farmers who inhabited his landscapes, and by the late 1840s, he had begun to look for compositional and pictorial solutions that would mitigate his own earnestness. In some of his most highly regarded canvases of the late 1840s and early 1850s, Durand solved the problem of pictorial and compositional unity by avoiding it altogether. Rather than struggling to reconcile near and distant pictorial spaces, he emphatically asserted the foregrounds of his composition to the near exclusion of background information. His narrow slices through forest interiors, his massive rocky outcrops, and his screens of trees all either denied or limited visual access to the deeper recesses of illusionary space. Durand boldly thrust all his pictorial information to the surface of the canvas, where it could bask in the splendor of its own rich detail.[6]

Cole's gifted pupil Frederic Church struggled with a problem similar to that of Durand. But Church was not so much overly literal as he was possessed by pseudoscientific impulses and an eagerness to account for natural phenomena each in its unique specificity. In his youth, Church was justifiably enamored of his ability to render the physical world with both dazzle and sober convincingness, and he simply could not make his aptitude for detail the subordinate of generalization. Even in the early 1850s as Church matured into America's most important landscape painter, he found it difficult to separate his skills as an artist from the tempting challenge to render detail with the full flourish of his polished accuracy.

It was only as Church began to paint monumental canvases that he discovered the source of a deeper pictorial and compositional unity. After his first famous excursion to South America in 1853, Church came to view largeness not so much as an issue of format but as a vehicle of conceptual order. His pictures were physically big, but so were his subjects, and so were the distances he traveled to find them. Somewhere in the murky physicality of discovering, conceiving, and creating his grand manner subjects, Church came to equate the illusion of pictorial vastness with the great distances he traveled to find inspiration with the physical space he traversed in his own studio while walking back and forth before a ten-foot painting. That conceptual order and consistency became almost a second religion to Church, and the results were masterful meditations on formal unity beyond anything New York critics could have conjured in their wildest flights of imagination.

By the late 1850s, a younger generation of American writers had come to count unity among the supreme virtues of painting in any genre, but especially in landscape. Inspired by the holistic approach of the French Barbizon painters and by the persuasive reasoning of the English theorist John Ruskin, critics such as James Jackson Jarves and Clarence Cook, and later G. W. Sheldon and S. G. W. Benjamin hectored more naive forms of pictorial expression into the arms of calendar printers and chromolithography firms, banished forever from larger conversations about American art and its future. Initially a fairly radical fringe element, these writers became America's most influential tastemakers. They would eventually drive Hudson River School painting to its demise, a death it was utterly unprepared to face. But in the late 1850s, these critics were little more than a loud vanguard voice. Still, even established painters seem to have heard their cries for formally unified canvases.[7]

Probably less in response to America's younger critics than to the broader zeitgeist of international artistic ambition, Frederick Kensett, Sanford Gifford, Martin Johnson Heade, and others moved pictorial unity into the upper register of their aesthetic concerns. What Cole had discovered through optics and Church conveyed through scale, these painters found in chromatic uniformity, harmonic tonal relationships, the painted illusion of natural light, and a consistently polished surface quality. Their diffuse morning or evening sunlight, playing across still water or upon open fields, lent a serene and at times an almost monochromatic order to their work. Insistently horizontal and increasingly void of extraneous detail, these brilliantly unified compositions were austere, but mesmerizing in the sensitive order of their luminescent atmosphere.

Kensett, Gifford, and Heade solved the issue of unity in wholly original terms by changing the means through which their landscape and seascape subjects could be visually navigated. The optical logic of Cole's foreground anchor was utterly forsaken as viewers were induced to remain in nearly constant visual motion, skating across surfaces so pristine they were not easily penetrated. Their manipulation of finely modulated color, shifting in nearly imperceptible tonal increments, encouraged active attention to surface, and a vision that found as much satisfaction in exquisite patina as in the illusion of depth. There were yet distinct foregrounds, middle distances, and backgrounds. But rather than allowing the viewer to plummet headlong into an illusion of receding space, Kensett, Gifford, and Heade introduced sparse compositional elements as syncopated stepping stones for dipping into and darting out of consistent, enveloping atmosphere. And that luminous air was the source of the most persuasive pictorial unity yet devised by American artists.[8]

[The mahlstick falls. Rising, the painter circles behind the chair, eyes locked on the surface of the canvas. Still holding the palette and brushes, his feet shuffle backward, and with each step, details coalesce. The specificity at the painting's surface, the insistent particularity, dissolves. Is that pictorial unity or the limitations of the human eye? It is both. It seems clear from eight feet away that unity is the opposite of clarity. But of course that is a very truly factual fictional lie.]

PICTORIAL UNITY WAS OF COMPARATIVELY little consequence to period still-life painters, who proudly reveled in the meticulous fuss of their unencumbered detail, each petal on a flower, each dewdrop on a melon. By the same token, unified compositions were much less critical to the livelihoods of successful portraitists than the particularity of passable likenesses. A larger sense of order was especially important to landscape painters in part because America's wilderness and even its rural areas were powerful subjects ripe with metaphor and dense with associated meanings. America was not just scenery. The sheer greatness of the land held every kind of prospect for Americans and every kind of personal and collective desire, from humble agrarian incomes to the promise of enormous wealth, from simple basic freedoms to epic frontier adventure, and from the power of personal liberty to the power of states united. For American landscape painters to articulate those expansive hopes and dreams persuasively, their paintings had to communicate something grander than the sum of isolated parts. Ironically, in the midst of a democratic experiment that exalted the individual, it took the unity of a forest to capture America's principles and optimism. A single tree or a hundred single trees were simply inadequate for that purpose.

If America's endless bounty of continuous virgin wilderness bore the weight of a young nation's diverse secular and material ambitions, it exerted a profound moral force as well. Untouched and unplowed by the hands or the implements of men, the American landscape was seen as a closer expression of God's mighty intention, nearer in a way to the very miracle of creation itself. In the nineteenth century, most of the United States and certainly its contiguous territories remained in the untrammeled state that God had left them, "undefiled works," as Cole described America's remote frontiers.[9] For a nation as relatively young as the United States, lacking entirely in the mythic and cultural traditions that only centuries can sanctify, the spiritual gift of a vast and pristine wilderness was an enormous consolation. To have been so blessed by the Creator of such extraordinary natural wonders was justification enough for America's unshakable faith in its own moral authority.

For landscape painters of even token religious sentiment, to stand alone in America's magnificent forests, its vast prairies, before its formidable mountains, and under its endless skies was to experience the very divinity of God and to hear spiritual truths whispered nowhere else in the world. The profundity and the accepted holiness of America's perfect wilderness shaped America's

expectations for landscape painting, as it struck at the very fiber of its philosophical being. The unity
and order that Cole, Durand, Church, and others distilled from the seeming randomness of the
natural world was more than an aesthetic concern, it was an expression of God's omnipotence and
omnipresence over creation. Even if that order was not easily decipherable or understood by man,
or even meant to be, Americans believed that God's world was not a random or unreasoned place and
neither should be the landscape paintings that described it.

In his famous essay "Nature" of 1836, Ralph Waldo Emerson, the Sage of Concord and
perhaps America's most original mind of the nineteenth century, wrote:

> *When we speak of nature…we have a distinct but most poetical sense in mind. We mean the integrity*
> *of impression made by manifold natural objects.… The charming landscape which I saw this*
> *morning is indubitably made up of some twenty or thirty farms. Miller owns this field, Locke that,*
> *and Manning the woodland beyond. But none of them owns the landscape. There is a property*
> *in the horizon which no man has but he whose eyes can integrate all the parts.* [10]

Emerson was thinking more of poetry than of visual arts, but his poetics of the American
landscape aptly summarized and no doubt deeply influenced the philosophical exegeses of nineteenth-
century American landscape painting. Before Cole, no American painter had achieved Emerson's
"integrity of impression made by manifold natural objects" and none possessed the imagination or
the ambition to "integrate all the parts."

Thomas Cole died suddenly in 1848, just days past his forty-seventh birthday. He did not
live to see the quest for pictorial unity that he had set in motion exalted as an expressive vehicle
in its own right. Cole had no lack of grand manner ambition, and he produced religious and literary
landscapes that depended heavily upon compositional order to maintain the legibility of his epic
and even grandiose themes. But that was not the same as allowing broad compositional unity to speak
for itself, to represent the larger values, beliefs, and ambitions that occupied the ideals of most
nineteenth-century Americans.

By the 1850s, the painters who would become known as the Hudson River School, Durand,
Kensett, Church, Gifford, Jasper Cropsey, Worthington Whittredge, Albert Bierstadt, and others

inherited from Cole a mature landscape idiom through which they would make no small statement about American soil and the American experience of it. In the 1850s, the closing decade of delirious Jacksonian expansionism, the era of Manifest Destiny, and the last heady hours of innocent and youthful optimism before the Civil War, the painters of the Hudson River School emerged as America's most hopeful voice of cultural authority and the chroniclers of a vital American age. And regardless of how each arrived at his particular sense of pictorial and compositional unity, those qualities were by then essential components of any expression of American identity, and they were here to stay.[11]

[Returning slowly, almost reluctantly, to the surface of the canvas, to the hard wooden chair, the painter sits and considers the information gathered from eight feet away. How to take so many diverse details and forge them into a coherent composition? Is it a question of color, of perspective, of optics, of scale? Is it a question at all? There are a thousand solutions, but only one answer. What will it be?]

PICTORIAL AND COMPOSITIONAL UNITY ENDOWED Hudson River School painting with the physical importance and the moral force to comment broadly on the American experience. It lent to the canvases of Durand, Church, and Kensett a resonant baritone that sang of matters far more consequential than attractive scenery and pleasant woodland strolls. But that unity came at a price. It established a format of formidability that was capable of draining the intimacy or anything even remotely engaging from their compositions. The sheer scale of their work, the monumentality of their subject matter, and the grandiloquence of their dramatic themes held awe-struck viewers at bay. And at such a remote distance, it was impossible to experience the creative individuality that was the artist at work.[12]

In some cases, the grandeur of mid-century landscape painting was perfectly consistent with the great personal ambition of many of the Hudson River School painters, particularly Church and his younger rival Bierstadt. Distance was little more than the price great artists paid to make grand statements of global or at least hemispheric consequence. Leave charm and intimacy to the genre painters. But that was not easy to accept even for Church and Bierstadt. Those two great artists produced monumental canvases that were known even in their own time as "machines," but they still painted their wholly unified epic landscape subjects one careful stroke at a time. Some of those strokes were more delightfully executed than others, and it was only through the intimate examination of the painted surface that anyone would recognize the distinction.[13]

The nineteenth-century French novelist Gustave Flaubert said "Le bon Dieu est dans le detail" — God is in the details.[14] For the Hudson River School, that sentiment may have characterized their feelings about landscape painting as it was practiced in America. Having created the world, so to speak, or at least having established an overarching compositional unity that stood for the world as it existed on their ever-expanding canvases, the details they introduced were much like tiny Adams and Eves set loose in paradise.[15] Those details were quite often human figures, and even when they were not, they were intended to engage the viewer on a human level and on a relatively human scale. The details were also the painter's one hope of attracting close inspection, and that in turn was the one opportunity for the viewer to know the painting as the artist knew it, and to share in the experience of its creation. For a modest artist, it offered a moment of empathy. For the ambitious, it was when mortals were allowed to commune with the gods.

The small details of Hudson River School paintings were frequently pungent with information about the lives of the artists themselves. In Durand's panoramic *June Shower* (figs. 1–3) of 1854, a woodsman guides two oxen pulling a wagon loaded with timber. A fierce thunderstorm gathers over the distant mountain and lightning has already struck the village that huddles in its shadow. But the woodsman remains unhurried by the threatening weather, and in a sense, he could be Durand himself, a patient and workmanlike figure, who similarly earned his livelihood from a symbiotic relationship with the land. For Durand, the storm might have been an allusion to the critics and the rush of younger artists seeking to usurp his position as elder statesmen of the American landscape movement. If the title *June Shower* seemed to understate the painting's violent sky and the ominous tone, Durand, like the unfazed woodsman, had no doubt seen worse storms (literal and metaphoric) in his nearly sixty years, and probably fretted little at so much blow and fuss.[16]

Figure 1:
Asher Brown Durand (1796–1886)
June Shower
1854
Oil on canvas
Manoogian Collection
Cat. 6

Figures 2 and 3:
Asher Brown Durand (1796–1886)
June Shower (details)
1854
Oil on canvas
Manoogian Collection
Cat. 6

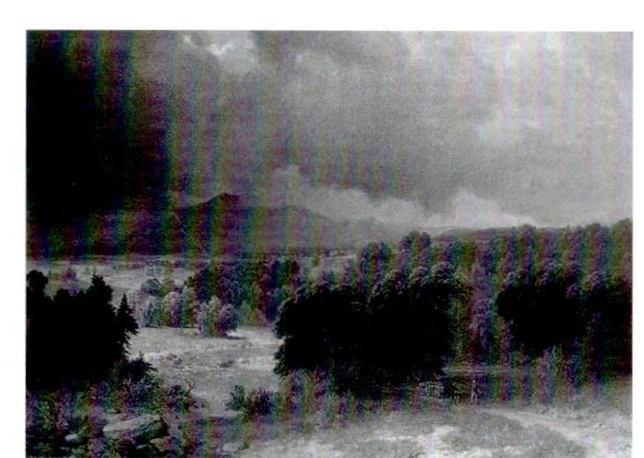

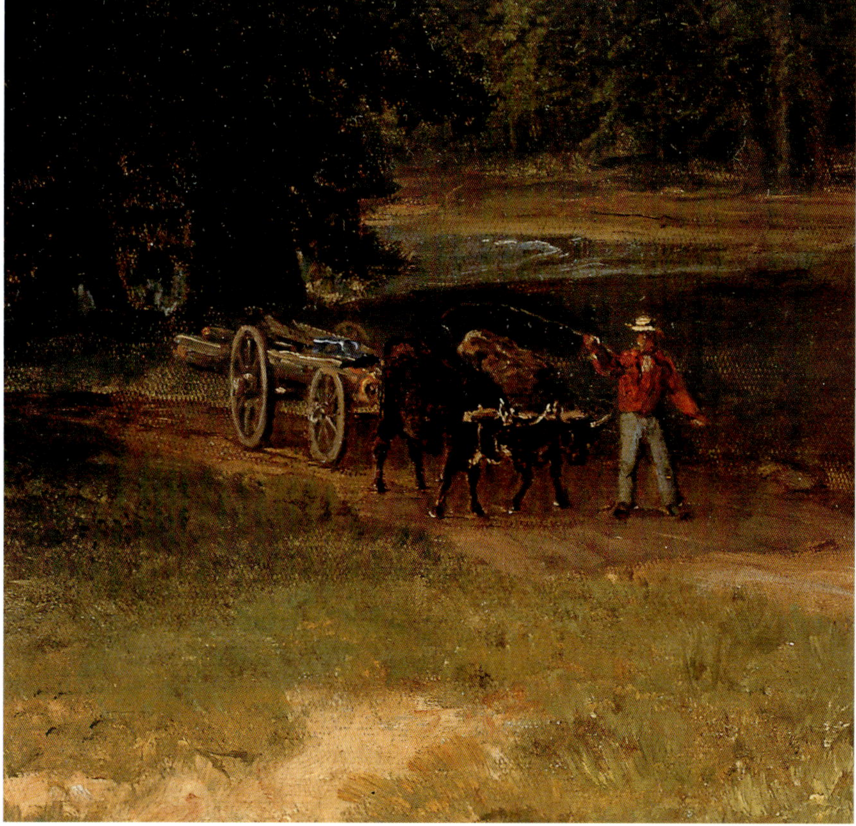

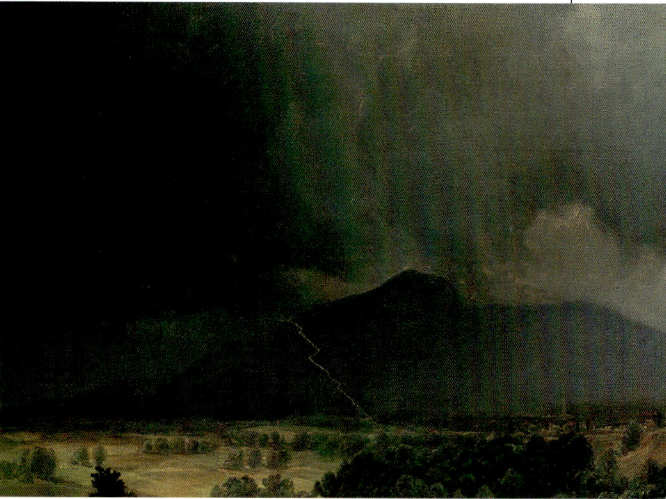

Figure 4:
Jasper Francis Cropsey (1823–1900)
The Backwoods of America
1858
Oil on canvas
Manoogian Collection
Cat. 9

Figure 5:
Jasper Francis Cropsey (1823–1900)
The Backwoods of America (detail)
1858
Oil on canvas
Manoogian Collection
Cat. 9

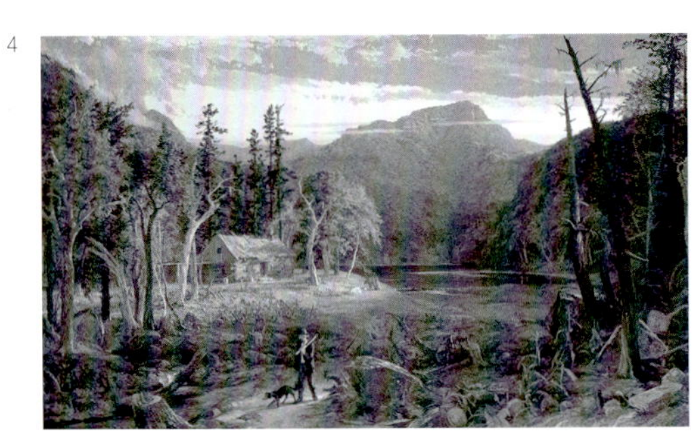

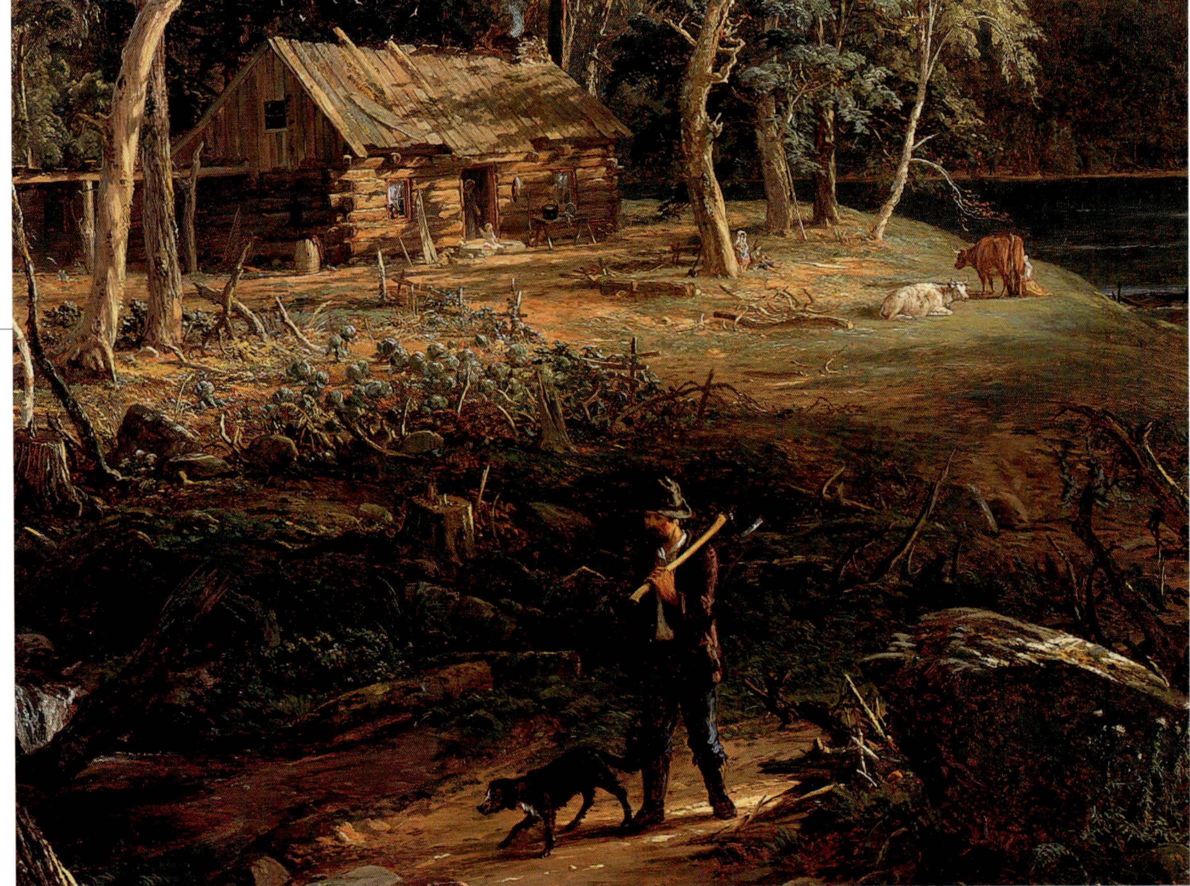

Similarly, in Cropsey's *The Backwoods of America (figs. 4–5)*, the man and his loyal hound
in the foreground may allude to concerns personal to the artist as it reinforced the work's larger
meditation on wilderness life. Painted in England in 1858, when Cropsey was struggling to establish
a market for his American landscapes in Great Britain, the large canvas was meant to introduce the
English to authentic American frontier life. *The Backwoods of America* is rife with details that ani-
mated pioneer existence, including primitive tools, makeshift fences, the scattered gardens, and a
ramshackle cabin, all of which flavored the picturesque and slightly harsh landscape the wilderness
family inhabit. But in the foreground, the dog has clearly spotted something that poses an unseen
threat, and it lowers its head in a defensive posture. Whatever it is, the woodsman sees it too. In addition to its many difficulties and hardships, the American wilderness was a place fraught with peril.
Cropsey's canvas illustrated the urgency of remaining always on the alert amid such lurking dangers,
and perhaps the same could be said for the life of a struggling artist, whether in America or in
England.[17]

Albert Bierstadt painted *Peace and Plenty, North Conway, New Hampshire (figs. 6–7)* in
1864, not long after returning with his friend Fitz Hugh Ludlow from his second great excursion
into the American West. The impressive views that resulted from Bierstadt's first trip to the Rocky
Mountains had already excited the imagination of the American public, who waited expectantly
for his next grand manner canvas to debut. In the relatively short interval between Bierstadt's return
from the West and the completion of his first monumental Western landscape, he produced a large
and ambitious but relatively serene haying scene set in New Hampshire's White Mountains. *Peace and
Plenty* reflected the larger issues of community and collectivity during the late stages of the Civil
War, but for Bierstadt the subject probably registered on a personal level as well. In the foreground,
two oxen pull a wagon heavily loaded with harvested hay. On top, two young lovers steal a private
moment from the family and neighbors who have gathered on harvest day. At that moment in 1864,
Bierstadt was in love with Rosalie Ludlow, the wife of his friend and traveling companion. She
would eventually leave her husband and marry Bierstadt. That foreground element in *Peace and Plenty*
may reveal Bierstadt's tender feelings for Rosalie even as he wrestled with the burden of devastating his friend.[18]

Figure 6:
Albert Bierstadt (1830–1902)
Peace and Plenty, North Conway,
New Hampshire
1864
Oil on canvas
Manoogian Collection
Cat. 16

Figure 7:
Albert Bierstadt (1830–1902)
Peace and Plenty, North Conway,
New Hampshire (detail)
1864
Oil on canvas
Manoogian Collection
Cat. 16

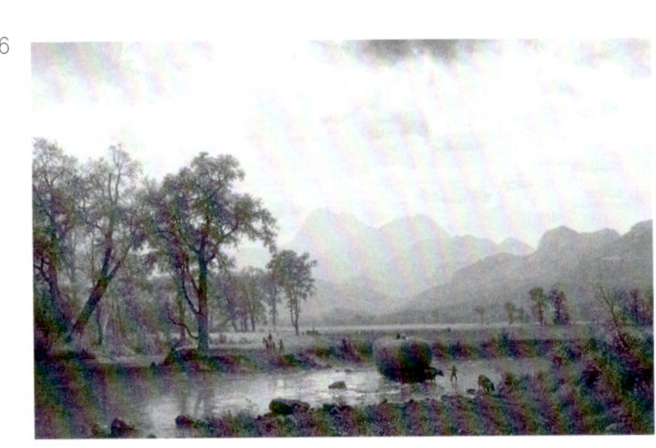

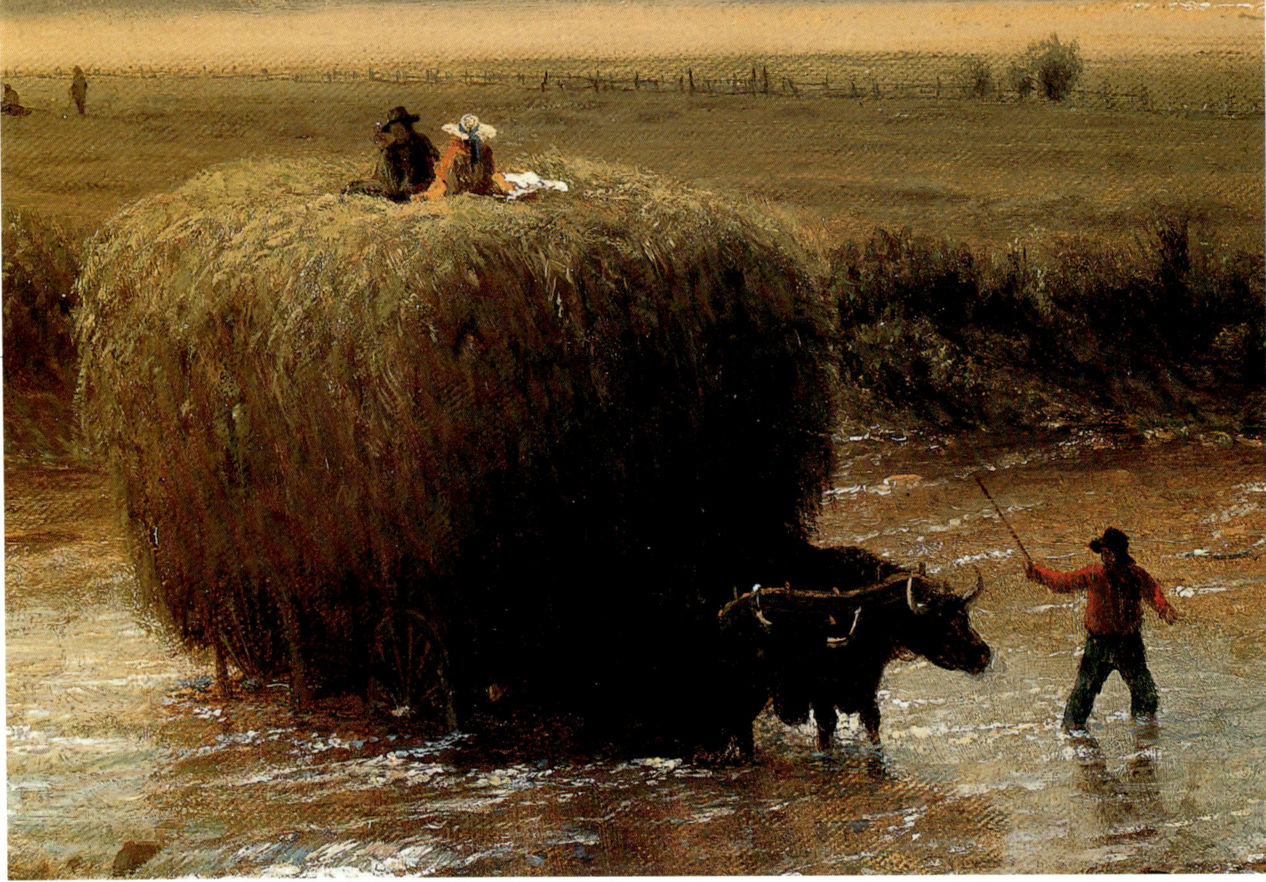

The Hudson River School painters employed small details to personalize and append engaging narratives to the grandeur of their often imposing canvases. Typically, they applied those details as distinct points of accent to physically and psychically interrupt the larger compositional and pictorial unity of their landscapes. But curiously, some artists found those same disruptive features useful in thematically reconfirming the very pictorial order they had interrupted. In Gifford's *Mount Mansfield (figs. 8–10)* and Whittredge's *Twilight on the Shawangunk Mountains (figs. 11–12)*, woodsmen (or more likely, artists dressed as woodsmen) build or feed small fires as they are shrouded in the larger light of glowing sunsets. The very reasonableness of their task, building fires before the sun goes down, rendered their activity so blandly logical as to almost delete its meaningfulness. But in both canvases, the meagerness of man's small fire compared to the magnificent blaze of the evening spectacle sent the unmistakable message that humanity's most capable efforts would always be dwarfed by the awesome and unifying power of nature.[19]

The more prominent detail in Gifford's *Mount Mansfield (fig. 9)* is the small figural and canine grouping at the lower center of the composition. By the 1850s, the placement of human figures contemplating scenic vistas had been an effective device of landscape painting for at least two centuries.[20] In *Mount Mansfield*, the figure leaning on his rifle more or less duplicates the visual experience of the artist, and by extension, that of the viewer of the painting, creating a powerful unity of purpose between painter, subject, and audience. Moreover, the seeming neutrality of that small detail was capable of embodying a nearly unlimited range of human dreams, desires, and emotions that were ultimately projections of the dreams, desires, and emotions of the viewer. On the one hand, the figure atop Mount Mansfield may have been contemplating his utter insignificance in relation to the greatness of nature, of God, of the Green Mountains, or of this particular sunset. On the other, he could have been calculating the profits the many miles of timber below him might generate. But whether a benign or an active influence over the landscape, the watching figure in Hudson River School landscape paintings was external to the overall unity of the painting, and thus from the larger order of nature's rhythms and majesty. If only to function successfully as distinct compositional detail, the gaze of the observer almost had to be magisterial. It almost had to be the colonizing look that signaled the end of the landscape's pristine era.[21]

Figure 8:
Sanford Robinson Gifford (1823–1880)
Mount Mansfield
1859
Oil on canvas
Manoogian Collection
Cat. 10

Figures 9 and 10:
Sanford Robinson Gifford (1823–1880)
Mount Mansfield (details)
1859
Oil on canvas
Manoogian Collection
Cat. 10

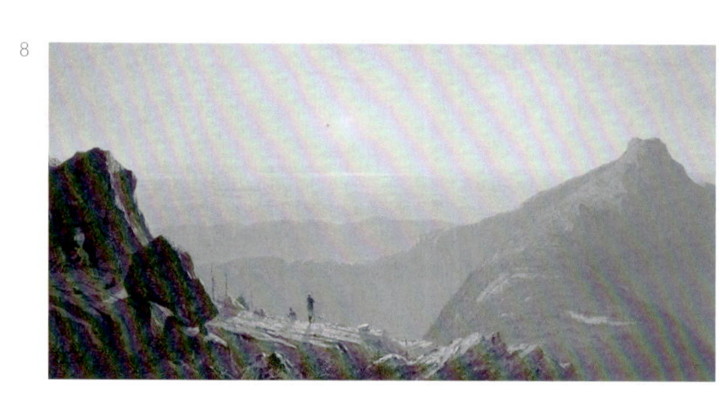

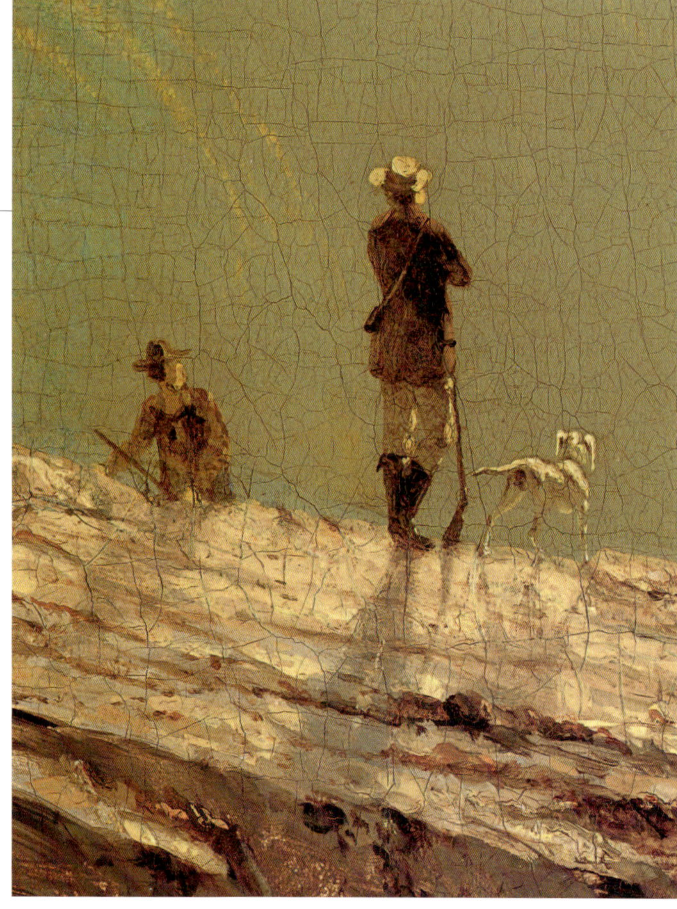

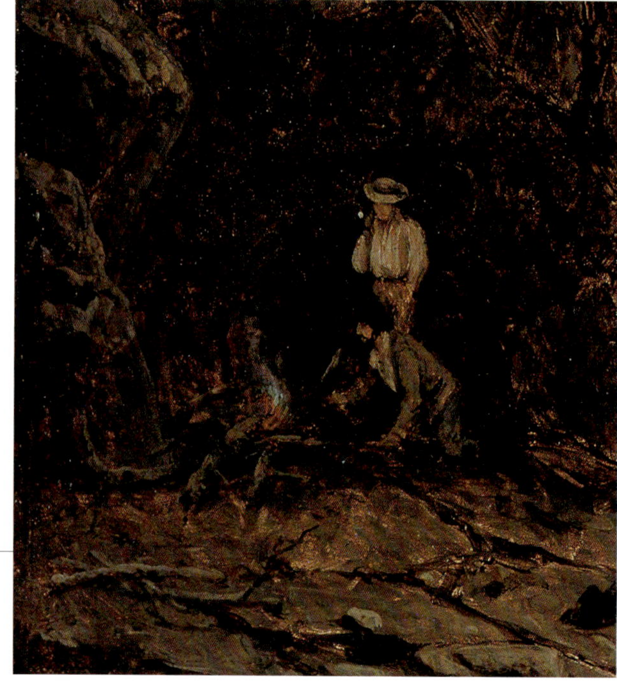

Figure 11:
Thomas Worthington Whittredge
(1820–1910)
Twilight on the Shawangunk Mountains
1865
Oil on canvas
Manoogian Collection
Cat. 22

Figure 12:
Thomas Worthington Whittredge
(1820–1910)
Twilight on the Shawangunk Mountains
(detail)
1865
Oil on canvas
Manoogian Collection
Cat. 22

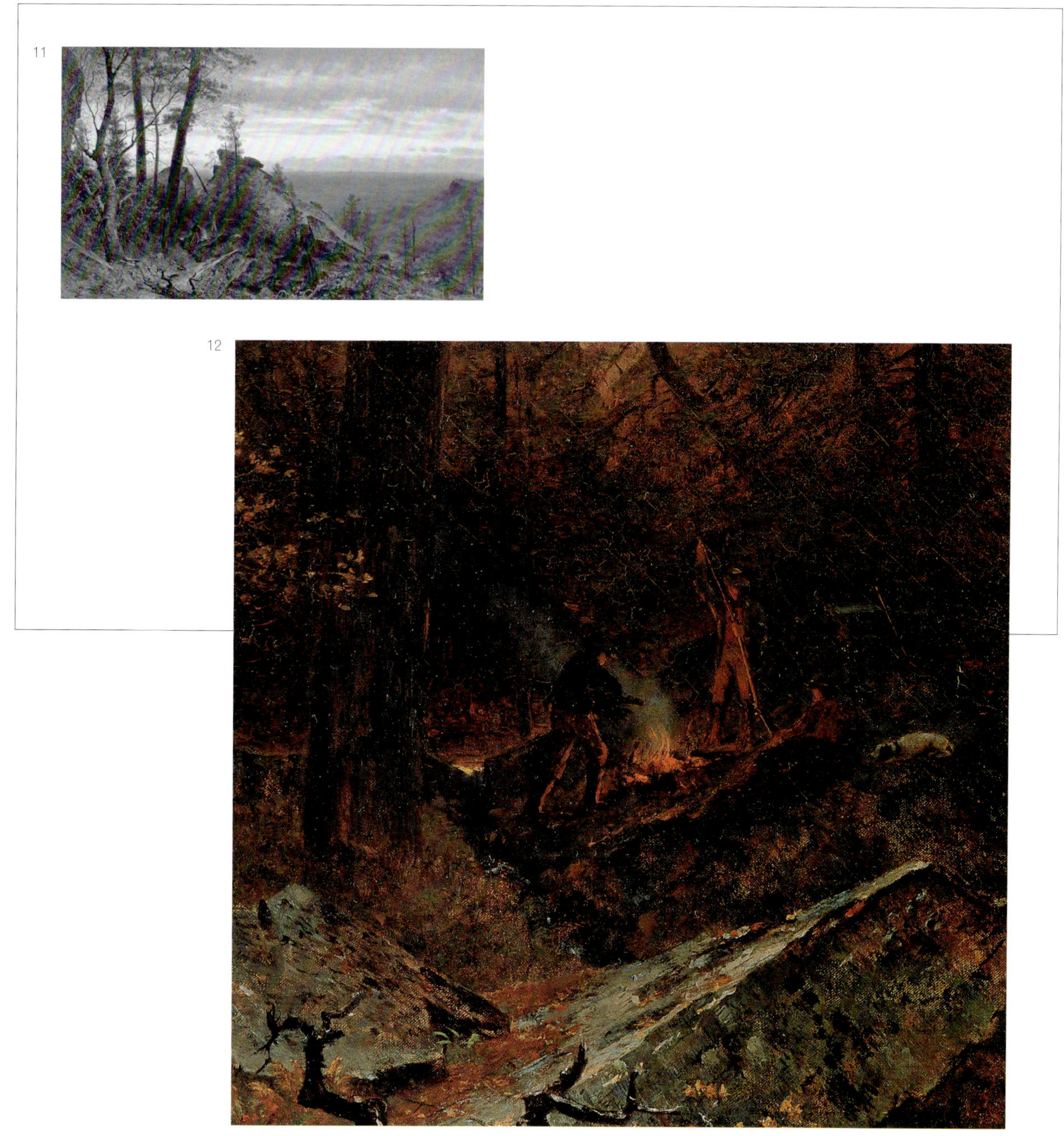

The work of Gifford, Whittredge, and others was largely a project of divining pictorial
order from wilderness subject matter not unlike Cole had done decades earlier. But some artists
preferred layered consistency to dialectic opposition, and found New England's neat farms and
well-cultivated rural areas in closer conceptual harmony to the pictorial unity they hoped to achieve
on canvas. George Henry Durrie was best known for the engaging genre scenes set in snowy
Connecticut landscapes that he produced for the New York publishing firm of Currier & Ives. In
The Half-Way House (figs. 13–14), a painting of 1861, Durrie approached the landscape with greater
compositional ambition than he generally attempted in his overtly commercial work. But having
created such a persuasively unified landscape, it was seemingly impossible for Durrie to resist filling
that pleasant and well ordered idyll with contented inhabitants. Moving vertically through the center
of the painting from bottom to top, Durrie placed an excited dog running alongside a sleigh full
of well-bundled travelers. In the distance, a single figure watches children throwing snowballs on
a frozen lake, and beyond them a church steeple rises from a protective wood. Durrie was aware
of the pictorial and thematic strategies of America's most advanced landscape painters, especially
his fellow Connecticut natives, Church and Kensett. But for all his ambition, Durrie was unwilling
or unable to separate the pleasing order he found in cultivated landscapes from the lives that
brought order to the land in the first place and from his search for formal unity on the surface of
the canvas.[22]

Among the most original artists of the nineteenth century, Martin Johnson Heade nearly
always enlarged the intellectual scope of whatever genre he tried. His atmospheric salt marsh landscapes were already a departure from the sublime or beautiful or picturesque scenes his colleagues
painted in the mountains or on sandy shorelines. Like most of his salt marsh subjects, *Sunset on
the Marshes (figs. 15–16)* is a broadly horizontal composition, bathed in a generalizing light and
atmosphere, and punctuated by carefully placed details. For Heade, those details were an abstract
concern more than an opportunity for autobiography or anecdote, and he placed intensely red
strokes of paint on the foreground foliage, on the duck's back, on the watery reflection of a haystack,
and on the man in the boat. These red highlights were carefully placed markers leading directly to
the setting sun that was their source. Similarly, the two stacks of hay, whose rounded forms rhyme

Figure 13:
George Henry Durrie (1820–1863)
The Half-Way House
1861
Oil on canvas
Manoogian Collection
Cat. 12

Figure 14:
George Henry Durrie (1820–1863)
The Half-Way House (detail)
1861
Oil on canvas
Manoogian Collection
Cat. 12

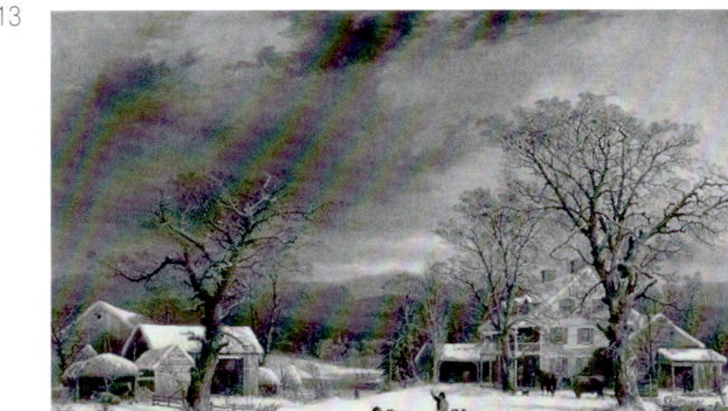

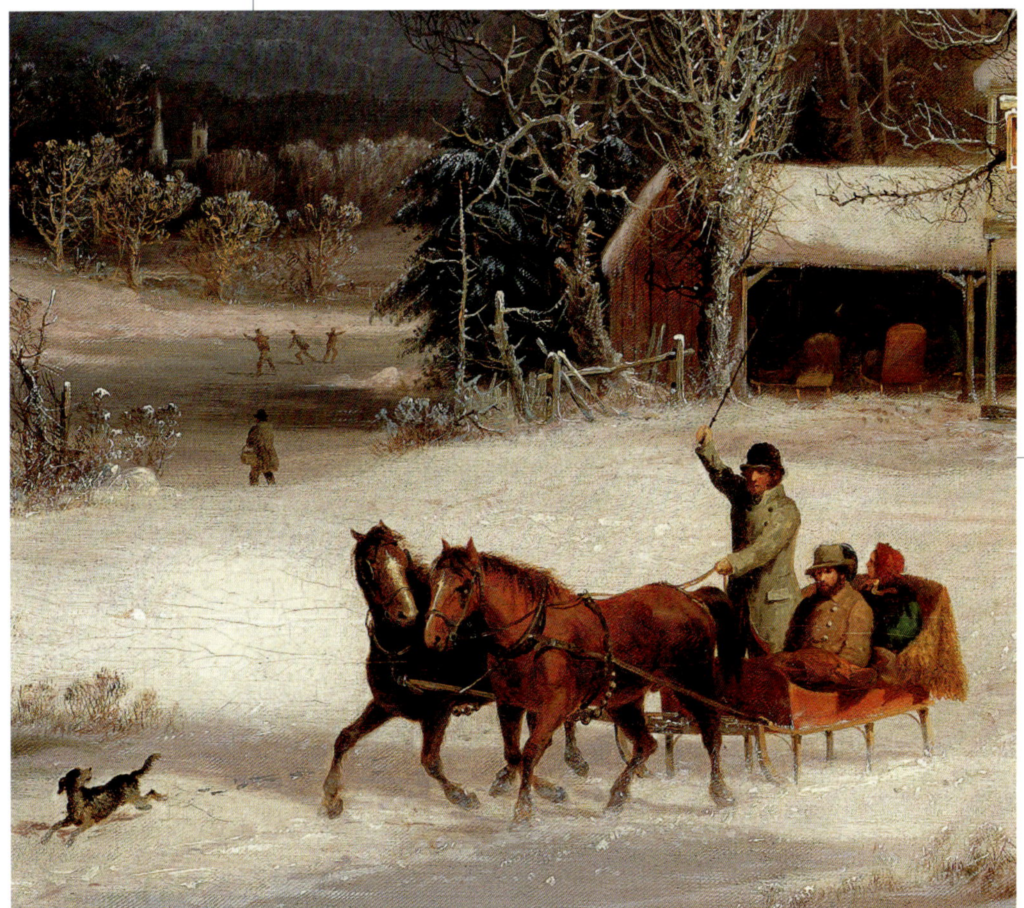

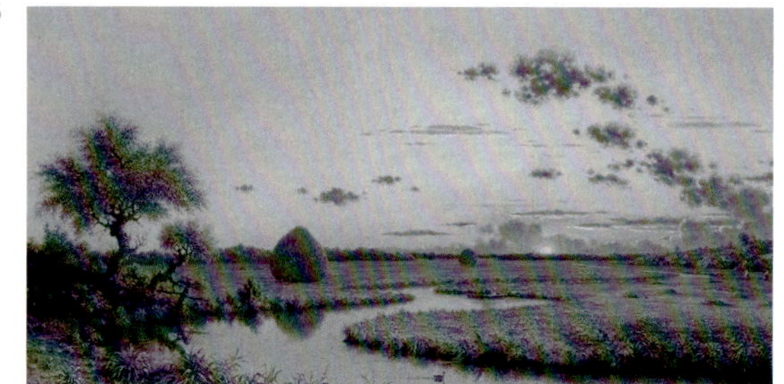

15

16

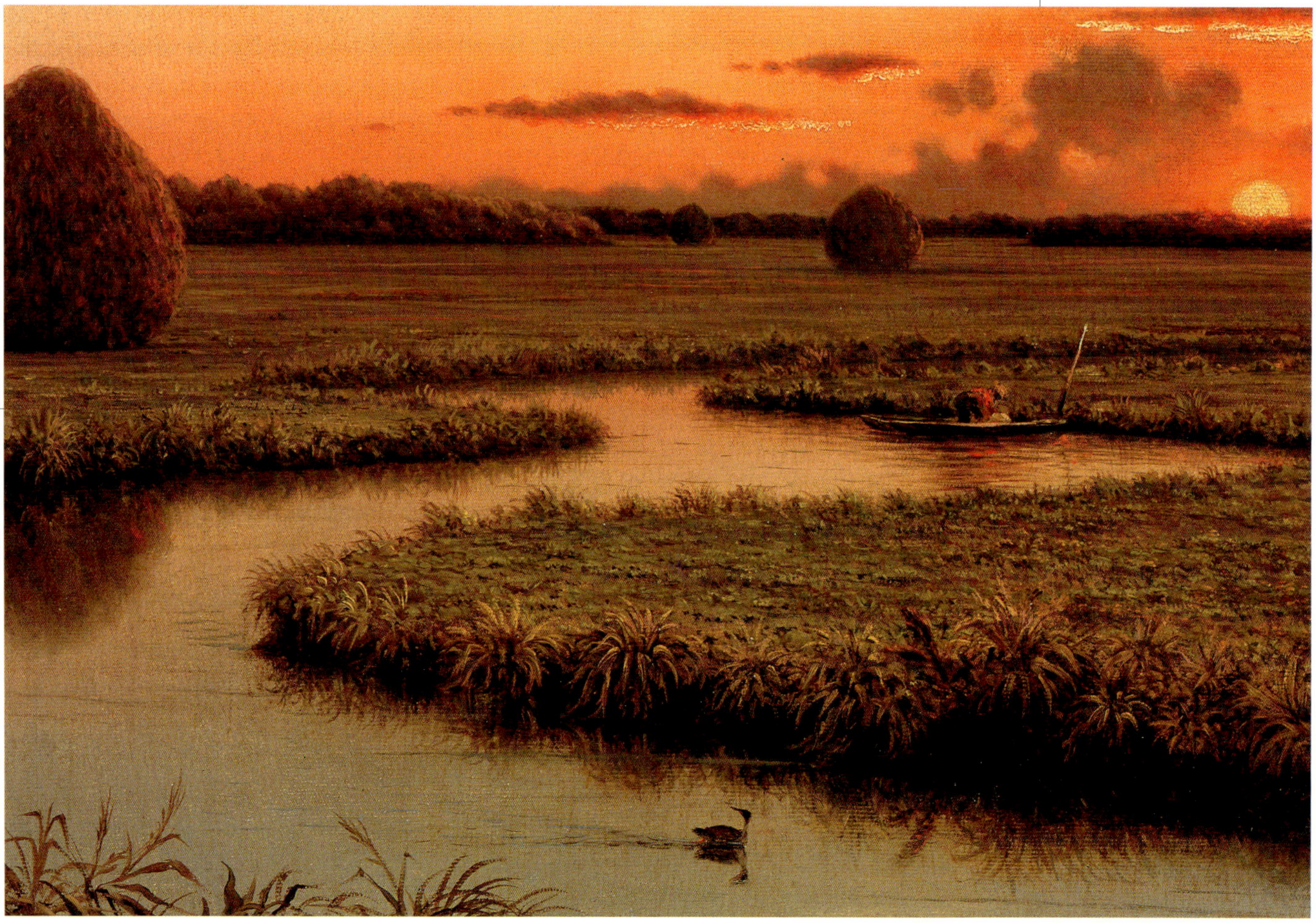

with the disappearing orb, also point to the light source. Bringing the work into brilliant formal and thematic agreement, the cadence of receding haystacks culminating at the setting sun established a quickening pictorial rhythm that captured the fleeting nature of twilight itself.[23]

Heade made extraordinary formal use of pictorial details in his marsh landscapes, but he was even more original in his South American subjects. In his paintings of hummingbirds and orchids before verdant tropical backdrops, Heade inverted the conventions of composition by making the tiny fluttering birds and delicate flowers bear the responsibility for pictorial unity, while the landscape was little more than accent or supporting detail. In *Cattleya Orchid, Two Hummingbirds and a Beetle (figs. 17–18)*, a hybrid genre made up of roughly equal parts landscape and still life, Heade painted the smallest individual elements at life size before the implied vastness of miniature tropical landscapes. The strategy helped Heade come closer to finding God in the details than any other painter in nineteenth-century America. For all of the recent efforts to shoehorn Heade into the world of Darwin and evolutionary science, his orchids and hummingbirds appear less evolutionary than having been just released by a creator into the garden of great beyond.[24]

Heade effectively captured the hothouse beauty of the tropics, but it was Frederic Church who put the most indelible stamp on South American subject matter. Church made his first trip to New Granada (now Colombia) and Ecuador in 1853, and was preparing for a second journey in 1857 when he completed *View on the Magdalena River (figs. 19–20)*. At that point, he had yet to produce any of his grand manner South American masterworks, such as *Heart of the Andes* or *Cotopaxi*, and he rightly believed that a return to South America was essential to capturing its magnitude and force.[25] By early 1857, Church had made plans to travel to the tropics with his fellow landscapist Louis Rémy Mignot, who was in almost every respect his mirror opposite. Mignot was of southern birth and expansive temperament, he was a Catholic, the child of immigrants, and he possessed only slender connections to his birthplace in Charleston. Church, on the other hand, was a pious, protestant Connecticut Yankee, who traced his family's origins in America to the early sixteenth century. Four years later, the Civil War would transform friendships like the one between Church and Mignot into an utter impossibility. But in 1857, the differences between the two men may have done little more than to give Church pause to ponder the nature of difference in other contexts.

Figure 17:
Martin Johnson Heade (1819–1904)
*Cattleya Orchid, Two Hummingbirds
and a Beetle*
c. 1875–1890
Oil on canvas
Manoogian Collection
Cat. 30

Figure 18:
Martin Johnson Heade (1819–1904)
*Cattleya Orchid, Two Hummingbirds
and a Beetle* (detail)
c. 1875–1890
Oil on canvas
Manoogian Collection
Cat. 30

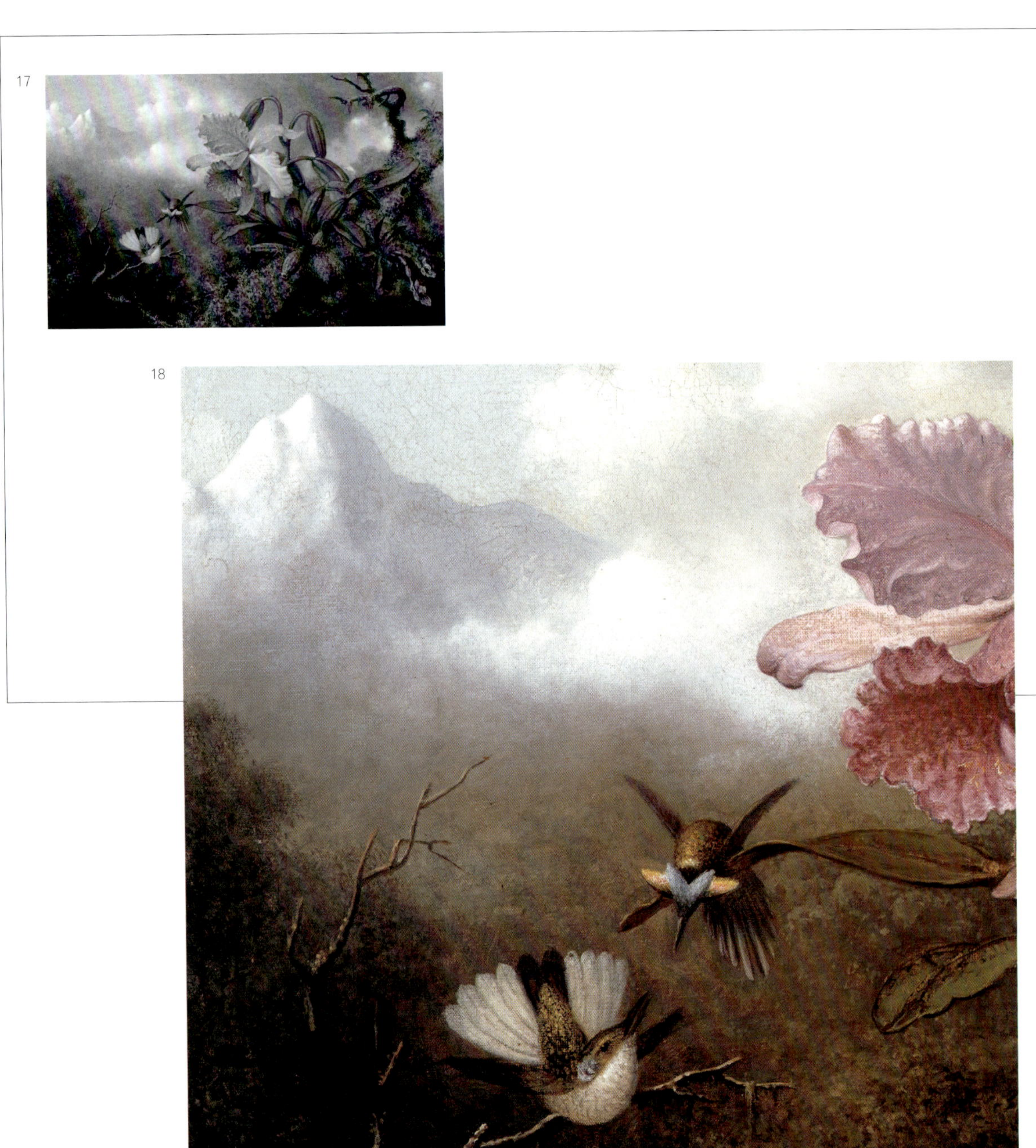

Figure 19:
Frederic Edwin Church (1826–1900)
View on the Magdalena River
1857
Oil on canvas
Manoogian Collection
Cat. 8

Figure 20:
Frederic Edwin Church (1826–1900)
View on the Magdalena River (detail)
1857
Oil on canvas
Manoogian Collection
Cat. 8

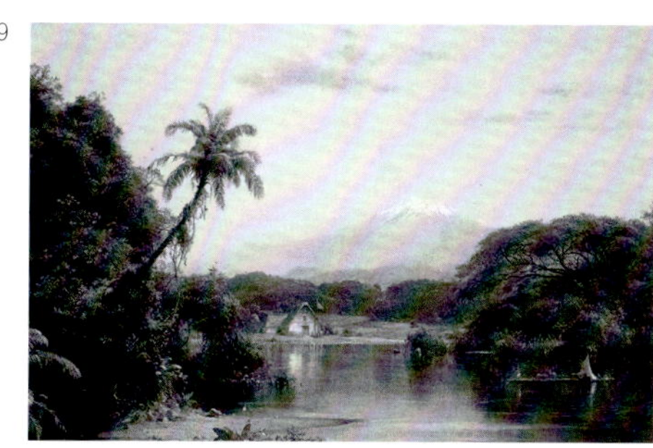

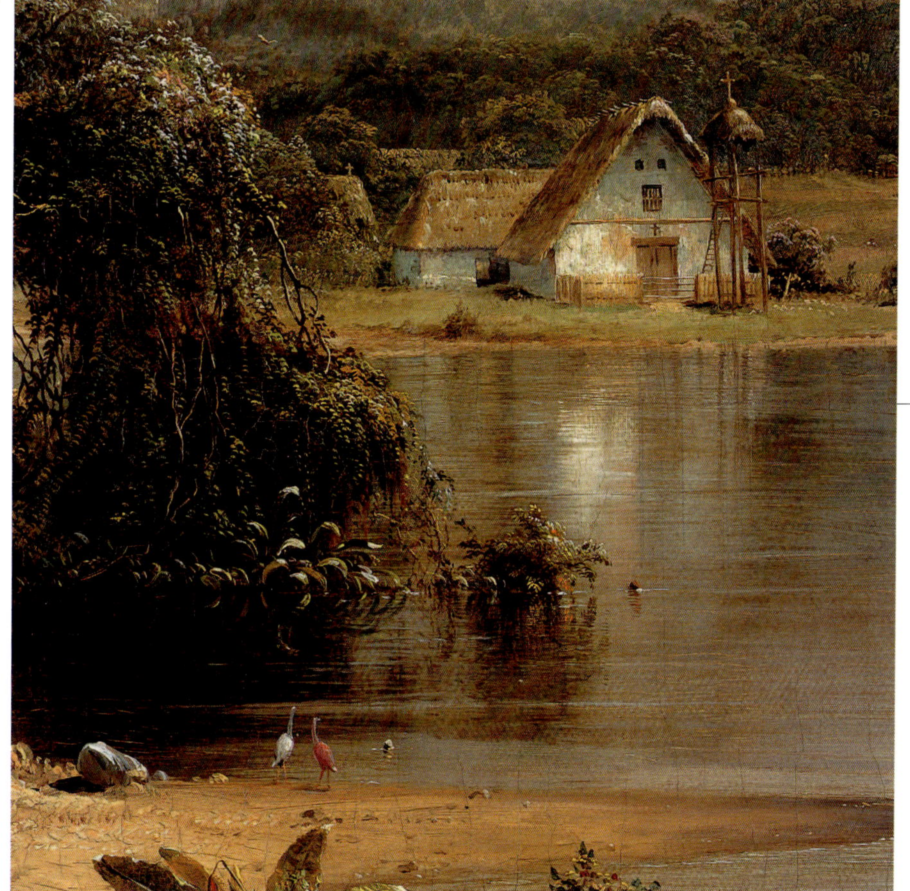

In *View on the Magdalena River*, Church planted a mission chapel squarely on the bank
of the wide estuary. He had sketched that chapel from a variety of angles on his first journey to New
Granada in 1853, and it had appeared in more than one of his paintings. But as Church planned his
second trip into the Southern Hemisphere with Mignot, he may have contemplated the many differences that separated his world from the remote tropical regions to which he was returning. Church
knew that the tropics would play an enormously significant role in his painterly ambitions, pictorial
strategies, and his professional successes. Regardless of how different and unfamiliar they were to the
world in which he was raised, to the world he inhabited, and to the world as he knew it, the tropics
would become very much a part of him. It was no coincidence that as Frederic Church awaited his
return to South America in 1857, amid the unifying humidity of tropical air, he placed a church on
the Magdalena River, a pictorial signature and a clever detail that claimed the territory for his own.[26]

[The painter again rises, and drags the chair on two hind legs in three, four, five steps backward from
the easel. The view is unencumbered. This look, this take on the finished picture framed on the
easel, this chance to understand it, and to remember it forever depends upon this look, this take on
the finished picture framed on the easel, this chance to understand it, and to remember it, etc.
For all the adventurous travel to the mountains, the sea, the American West, and even South America,
perhaps the most important distances covered by the artist are the few paces in a New York studio
that separate the close work of painting from a general overview of its results. Back and forth and back
and forth again. Finally and utterly satisfied that the painting is complete, convinced beyond doubt
that the work is done, the painter returns to the easel and adds a touch of intensely red paint to the
back of a duck.]

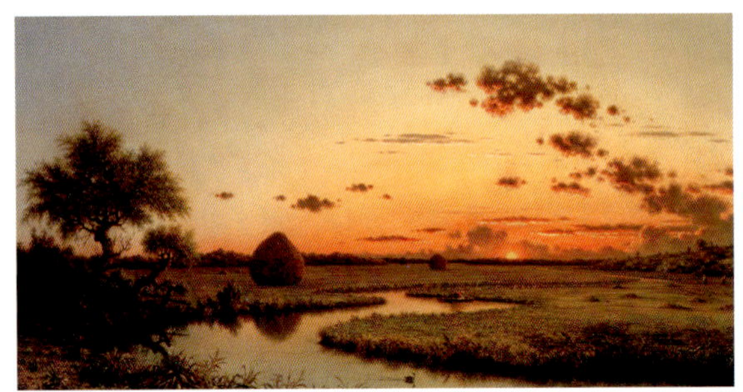

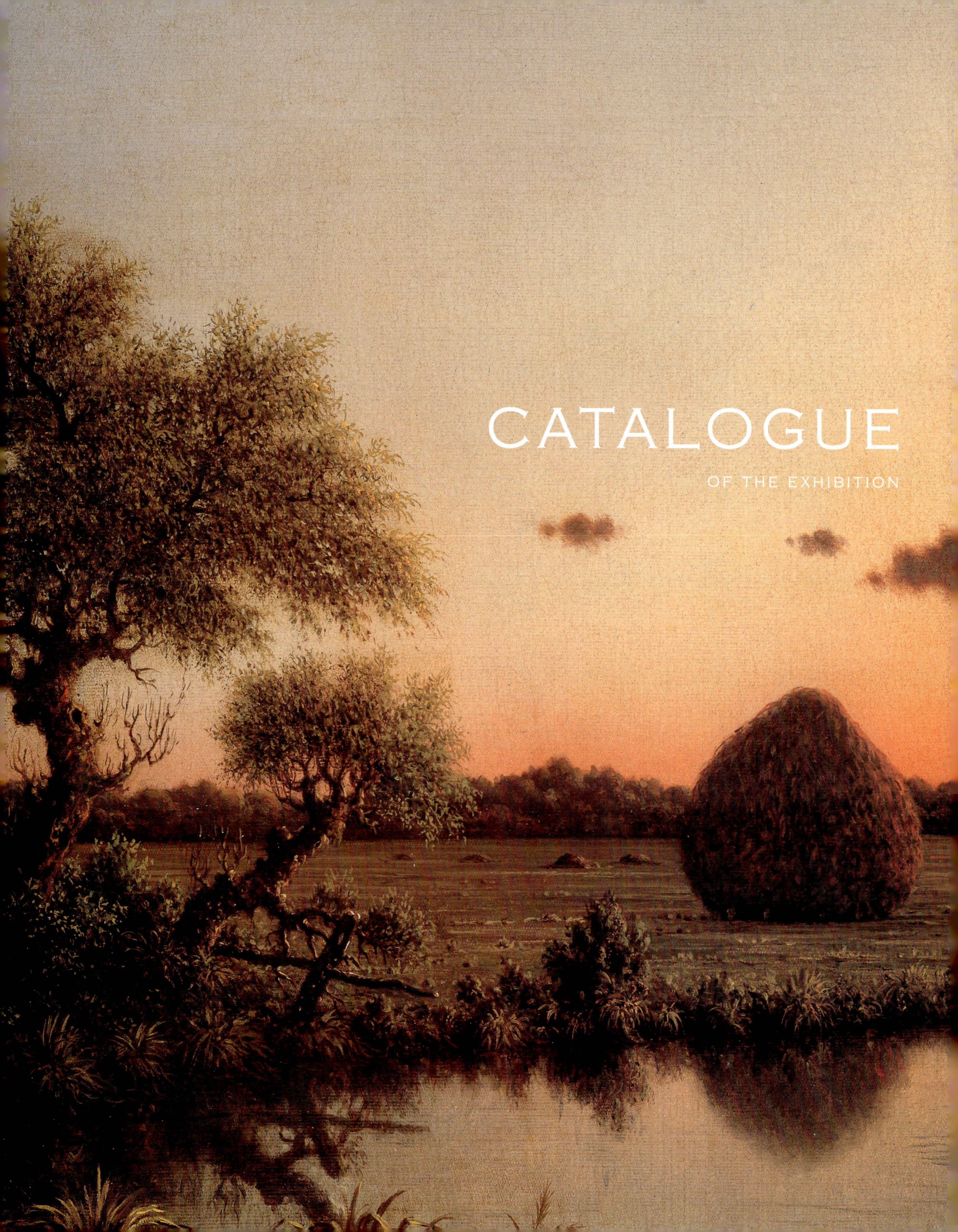
CATALOGUE
OF THE EXHIBITION

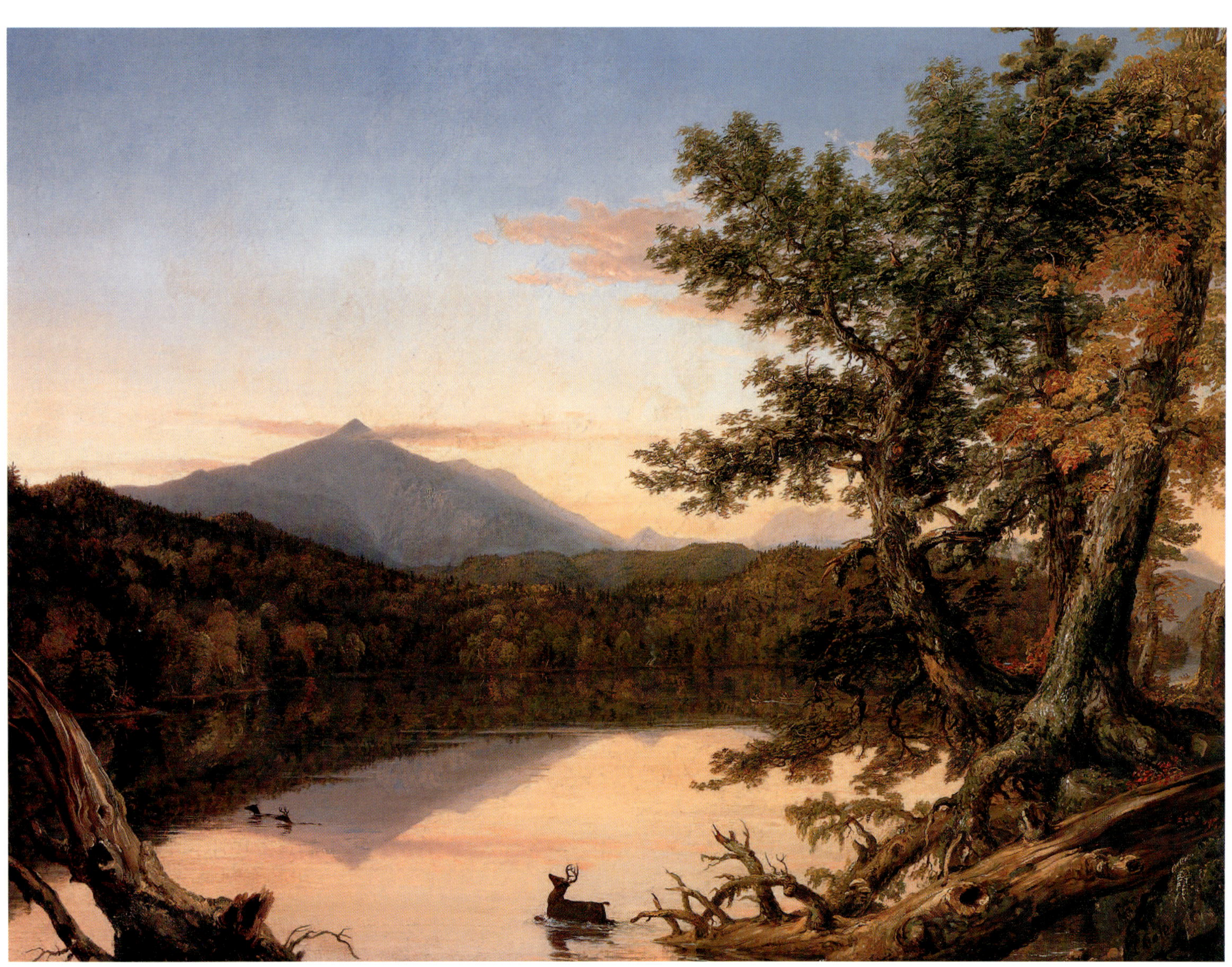

c. 1837–38 (painted when the artist
was 35–37 years old)
Oil on canvas
34 ⅛ x 46 ⅛ in. (86.7 x 117.2 cm)
Signed at lower right: *T Cole*

Early provenance: From the artist, Catskill, N.Y., c. 1837–1848; to Maria Bartow Cole, the artist's widow, Catskill, 1848; (sold, possibly with the help of Frederic Church) to William Earl Dodge Jr., New York, mid 1850s.[1]

References: Manoogian, 1989, no. 2, pp. 16–17. Manoogian, 1997, no. 1, pp. 26–29 and 186.

In the autumn of 1835, when Thomas Cole first visited Schroon Lake in the Adirondack Mountains, he had been America's most admired landscape painter for more than a decade. His canvases had impressed collectors, writers, and colleagues since 1825, when the then-unknown Cole emerged from the Catskill wilderness with a well developed style that communicated the sublime beauty of America's frontier and the idealism of a young nation poised for greatness. Even such an important painter as John Trumble marveled at Cole's precocity, as he bought a canvas for his own collection and confessed, "This youth has done what I have all my life attempted in vain."[2]

For all of Cole's early ambition and accomplishment, as he rowed a small boat to the widest part of Schroon Lake in the autumn of 1835, some of his most notable achievements lay just ahead of him. Within months of seeing the "beautiful sheet of water, shadowed by sloping hills clothed with heavy forests," Cole would complete his *View from Mount Holyoke, Northampton, Massachusetts after a Thunderstorm (The Oxbow)*, which represented the visual equivalent of the artist's most complex ideas about the American landscape and the painting of it. Later in 1836, he finished a cycle of five paintings called *The Course of Empire* for his friend, the dry goods millionaire Luman Reed. Cole's exhibition of the series at the National Academy of Design in the winter of 1836 was a popular and critical success that vaulted the painter to an even higher level of esteem.[3]

Cole's 1835 visit to Schroon Lake was brief, but the scenery made a deep impression. Upon returning to New York in early October, he wrote in his journal:

*In the neighborhood of Schroon the country is more finely broken.…
On both hands, from shores of sand and pebbles, gently rise the
thickly-wooded hills: before you miles of blue water stretch away:
in the distance mountains of remarkable beauty bound the vision.
Two summits in particular attracted my attention: one of a serrated
outline, and the other like a lofty pyramid. At the time I saw them,
they stood in the midst of the wilderness like peaks of sapphire. It is
my intention to return to this region at a more favourable season.*[4]

Cole made only a few cursory sketchbook notations during his first trip to Schroon Lake. The most considered of these drawings *(fig. 1)* captured the wide expanse of water with mountains rising in the distance, and although the sketch is slight, it is rich in information. The drawing bears several descriptions of color, references to the relative distance of each summit, and a note that he had drawn the highest peak of Schroon Mountain (now Hoffman Mountain) "too low." The foreground of Cole's sketch is empty except for the lightly limned boat that he described "rowing north for half an hour or so" until "the lake expanded to the breadth of two or three miles. Here the view is exceedingly fine." And it was here that Cole likely made the drawing in his sketchbook that eventually became the painting *Schroon Lake*.[5]

It was not until late June 1837, in the company of his new bride, Maria Bartow, and his friends, Mr. and Mrs. Asher B. Durand, that Cole fulfilled his promise to return to Schroon Lake. He brought the same sketchbook he had carried in 1835, filling considerably more pages during his second visit. Cole made graphite sketches of the lake, the mountains, and a nearby pond, and inscribed careful notes on most of the leaves, indicating on which side of the lake he was working and the direction he was looking. His memory of the picturesque scenery had not failed him, and the travelers enjoyed pleasant weather. Cole wrote on one drawing dated 30 June 1837 that "the day was brilliant[,] clear atmosphere & flying clouds and the effects of light and shade striking[;] the finest effect was when the dark parts of the distant mountain was [sic] in the shadow of clouds and the bright ledge of rock in sunlight."[6]

Early in the second journey, Cole became intrigued by the cedar trees, fallen and standing, that lined the shore of Schroon Lake, and he made three drawings of the scruffy evergreens. The first he labeled, "Cedar Streching [sic] over the water … " On the second drawing, he wrote "White Cedar" and described "a multitude of branches mossy and broken with sparse foliage." The third drawing of an ancient log that had fallen on its side and lain there for a year or more was simply marked "Cedar." None of Cole's sketchbook drawings of cedar trees relate directly to the mossy evergreen that curves over the water in the finished painting, nor the skinned log with the twisted branches that rests at the right foreground. But given the keen interest Cole took in these trees during his second trip to Schroon Lake, and the prominence they are afforded in the finished painting, the artist may not have started the canvas until after the summer of 1837 at the earliest.[7]

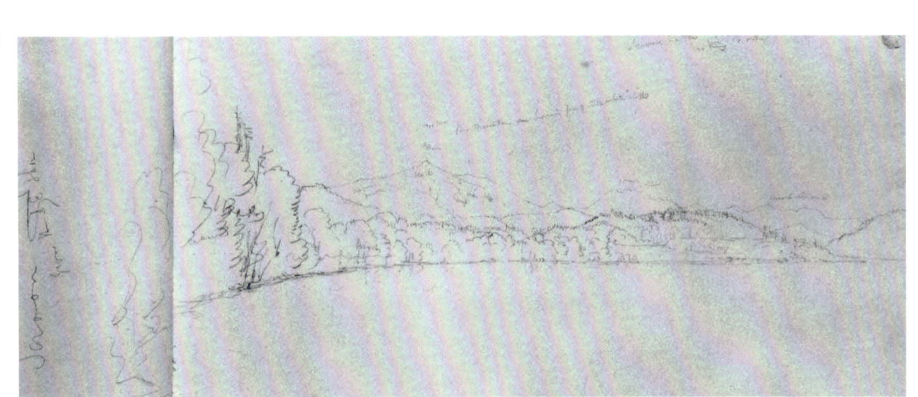

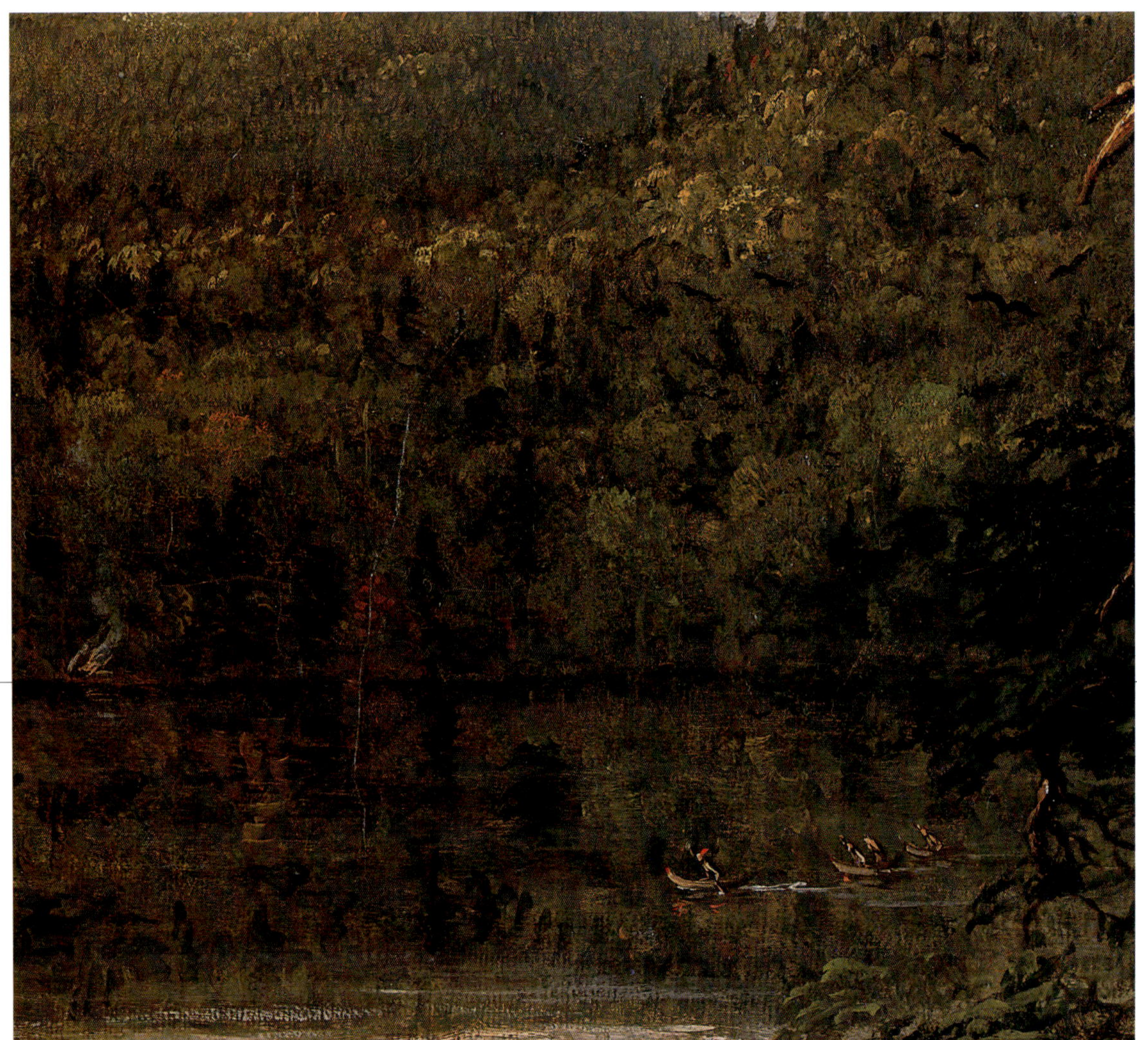

In the most fully resolved compositional study for *Schroon Lake*, a drawing that Cole probably completed in the studio, a Native American stands amid the trees at right and aims an arrow at the large deer in the foreground.[8] Cole chose to eliminate the hunter in the finished painting, but he introduced a more subtle if no less menacing threat to the otherwise calm of the quiet mountain lake. Four deer have taken to the water, and the very unnaturalness of their swim is disturbing even though the crawl to a safer shore is from a danger not immediately evident. Barely noticeable in the shadowy center of the lake, three small canoes bearing Native Americans race across the still water *(fig. 2)*, but they do not travel in the direction of the deer, which they have no hope of catching and seemingly no desire to. Nor do they turn toward the wisp of smoke lifting from a fire on the distant shore of Schroon Lake. The canoes paddle straight ahead with a clear sense of urgency, as a flock of twenty or more large black birds circle overhead and betray their position.

Only months before making his first trip to Schroon Lake, in May 1835, Cole had presented a lecture entitled "Essay on American Scenery" at the New York Lyceum. The essay was his most important public statement to date about the increasingly traveled American wilderness, and it was a turning point in the nation's growing passion for landscape painting. Cole was concerned about American culture's civilizing influence on the native frontier, and he urged a more measured use of its bounty and a more stalwart protection of its unique beauty:

> *In this age, when a meager utilitarianism seems ready to absorb every feeling and sentiment, and what is sometimes called improvement in its march makes us fear that the bright and tender flowers of the imagination shall all be crushed beneath its iron tramp, it would be well to cultivate the oasis that yet remains to us, and thus preserve the germs of a future and a purer system.[9]*

But Cole had little reason to expect any enlightened exaltation of the imagination, let alone the preservation of wild and isolated scenery that spurred it into flight. By 1836, the rush of industrial progress had already made its way to within a short walk of Cedar Grove, his home and studio in Catskill, New York. The construction of the Catskill and Canajoharie Railroad cut a wide path through Cole's beloved valley of Catskill Creek. In a furious letter to Luman Reed, the artist made his position clear in terms that were far less poetic than the elegant language he had used in his essay:

> *The copper-hearted barbarians are cutting all the trees down in the beautiful valley on which I have looked so often with a loving eye — this throws quite a gloom over my spring anticipation — tell this to Durand, not that I wish to give him pain, but that I want him to join me in malediction on all dollar-godded utilitarians.[10]*

At the far right edge of Cole's *Schroon Lake*, in a small wedge of water glimpsed between the trees, yet another canoe appears, carrying two or perhaps three men. Although little more than a smear of thin brown paint, the mark was no afterthought on Cole's part. Indeed, it may hold the key to *Schroon Lake*. Still angry about the invading railroad, Cole ultimately produced a profound meditation on civilization's encroachment upon wild and remote locations. Against the pristine backdrop of Schroon Lake and the mountains he so admired, Cole captured the region's natural and cultural history in one panoramic sweep. First came the animals, then the indigenous people, and it seems likely that the tiny canoe at the far right of the composition — a presence that has driven deer into the lake and Native Americans to step up their paddling — may represent the approach of civilization and all that would come with it.

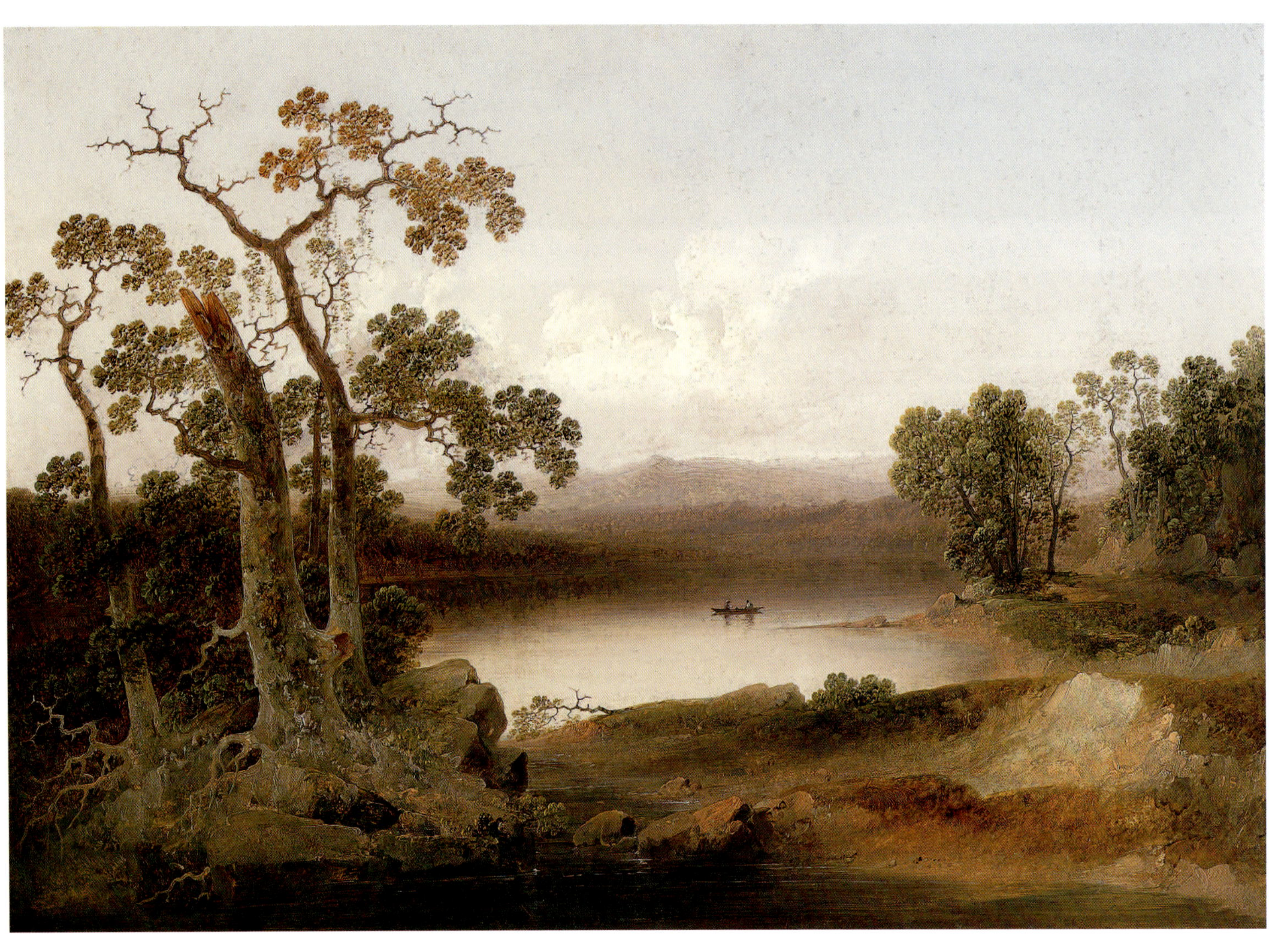

Joshua Shaw was a capable English artist who worked in London during the late eighteenth and early nineteenth century, painting romantic and literary inspired landscapes in the manner of Claude Lorraine. Despite his skill in the landscape genre, the competition for patronage in London was stiff, and any hope of commercial success was decidedly limited. After years of struggle to midlife and mid-career, an opportunity presented itself in 1817, when Benjamin West hired Shaw to accompany his painting *Christ Healing the Sick* on the long Atlantic crossing from London to Philadelphia. Upon his arrival, Shaw immediately recognized the wonder of the American landscape, and realized that his prospects were far more promising in Philadelphia than he could ever hope them to be in London. He remained in the United States for the rest of his long career.[1]

Shaw was based in Philadelphia, but he was drawn to the American wilderness, and traveled from the rugged Catskill Mountains to the more pastoral regions along Pennsylvania's Schuylkill and Susquehanna Rivers. Although he rarely transcended the landscape formulas he had learned in England, Shaw understood that the American frontier demanded a means of expression that was as unique in character as the awesome landscape itself. For a published series of intaglio prints based on his watercolor drawings, Shaw included a letterpress statement that suggested the differences between the American and the European countryside, and the opportunity presented by the former:

> *Striking however and original as the features of nature undoubtedly are in the United States, they have rarely been made the subjects of pictorial delineation. Europe abounds with picturesque views of its scenery. From the mountains of Switzerland to the tame level of the English landscape, every spot that is at all capable of exciting interest is familiar to the admirers of nature, while America only, of all the countries of civilized man, is unsung and undescribed.*[2]

Although he recognized its rich potential, Shaw never fully embraced America's landscape subjects, never followed his own prescription, and his letterpress statement remained little more than eager salesmanship. Ironically, he became best known for feeding Philadelphia's hungry market for English coastal scenes, which he produced from memory during his more than four decades in the United States. By the 1830s, the English shorelines that he submitted to exhibitions in Philadelphia and New York betrayed the growing influence of genre painting, no doubt inspired by the expanding American market for subjects of human interest. But for all of the artist's unapologetic attempts to produce saleable paintings, his most compelling canvases were the few unself-conscious American landscapes that he based on careful examinations and drawings made from nature.

Shaw's *View of the Susquehanna* of 1838, painted when the artist was past his sixtieth birthday, revealed his skill, his versatility, and how thoroughly he understood the American landscape idiom that Thomas Cole had invented in the 1820s. Shaw carefully delineated the oak trees on the left side of the composition, in some respects still following the English manner, but he applied the thin paint more honestly and vigorously than is typical of his work. His emphatic articulation of the exposed root structures and the twisting upper branches, reaching skyward like gnarled fingers, is reminiscent of Cole's most expressionistic trees of the same period. The blasted trunk in the foreground was also a common device of Cole, and could have been lifted directly from one of his Catskill paintings were it not so earnestly observed and integrated along the bank of the Susquehanna River.

In selecting an almost muddy vista, and recording it in thin washes of monochromatic oil paint, Shaw intelligently reconciled the form and the content of *View of the Susquehanna*. He achieved an honest, uncontrived quality, and in some areas of the painting, such as the horizon glimpsed between the foreground trees, he brushed the paint so economically that the pencil drawing is visible beneath it. But the freedom, the freshness of execution and the integrity of *View of the Susquehanna* would not have made it any more appealing to Philadelphia collectors. If Shaw displayed *View of the Susquehanna* during his lifetime, it does not turn up in the records of any major exhibitions, and if he managed to find a buyer for the canvas, it is unknown when it left his studio.

3   JULY SUNSET   Frederic Edwin Church (1826–1900)

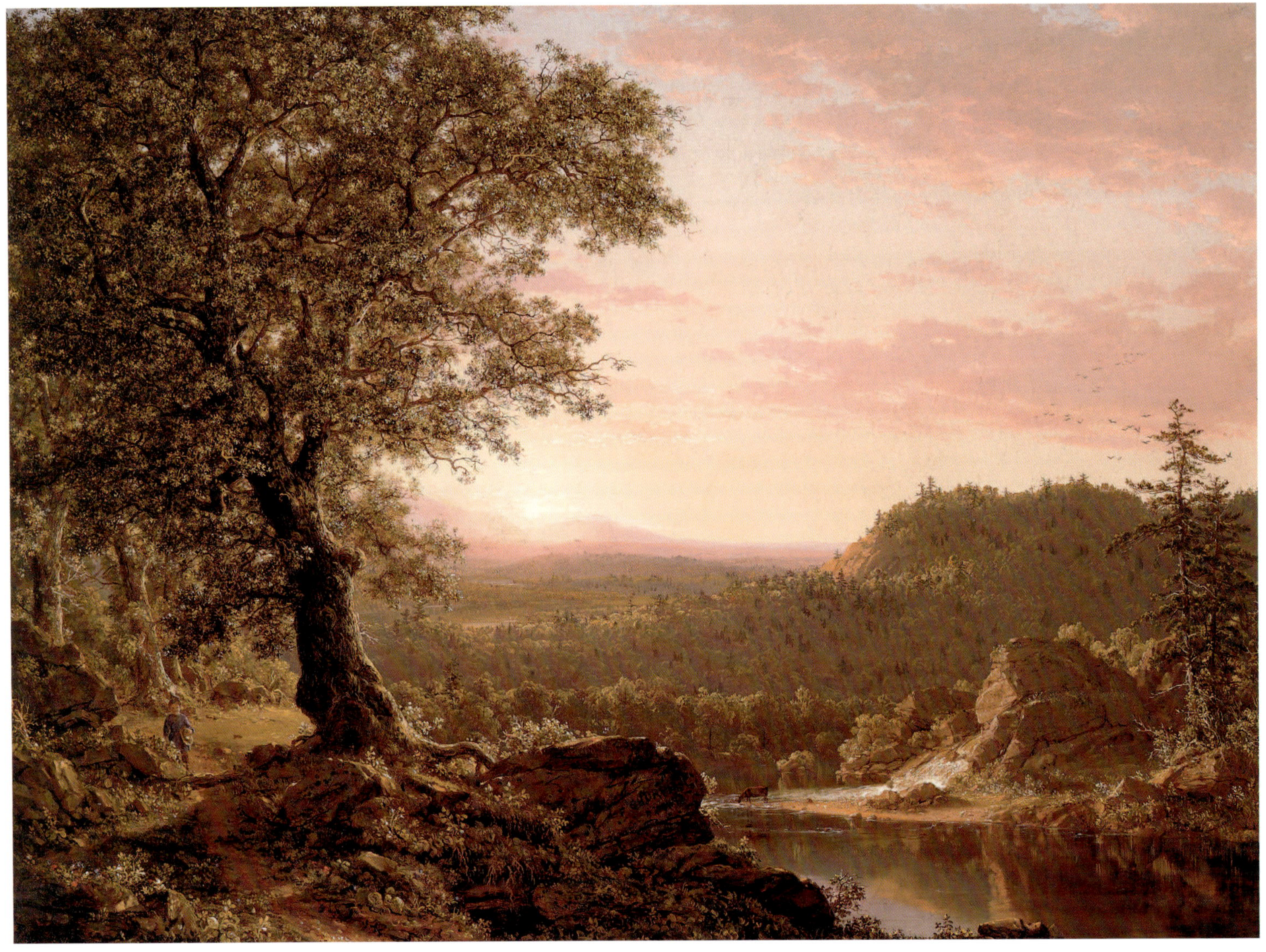

1847 (painted when the artist was 20 years old)
Oil on canvas
29 x 40 ⅜ in. (73.7 x 102.6 cm)
Signed and dated at lower center:
F Church 1847

Early provenance: From the artist, New York, 1847; (probably sold) to Adrian Janes (uncle of the artist on his mother's side), New York, 1847.

Early exhibition history: *Twenty-second Annual Exhibition of the National Academy of Design*, New York, spring 1847, no. 173.

Early publications: "The Fine Arts. Exhibitions at the National Academy. Second Saloon," *The Literary World*, 5 June 1847, p. 419.

References: Manoogian, 1989, no. 3, pp. 18–19. Manoogian, 1997, no. 2, pp. 30–31 and 186. Manoogian, 1999, no. 9, pp. 36–37.

Frederic Church was barely eighteen years old in June 1844, when he traveled from his hometown of Hartford, Connecticut, to Catskill, New York, to become the student of Thomas Cole.[1] Recommended by one of Cole's more reliable patrons, the Hartford collector and philanthropist, Daniel Wadsworth, Church spent two years training with the great landscapist at Cedar Grove, his home and studio near Catskill. Although he was young, Church understood that he was studying where American landscape painting had been reinvented, and he traced the footsteps that Cole had left in the region for nearly twenty years. Church drew subjects Cole had drawn, hiked along the Hudson River and Catskill Creek, and made more than one excursion with his teacher to the Catskill Mountain House and to Kaaterskill Falls. Predictably, the pencil drawings, oil sketches, and modest studio landscapes that Church produced during his stay at Catskill owe much in method, style and content to the influence of Cole. But that same body of early work also reveals a maturing artist of incontestable talent, whose vision was already beginning to reflect his own interests, temperament, and considerable ambition.[2]

In 1846, under the tutelage of Cole, Church produced two significant pictures – an historical landscape based on his own ancestry, *Hooker and Company Journeying through the Wilderness from Plymouth to Harford in 1636*, as well as an interpretation after Cole's much admired *The Oxbow* of 1836.[3] For his public debut in New York, Church contributed *Hooker and Company* to the spring 1846 exhibition of the National Academy of Design, where the painting was seen by Daniel Wadsworth and acquired for the new Atheneum that bore his name in Hartford. Wadsworth took an interest in Church's development in part because they were both sons of prominent Hartford families who traced their history to the founding of the Connecticut capital in the mid seventeenth century. Hartford was central to both of their identities, and would continue to exert an influence on the young artist for much of his early career.[4]

Church left Cole and Catskill in June 1846, and before the end of the year, he had rented a studio in the American Art-Union Building in Manhattan. By the spring of 1847, he had completed a handful of major paintings, including *Christian on the Borders of the 'Valley of the Shadow of Death,' Pilgrim's Progress* and *July Sunset*. Both pictures were indebted to Cole's example and aesthetic principles,

and both were suggestive of the scenery around Cedar Grove and Catskill.[5] In *July Sunset*, Church assembled a composite view of Catskill Creek that was largely based on drawings he had produced in the valley near Cole's studio. But the impressive oak tree that anchors the foreground and fills the entire left side of the canvas probably derived from drawings Church made of the Charter Oak, an arboreal landmark situated in Hartford rather than in Catskill, and at that time, perhaps the most famous tree in America.[6] Church had probably sketched the tree many times, but he produced a significant composition drawing of the Charter Oak in the late summer of 1846 *(fig. 1)*. Writing to Cole in October of that year, he described the drawing, the tree, and his plan "to paint it on a pretty large canvas during the coming winter." And indeed he did produce two pictures of the Charter Oak in addition to the majestic tree in *July Sunset* that he transplanted from Hartford to the valley of Catskill Creek.[7]

Church submitted *Christian on the Borders of the 'Valley of the Shadow of Death,' Pilgrim's Progress* and *July Sunset* to the spring 1847 exhibition of the National Academy of Design. His choice of presentation pictures was quite deliberate and meant to demonstrate his abilities as a landscaper painter and his thematic range, but those two canvases also would have reminded his colleagues, as well as New York critics and collectors, that he was the favored protégé of the much revered Cole. It was widely known that Cole had spent much of 1846 working on, or at least contemplating, *The Cross of the World*, a proposed cycle of four paintings that, like Church's contribution to the National Academy show, was inspired by John Bunyan's novel *Pilgrim's Progress*.[8] But a reviewer for *The Literary World* also saw evidence of Church's close connection to Cole in *July Sunset*, noting that: "The first glance at this picture impresses one with the idea that it must be one of Cole's."[9]

The critic had a point. The setting sun, the distant foothills, the broad valley, and Catskill Creek, alternately slumbering in pools and tumbling over low cascades, had been painted by Cole many times in many variations.[10] Cole himself could almost have stepped from the familiar scenery of *July Sunset*, and indeed a Cole did. To the left of the massive oak tree appears a small boy in a blue smock with his hat removed as if Church wanted him to be recognized as Thomas Cole's young son, Theodore *(fig. 2)*.[11] Church had exhibited

Figure 1:
Frederic E. Church (1826–1900)
The Charter Oak, Hartford
1846
Ink and pencil on light gray paper
New York State Office of Parks and
Recreation, and Historic Preservation,
Olana State Historic Site,
Taconic Region (OL.1977.302)

Figure 2:
Frederic E. Church (1826–1900)
July Sunset (detail)
1847
Oil on canvas
Manoogian Collection

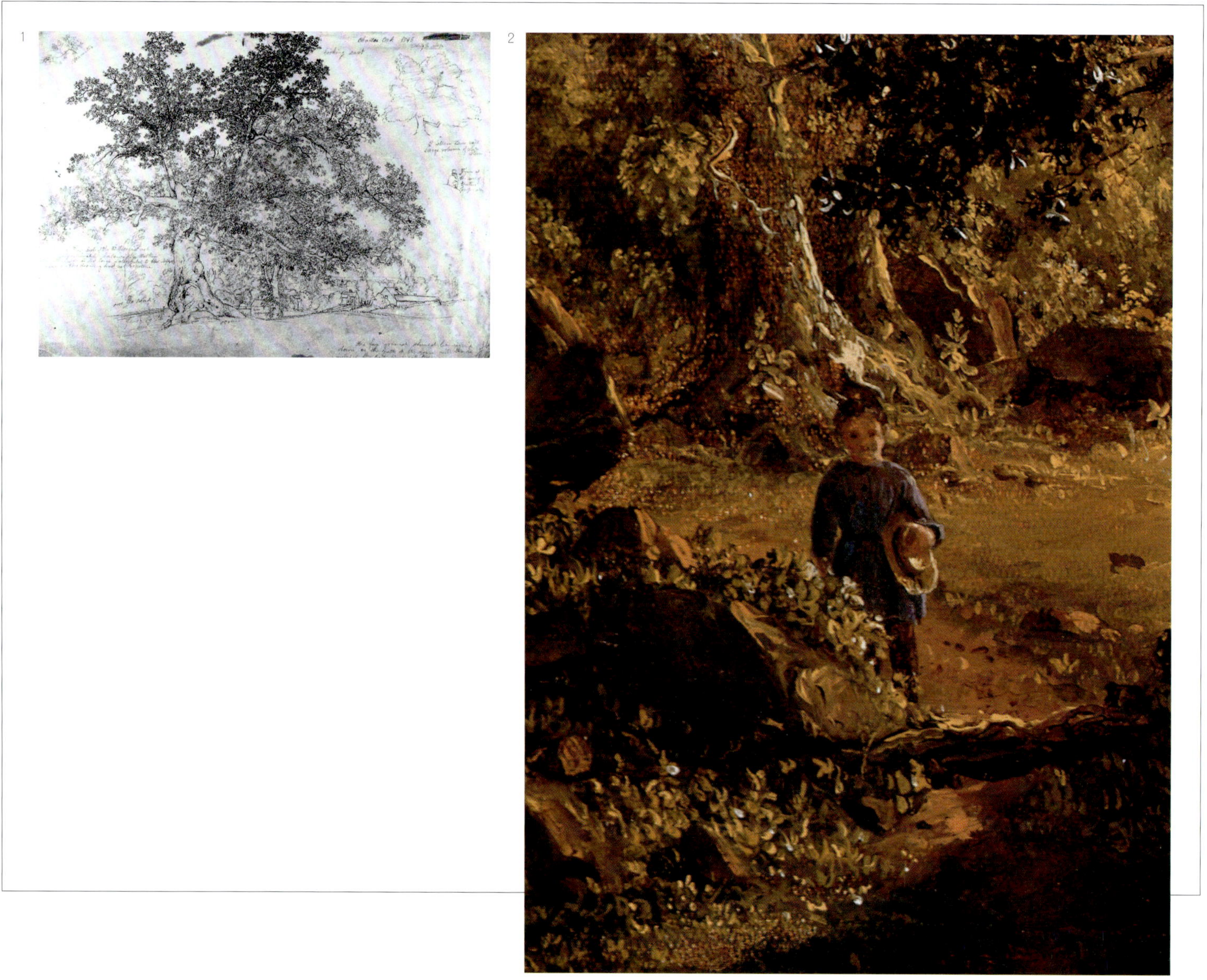

July Sunset at the Academy in 1847, in part, to establish an artistic lineage that would lead directly to Cole, but the compliment of *The Literary World* may have been more pointed than the young painter expected. *July Sunset* was no slavish copy, and Church had gone to some length to impose his own identity on the Catskill subject. He more or less proclaimed his entitlement to the region's scenery by planting a piece of his own native history right on the bank of Catskill Creek, a piece of Hartford, Connecticut, the mighty Charter Oak.[12]

No representative of the New York press noticed the Charter Oak. No writer recognized it as Church's proprietary claim to the Catskills, and no critic took it for the mild oath of independence that it was. And by electing to work in the Berkshire Mountains rather than at Cedar Grove during the summer of 1847, Church may have been conceding (for the time being) the Catskills to his famous teacher. Church completed his major Berkshires canvas, *View from Stockbridge, Mass.,* in late 1847, and made plans to show it at the spring 1848 National Academy of Design exhibition. But when Cole died suddenly in February 1848, a month before the Academy show opened, Church may have regretted distancing himself from his teacher. He still submitted *View from Stockbridge, Mass.,* but in May of 1848, Church painted *To the Memory of Cole,* an homage laden with his teacher's favorite devices, and no hint of Hartford. He visited Catskill in the autumn of that year, and remained a loyal and support-ive friend of the Cole family for the rest of his life.[13]

Church probably hoped that *July Sunset* would land in the home of some important New York collector, but it never got the chance. The press failed to notice the Charter Oak flourishing along-side Catskill Creek, but a Hartford native could scarcely have missed it. Before the 1847 National Academy of Design exhibition opened, Adrian Janes, Church's uncle on his mother's side, had already acquired the work. Like his nephew, Janes had recently moved from Hartford to New York, and *July Sunset,* part Catskills, part Hartford, part Cole, part Church, probably seemed resonant of his own chang-ing circumstances as well.[14]

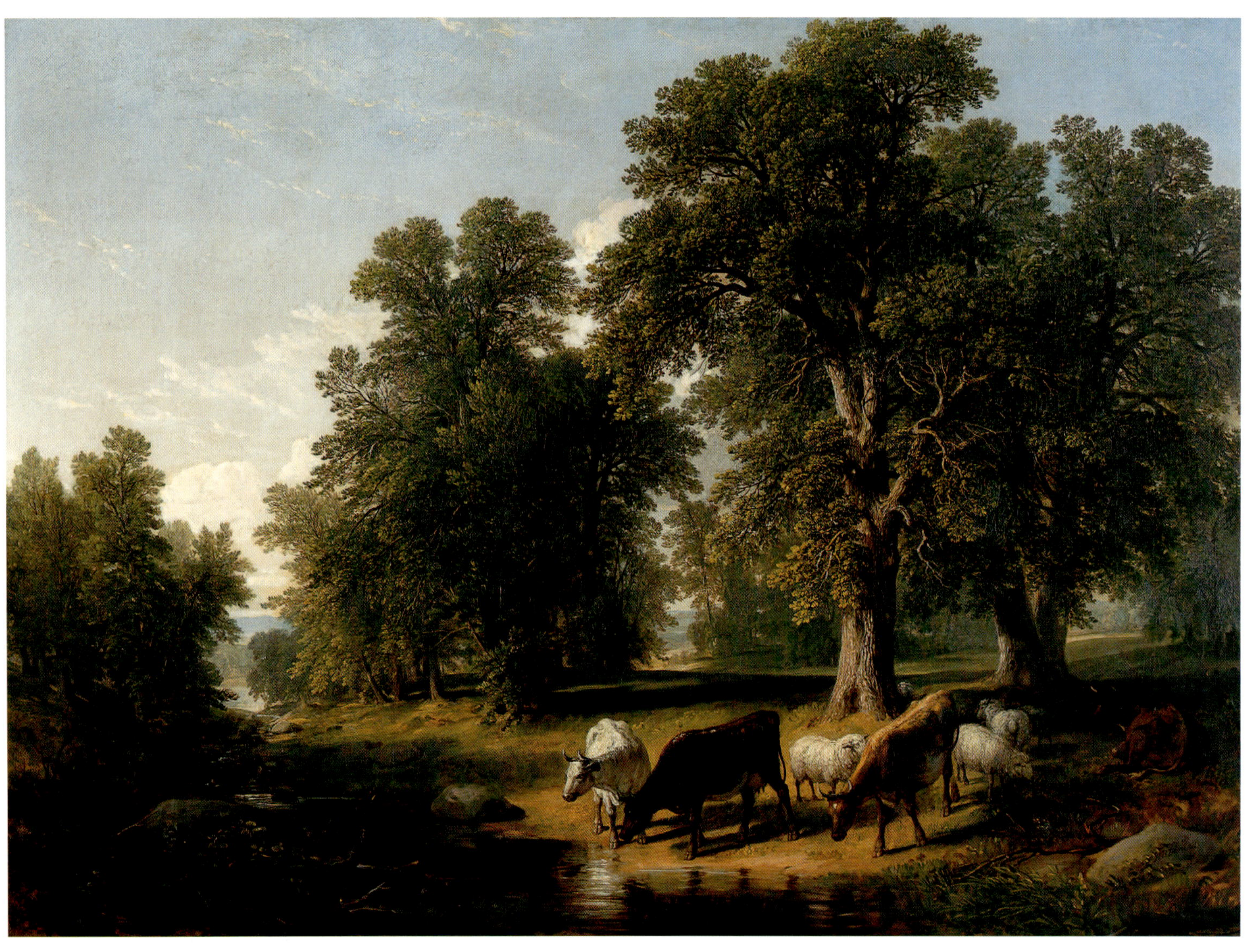

1849 (painted when the artist was
52–53 years old)
Oil on canvas
39 3/4 x 42 in. (101 x 106.7 cm)
Signed and dated at lower right:
A.B.Durand/1849

Early publications: Tuckerman, 1867, p.195.
References: Manoogian, 1996, p.21.

When Thomas Cole died unexpectedly after a short illness in February 1848, Asher B. Durand mourned the loss of one of his closest friends and his most supportive colleague. Cole's death also thrust Durand into a leadership position among the growing clan of landscape painters who were opening studios in New York. The role was not altogether unfamiliar to Durand. He had been a founder of the National Academy of Design in New York, and at the time of Cole's death, he had held the presidency for three years. But Durand could never have expected to become the authoritative voice of landscape painting in America. Although he was five years older than Cole, it was the younger artist who had forged the landscape aesthetic that had impressed artists and writers and seized the public imagination. Any painter attempting to capture America's picturesque scenery or rugged wilderness in the late 1840s, regardless of his age, had to acknowledge the example of Thomas Cole, and Durand had always done so willingly.[1]

Durand came late to landscape painting, having begun his professional life as an engraver. He owned or was a partner in a series of successful firms, but Durand aspired to be a painter, and by the time he met Cole in late 1825, he was already producing the occasional canvas. It was not, however, until the New York dry goods millionaire Luman Reed offered Durand a regular stipend in 1836 that he abandoned engraving altogether, and devoted himself solely to painting. And it was still a year later, after a sketching trip with Cole to Schroon Lake (see cat. 1) that Durand fully committed to the art of landscape. By then, he was forty-one years old.[2]

Durand spent the summer after Cole's death sketching in the Adirondacks and at Lake Champlain with his younger colleagues, John Casilear and Frederick Kensett. By early September 1848, the three artists had made their way back as far as Catskill, where they paid their respects to Cole's family and continued their sketching tour. While lodging at the Catskill Mountain House, Durand studied the nearby landmarks that Cole had helped to make famous in the 1820s – Fawn's Leap, Kaaterskill Clove, and Kaaterskill Falls. But he also wandered through the farmland on either side of Catskill Creek where it tumbles into Kiskatom Flats and the floodplain of the Hudson River.[3]

A Summer Afternoon was inspired by Durand's travels of 1848, and perhaps his walks along Catskill Creek. His handsome rural landscape attracted little attention when it was painted, but nearly twenty years later, the writer Henry Tuckerman gave it (or a work much like it) a fulsome description in his 1867 *Book of the Artists:*

'Summer Afternoon'…represents a quiet landscape, with water, meadow, trees, and cattle, all bathed in the soft, calm, and mellow light of a warm day, after the fierce heat of noon has subsided, and before the breeze of evening stirs the foliage. The sky and atmosphere, the vegetation, and especially the noble groups of trees, all breathe an air of quiet, brooding warmth and repose. All Durand's rare faculty appears in the latter, which are full of local character; the details of the scene are exquisitely true.[4]

While some writers chided Durand for painting scenes that were pleasant but lacked the drama of Cole's canvases or, later, those of Frederic Church, Tuckerman defended his friend's "patient study" and "industry." Tuckerman understood that Durand's steady nature and his careful scrutiny of the utterly familiar enabled him to produce canvases like *A Summer Afternoon,* in which he captured the sincerest truth in the most ordinary scenery and events. But in protesting Durand's workmanlike virtues so vigorously, Tuckerman may have underestimated the artist's powers of imagination and invention and inadvertently supported the arguments of his harshest critics.

In Durand's *A Summer Afternoon,* three cows leave the shade of a nearby grove to drink from a stream that may very well be Catskill Creek, while a fourth remains in shadow near a small flock of sheep. Just as Tuckerman suggested, Durand's pastoral scene convincingly suggested the stifling, airless lethargy of a late summer day in September. The water is still and the cows slink low as if to slide under the searing heat. All appears to be "exquisitely true," but as Durand wrote in 1848 of his stay in the Catskills:

With the exception of two days, the weather has been so cold that we have worked in overcoats and overshoes, and, in addition, have been obliged to have a constant fire alongside for an occasional warming, all of which I have endured pretty well, with no worse effect than a slight cold.[5]

John Frederick Kensett (1816–1872)

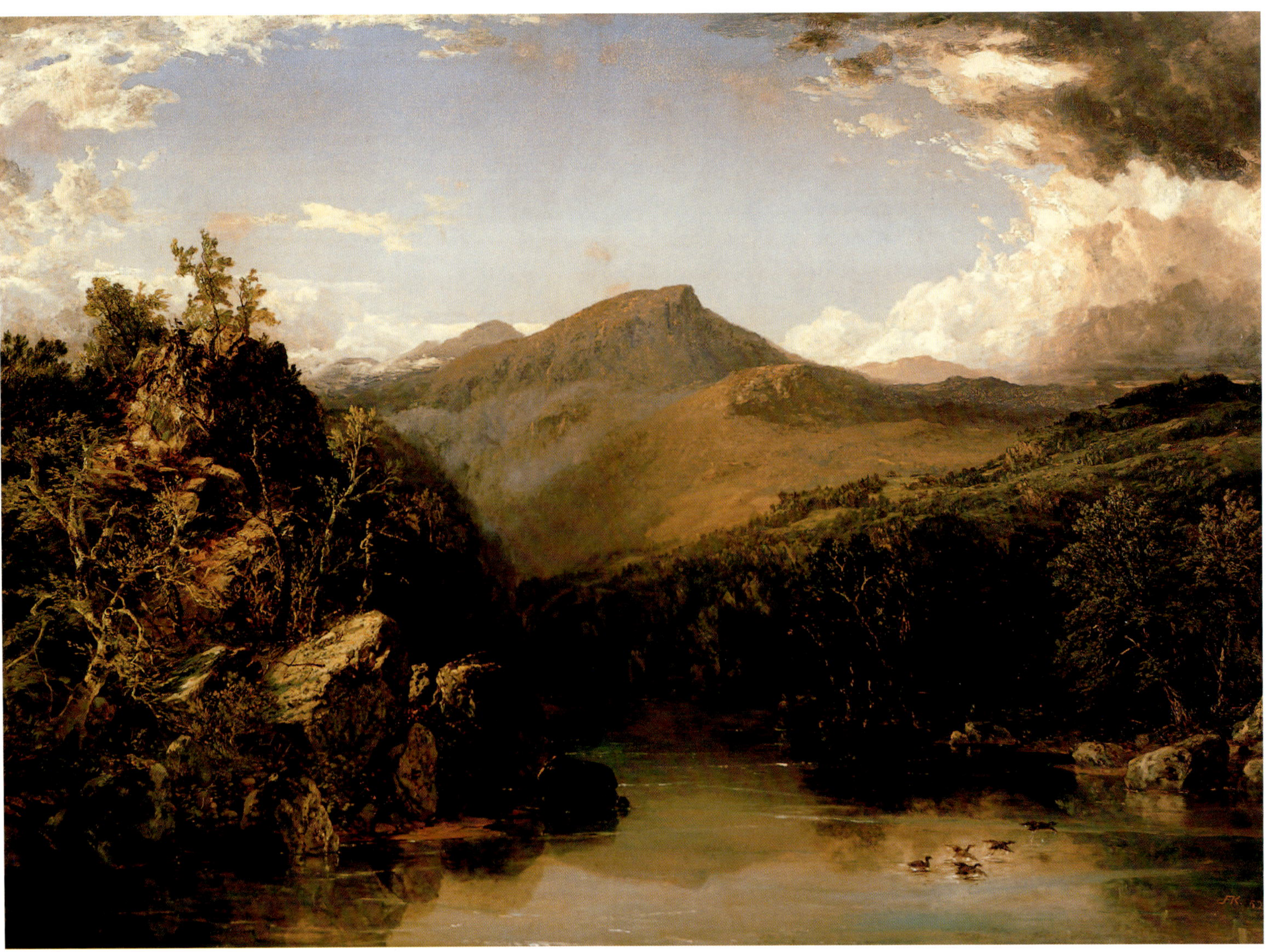

1852 (painted when the artist
was 35 years old)
Oil on canvas
35 ½ x 50 in. (90.2 x 127 cm)
Initialed and dated at lower right:
F. K. 52 (over earlier initials and date)

Early exhibition history: *Twenty-seventh Annual Exhibition of the National Academy of Design*, New York, spring 1852, no. 417.
Early publications: [George William Curtis], "The Fine Arts. Exhibition of the National Academy. II," *New York Tribune*, 1 May 1852, p. 3. Tuckerman, 1867, p. 511.

References: Manoogian, 1989, no. 4, pp. 20–21. Manoogian, 1997, no. 5, pp. 36–37 and 187. Wilton and Barringer, 2002, no. 6, pp. 80–81.

In the 1840s, landscape painting was poised to become America's first great artistic movement. The National Academy of Design, which had counted landscape painters among its founders in 1825, had become a mature institution in the 1840s, with a landscapist, Asher B. Durand, as its president. Civic leaders were increasingly eager to promote high culture in their communities. Such notable collectors of landscape paintings as Daniel Wadsworth in Hartford, Connecticut, and Jonathan Sturges in New York were among the first to champion art museums in the United States. The American Art-Union, a successful art subscription service and nationwide lottery, was founded in 1838, and proved an effective vehicle for marketing landscape paintings and broadening public appreciation for the arts. The Art-Union opened a gallery in New York, rented studios, published a periodical, and distributed countless engravings to its nearly 20,000 subscribers.[1]

In addition to institutional and commercial support, landscape painting benefited from Americans' increasing mobility. With improved roads and river travel and expansion of the railways, remote areas to which Thomas Cole and Durand had trekked in the 1830s became accessible destinations for a surging leisure class of American tourists. Innkeepers at Lake Champlain, the Catskills, the White Mountains, and Mount Desert Island all enthusiastically greeted growing numbers of visitors during the 1840s, and service industries developed to accommodate their every comfort and need. While modest excursionists contented themselves with small souvenirs and travel literature, wealthier pilgrims to these wilderness sites quickly became connoisseurs both of the picturesque scenery and of the paintings that captured its sublime beauty.[2]

Of course, the rising prestige of American landscape painting would have been unthinkable without talented artists to fill the demand for scenic subjects. Many of America's most revered painters of the 1850s spent at least part of the previous decade traveling or training in Europe. Even Durand, that quintessential American, made his one Atlantic crossing in 1840, while his younger colleagues, Frederick Kensett, Martin Johnson Heade, Richard William Hubbard, and Jasper Cropsey, spent much of the decade in Europe. When social unrest and talk of revolution began to percolate through France, Italy, and the Germanic states in 1847, many Americans artists returned to the United States before Europe's explosive year of 1848. Most opened studios in New York, joining younger colleagues like Frederic Church and Sanford Gifford in creating a significant new school of landscape painters based in Manhattan.

By 1848, the streets of New York hummed with the ambition of talented young artists. But when the dean of American landscapists, Thomas Cole, died unexpectedly in February, some feared that the gathering momentum of the 1840s might dissipate without his leadership. Cole's untimely passing was deeply mourned by his fellow painters, but the loss of so great a figure reverberated well beyond his immediate circle. After William Cullen Bryant's moving elegy, the death of Cole came to be considered a national tragedy. As much as committed institutions, a well organized commercial structure, affluent patrons, and motivated artists contributed to rise of landscape painting in America, the death of Cole catalyzed a nation hungry for a cultural identity of its own. Far from marking the collapse of the genre, Cole's death reminded Americans that landscape painting was its noblest cultural pursuit.[3]

While in Rome, Frederick Kensett made impressive contributions to the 1845 and 1847 National Academy of Design exhibitions, and in 1846, he sold eight pictures to the American Art-Union, providing financial support as well as important public exposure.[4] But even as he remained in Europe, Kensett realized that the American wilderness held extraordinary potential for a landscape painter, and that his own future awaited him there. He wrote to his sister, "I long to get amid the scenery of my own country, for it abounds with the picturesque, the grand and the beautiful."[5]

Kensett was among the better known of the European-trained landscapists who returned to New York in 1847. Within months of his repatriation, he was in the company of painters, witnessing the impressive wilderness that he had extolled in Europe. With Durand and John Casilear, he traveled to the Adirondacks and Lake Champlain in the summer of 1848, and by September, he was in Catskill, paying homage to Cole. By the end of the year, Kensett was elected an Associate of the National Academy of Design, and made a full Academician in 1849. He opened a studio on Washington Square, and was invited to join the prestigious Century Club that Cole had helped to found in the late 1820s. In 1849, Kensett returned to the Catskills, and in 1850, he spent

Figure 1:
John Frederick Kensett (1816–1872)
*Landscape (Reminiscence of the
White Mountains)* (detail)
1852
Oil on Canvas
Manoogian Collection

Figure 2:
John Frederick Kensett (1816–1872)
*Camel's Hump from the Western Shore
of Lake Champlain*
1852
Oil on canvas
High Museum of Art, Atlanta, Ga.,
Gift of Virginia Carroll Crawford, 76.67

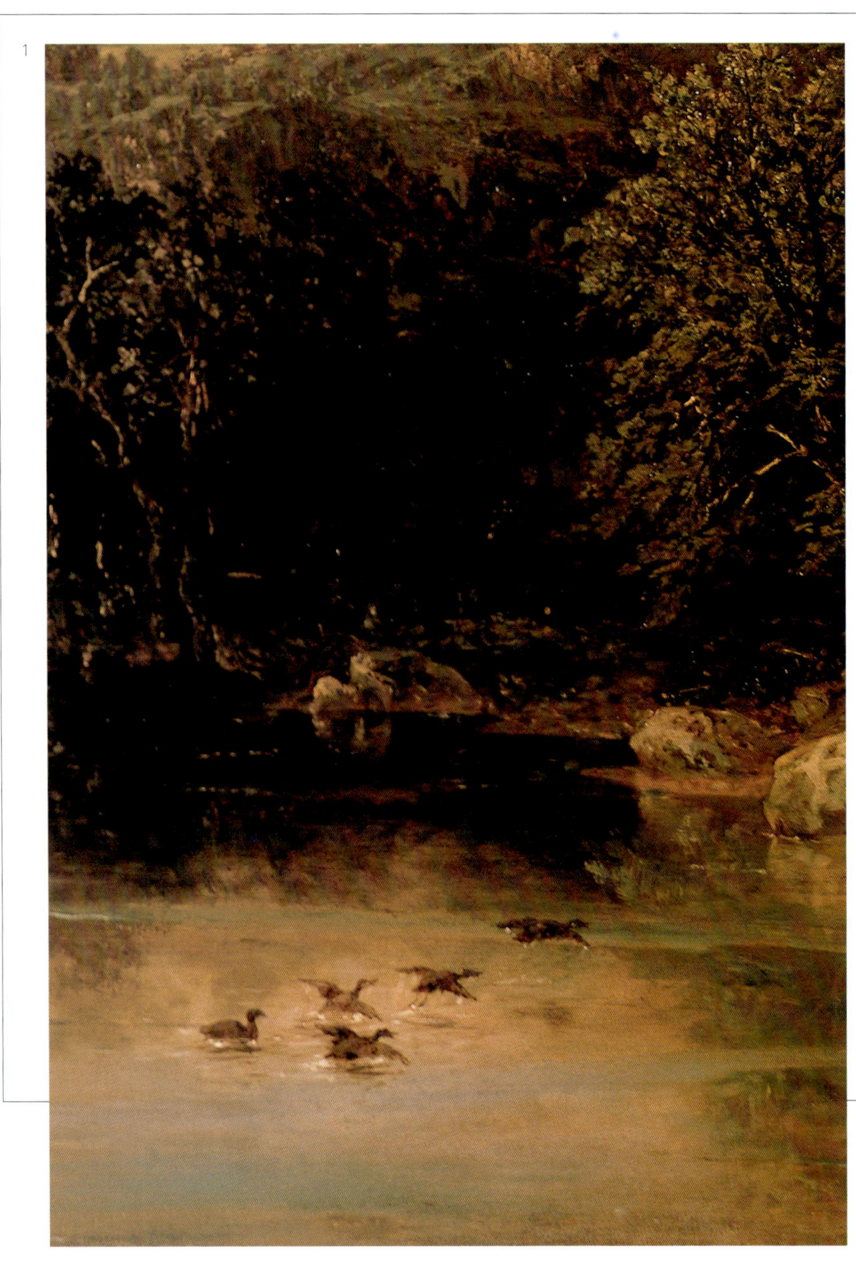

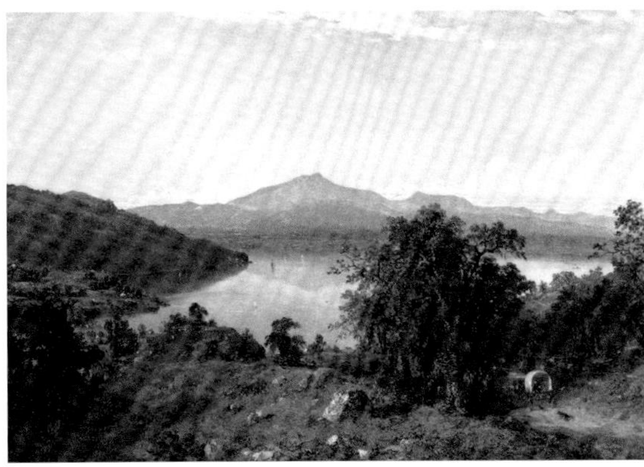

the summer with Casilear and Benjamin Champney in New Hampshire, where he first gazed upon the grandeur of the White Mountains.[6]

Kensett was hesitant to eliminate European subject matter from his repertoire. He had exhibited popular English and Italian views at the National Academy in 1848 and even in 1849 after his trip to the Adirondacks and the Catskills. In the spring of 1850, Kensett finally submitted American landscapes to the Academy exhibition, and by the end of the year he was at work on his largest painting to date, *The White Mountains – Mt. Washington*, which he presented in 1851. In addition to the profound Americanism of the subject matter, the painting was a statement of Kensett's mounting ambition. The picture was purchased by the American Art-Union, engraved by James Smillie, and printed by the thousands for the union's many subscribers.[7]

In the autumn of 1851, Kensett produced no fewer than seven major pictures, four of which were based on his recent travels to Lake Champlain, the Adirondacks, the Berkshires, and the White Mountains. Kensett's American landscape subjects of 1851 and early 1852 were derived from drawings and sketches that the writer Henry Tuckerman saw arrayed "on the walls of his room. The traveller [sic] recognizes localities at a glance."[8] But one work that may have confounded Tuckerman's tourist was a painting that Kensett based less on observation and sketches than on his memory and imagination. In the spring of 1852, among the works he exhibited at the National Academy was a canvas with the tantalizing title, *Reminiscence of the White Mountains.*[9]

The specific location that Kensett depicted from memory in *Reminiscence of the White Mountains* has been the subject of some discussion. Although he drifted to a reverie of the White Mountains, it has been suggested that Kensett was actually painting the peak known as Camel's Hump in the Green Mountains of Vermont. He had certainly seen Camel's Hump more recently than any of the White Mountain slopes, and at some point in 1852, he produced a substantial vista called *Camel's Hump from the Western Shore of Lake Champlain* (fig. 2). Kensett seemingly rendered the same range and the same high horizon in *Reminiscence of the White Mountains*, if from a much nearer vantage point. But even if so, it would be pointless to challenge the painting's title or to expect Kensett's suggestive distillation to be literal in its transcription of White Mountain scenery.[10]

More important than calculating the exact spot that Kensett remembered was his willingness to use memory as the bedrock for such a major landscape painting. By 1852, Romantic-era painters, poets, and composers had long argued for the creative virtues of dreams, memory, and the unconscious. Artists such as William Blake, Eugène Delacroix, William Wordsworth, Charles Baudelaire, Frederic Chopin, and in America, Edgar Allen Poe had quarried memory and the more mysterious recesses of the mind in the service of their particular expression. Kensett would have encountered any number of their ideas during his years in Europe. Certainly his paintings became increasingly meditative in the late 1850s, suggesting that the contemplative strain of Kensett's late marine subjects had a longer gestation period than is generally considered.

Kensett was aware too that American landscape painters were increasingly frustrated by the public hunger for geographic specificity. Even the accommodating Durand tried to reconcile the concepts of realism and idealism in landscape painting, insisting that the distinction was not as great as it seemed. When George Inness was asked about the specific locale of one of his landscapes, the painter barked, "[D]o you suppose I illustrate guide-books? That's a picture."[11] The decision then by Kensett to create a reminiscence of the White Mountains rather than a straightforward representation served more than one purpose. It allowed him to explore the deeper regions of his own imagination while avoiding the issue of literalness that plagued his contemporaries.

When Kensett exhibited *Reminiscence of the White Mountains* at the National Academy of Design in 1852, the painting was trumpeted by the critic George William Curtis as "one of the three finest landscapes in the exhibition."[12] Curtis was part of a growing enclave of young and outspoken New York writers, and he recognized that Kensett was not simply following the conventions of Cole. Although he said nothing of Kensett's use of memory or about the specific location rendered, Curtis understood that he was expanding the language of landscape painting as much with his intellect as with his brush.[13]

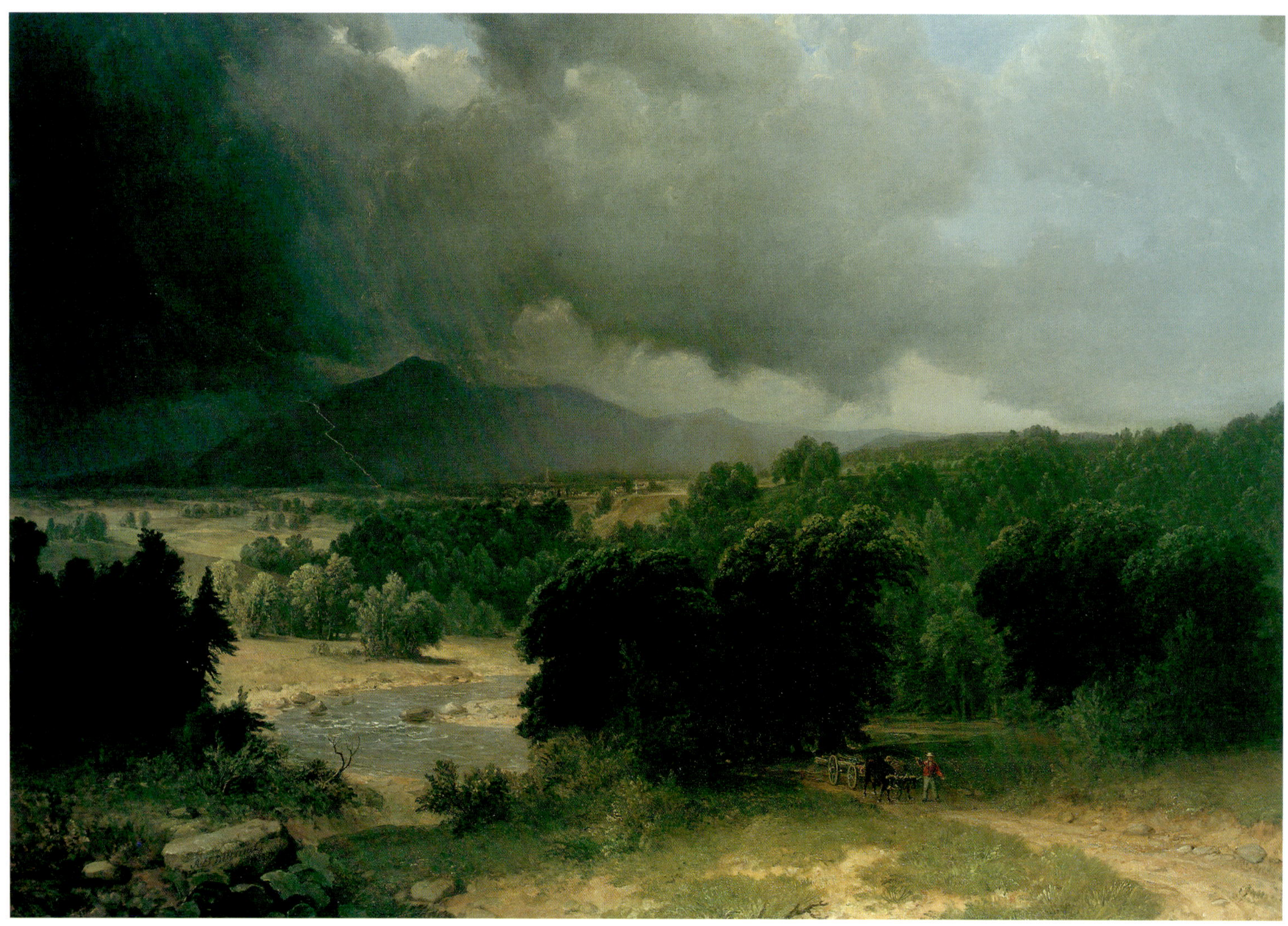

1854 (painted when the artist
was 57 years old)
Oil on canvas
33⅛ x 48⅛ in. (84.2 x 122.2 cm)
Signed and dated at lower left:
A B Durand/1854

Early provenance: From the artist,
New York, 1854; (probably sold) to H. K.
Brown, Newburgh, N.Y., 1854.

Early exhibition history: *Twenty-ninth
Annual Exhibition of the National
Academy of Design,* New York, spring
1854, no. 386.

Early publications: "Fine Arts.
National Academy of Design. II," *The
Albion,* 15 April 1854, p. 177. "The Fine
Arts. Exhibition of the National

Academy. II," *New-York Tribune,* 22 April
1854, p. 3. Tuckerman, 1867, p. 189.

References: Manoogian, 1989, no. 5,
pp. 22–23. Manoogian, 1997, no. 7, pp. 40–41
and 187–88. Manoogian, 1999, no. 14,
pp. 46–47.

By the 1850s, Asher B. Durand was the acknowledged leader of a growing school of New York–based landscape painters, who seemed to gain aesthetic ambition and commercial momentum with each new picture. He was by far the most senior of the group, and had helped to found the very institutions and organizations that his younger colleagues would have taken for granted, including the National Academy of Design and the Century Association. Unassuming by nature, Durand often appeared to be almost surprised by his own success amid so many talented young painters. But at the same time, he was also invigorated by their company and inspired by the challenge of their audacious talent.

In 1851, Jasper Cropsey and Frederic Church had both exhibited impressive storm scenes at the National Academy of Design, and Frederick Kensett's *Reminiscence of the White Mountains* (see cat. 5), with its threatening sky, was perhaps the most highly regarded picture at the 1852 show.[1] As president of the National Academy, Durand could not have overlooked the attention these storm scenes had attracted, and he may have painted and exhibited *June Shower* in 1854 to demonstrate his own facility in recording meteorological phenomena. But the storm in *June Shower* is merely the most obvious device among many, and while it may have reflected Durand's slim competitive instincts, it also served his larger meditation on man's ongoing quest for equilibrium in relationship to the natural world and its forces.

In *June Shower,* Durand divided his canvas horizontally into two nearly equal parts. The woods and farmers' fields take up one half of the composition, the gray mountains and sky fill the other. And like the earth and the sky, almost every other element in *June Shower* similarly confronts and engages its balancing counterpart. The storm has arrived, but has not reached the exposed vantage point of the viewer. The sky is dark, but nearly all of the landscape glows in bright sunlight. The scene's most compelling action, a bolt of lightning, strikes deep in the distant background, while the man in the foreground, leading two oxen and a wagon, is unhurried by the changing weather. The surface condition of the painting has probably been altered since Durand completed it, but the sky is glazed in a varnish that conveys convincing dampness while the pigment he used for the grassy plain is dry and almost chalky by contrast. An exercise in balance, *June Shower* could almost be a surrogate for Durand himself, a steady and patient figure, who, like the tranquil woodsman in the foreground, owed his living to the humble landscape in which he worked.

It is not surprising that Durand produced a painting of such conceptual sophistication in 1854. As he approached the twilight of a brilliant career, Durand thought a good deal about the tenets of American landscape painting, meditations that culminated in an 1855 series of letters published in *The Crayon.* In one of his more famous dispatches, he contemplated the American landscape both as a provider of human sustenance and as God's most brilliant work of art. Durand's use of contrasting dualities informed his well-conceived paintings of the 1850s, including *June Shower,* but it was also an effective rhetorical device that he adapted for his writings of the same period:

> *The external appearance of this our dwelling-place, apart from its wondrous structure and functions that minister to our well-being, is fraught with lessons of high and holy meaning, only surpassed by the light of Revelation. It is impossible to contemplate with right-minded, reverent feeling, its inexpressible beauty and grandeur, for ever assuming new forms of impressiveness under the varying phrases of cloud and sunshine, time and season, without arriving at the conviction*
>
> *— That all which we behold*
> *Is full of blessings —*
>
> *that the Great Designer of the glorious pictures has placed them before us as types of the Divine attributes, and we insensibly, as it were, in our daily contemplations,*
>
> *— To the beautiful order of His works*
> *Learn to conform the order of our lives.*[2]

Figure 1:
Asher Brown Durand (1796–1886)
June Shower (detail)
1854
Oil on canvas
Manoogian Collection

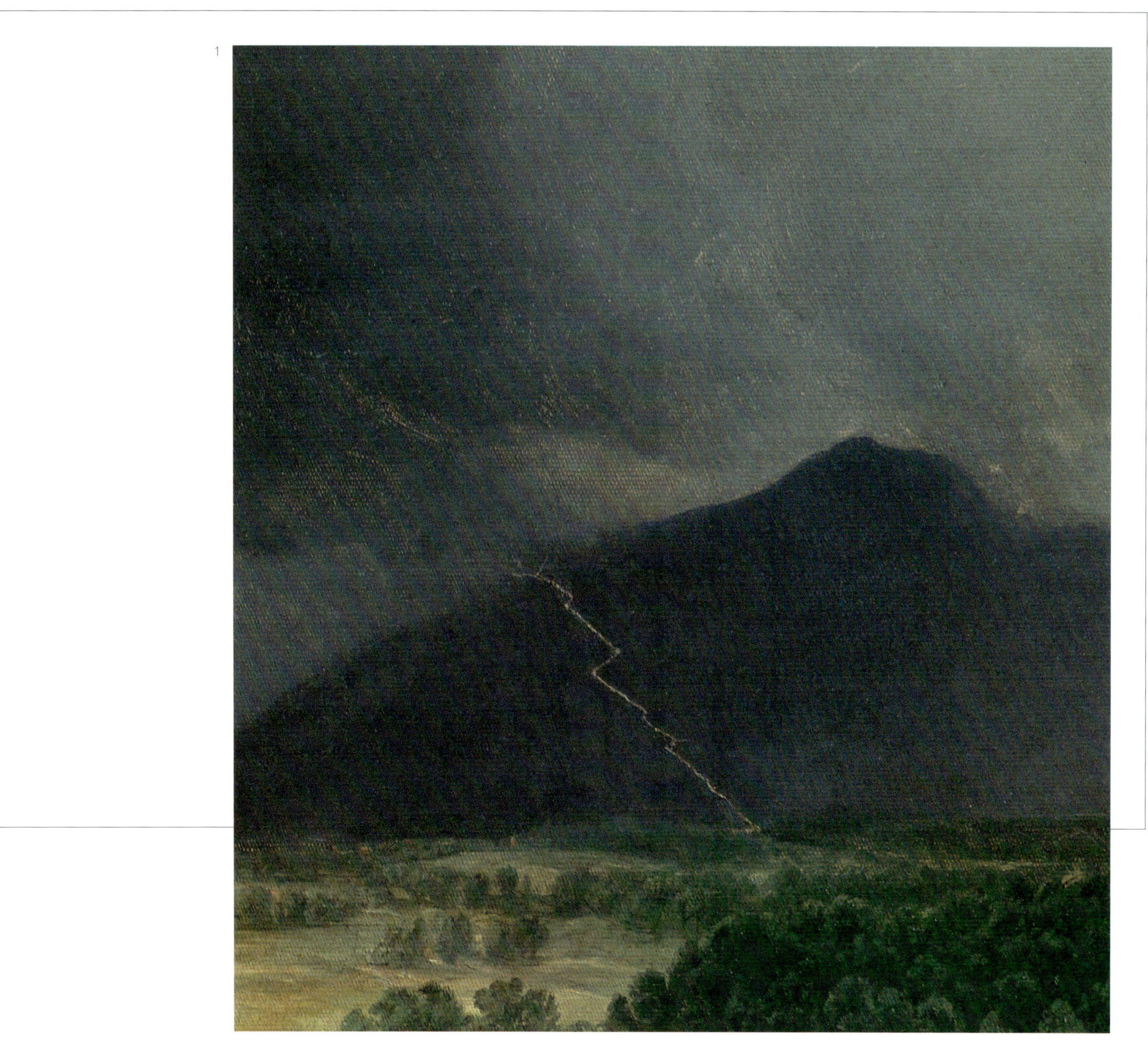

Years later, Henry Tuckerman remembered *June Shower* and described it in his essay on Durand in *The Book of the Artists.* While not speaking directly to the dialogue between pictorial elements, Tuckerman knew that balance and harmony were essential ingredients of Durand's finest works of art:

> *Whoever has watched the advent and discharge of a thunder cloud, in summer… will appreciate the perfect truth to nature, in the impending shadow of the portentous mass of vapor, as it falls on tree, rock, sward, and stream; and the contrasted brilliancy of the sunshine playing on the high ridge above.*[3]

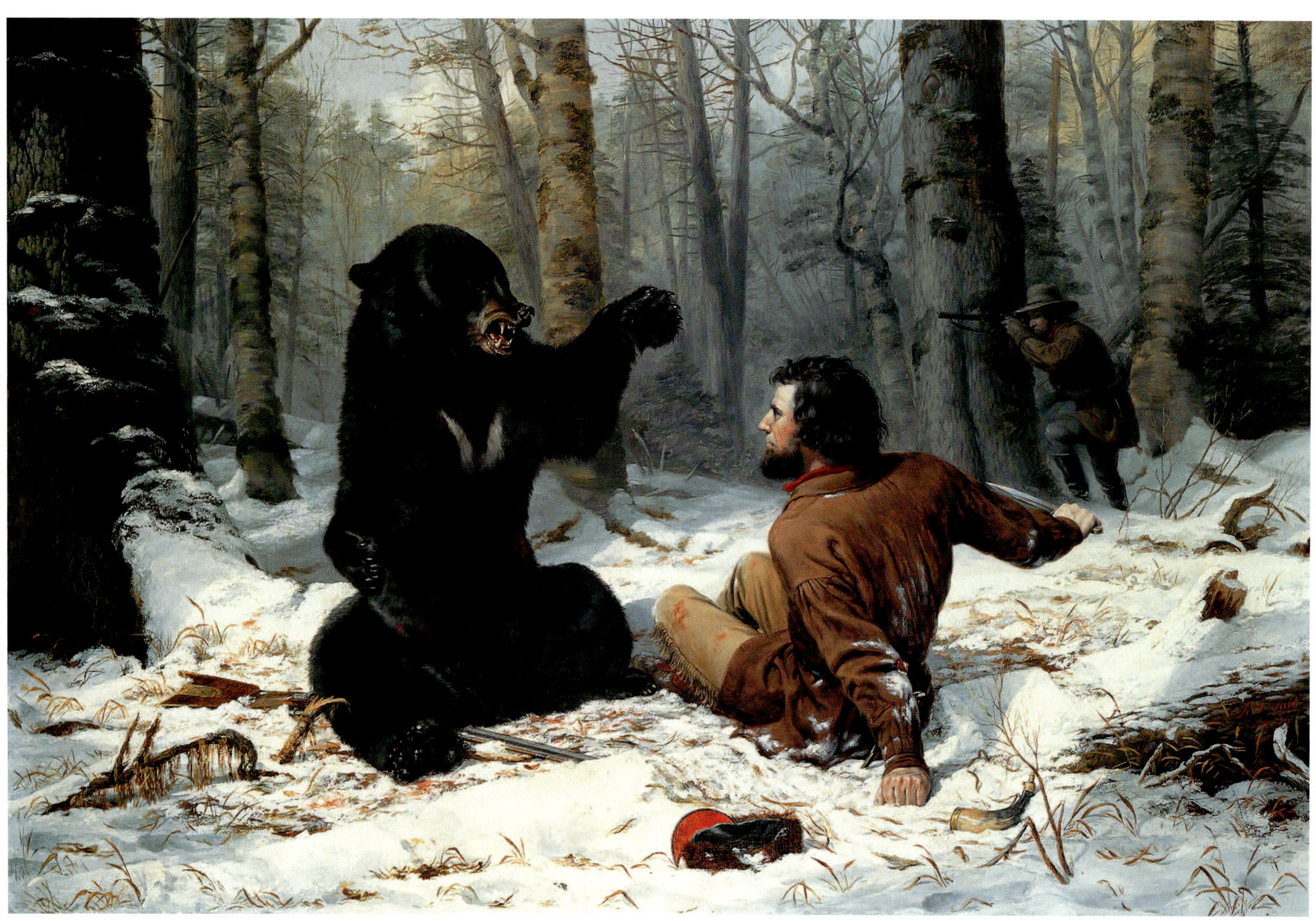

1856 (painted when the artist
was 36–37 years old)[1]
Oil on canvas
40 x 60 in. (101.6 x 152.4 cm)
Signed, inscribed and dated at
lower right: *A F Tait/N Y 56*

Early provenance: From the artist,
New York, 1856–58; (sold) to J. Campbell,
California, 1858.
Early exhibition history: *Thirty-third
Annual Exhibition of the Pennsylvania
Academy of the Fine Arts*, Philadelphia,
1856, no. 14 as *A Critical Moment*. *Thirty-
third Annual Exhibition of the National
Academy of Design, New York*, spring 1858,
no. 182.

Early publications: *New York Herald*,
23 April 1858, p. 3. *New York Morning
Express*, 4 May 1858. *New York Morning
Express*, 8 May 1858. *New York Daily
News*, 13 May 1858, p. 1. *Harper's Weekly*,
15 May 1858, p. 320. *The Crayon*, vol. 5,
1858, p. 177.
References: Manoogian, 1989, no. 29,
pp. 78–81. Manoogian, 1997, no. 28, pp. 96–97
and 194. Manoogian, 1999, no. 46, pp. 110–11.

Although Arthur Fitzwilliam Tait enjoyed some success as a journey-man painter and a lithographer in his native Liverpool, England, he sailed for the United States in 1850, believing that his prospects were more promising in America.[2] Tait's gamble paid dividends almost immediately. He arrived in New York at a moment when the visual arts were flourishing in the city, and indeed throughout much of the nation. His advanced technical knowledge of lithography made him an appealing artist to the publishing firm Currier & Ives, and their enormously successful ventures of the 1850s translated into instant acclaim and handsome remuneration for Tait. Moreover, his genuine interest in hunting, fishing, and sporting expeditions to America's abundant frontier coincided with a nationwide surge in leisure tourism, including an onslaught of visitors to upstate and western New York.[3]

If Tait was quickly absorbed into New York artistic circles, he was just as rapidly embraced by the culture of hunters, guides, and lodge owners who earned their livings in the Adirondacks. Tait genuinely enjoyed their rugged companionship, and by the mid-1850s, had developed an interesting symbiotic relationship with these outdoorsmen. Tait traded on their rustic existences for his most desirable subject matter, while his popular paintings, in turn, advertised their capable services to thousands of leisure sports-men in New York and across the country. Tait first began to paint the colorful figures of the Adirondacks in 1854, when he produced *Arguing the Point: Settling the Presidency*, which included a local guide, Anthony Sprague, a popular hotel owner at Chateaugay Lake, Jonathon Bellows, and other members of the Bellows household. The following year, he included himself and possibly the photog-rapher Mathew Brady as satisfied sportsmen delighted by the Adirondack bounty in the painting *Still Hunting on First Snow: A Second Shot*. The canvas was Tait's largest and most ambitious to date, and was met by nearly unanimous acclaim at the 1855 National Academy exhibition. Largely on the strength of the picture, he was elected an Associate of the Academy that same year.[4]

The perilous circumstance that Tait depicted in *The Life of a Hunter: A Tight Fix* marked something of a departure for the artist, and he may have initially questioned the wisdom of its chosen subject matter. A buckskin-clad guide has been surprised by a black bear, and in the ensuing struggle both have been knocked from their feet. They glare at each other and gather for another assault as a second man in the background aims his rifle, but holds his fire for fear of hitting his companion. It was a compelling contretemps between man and beast, but Tait may have come to view it as more dire than dramatic, and perhaps doubted the scene's potential appeal to his audience of sportsmen. Tall tales of harrowing encounters between men and bears were famous and even popular by 1856, but in almost none of these stories does the bear emerge the victor. When going up against Daniel Boone, Davey Crockett, or a variety of otherwise anonymous Adirondack woodsmen, the best a bear could usually hope for was a draw. Tait certainly understood the narrative arc of bear tales, and would have realized that his tableau was situated well outside its usual conventions.[5]

It was not until 1858, two years after it was completed, that Tait finally submitted *The Life of a Hunter: A Tight Fix* to the National Academy of Design in New York. By then, the crowd-pleasing Tait had made modest but significant changes to the canvas to suggest that the knife-wielding hunter held the upper hand over his ursine opponent. Well after the painting was finished and the impasto that described the bear's fur had dried, Tait returned to the picture and introduced strokes of red pigment to indicate three bloody wounds on the animal's great torso (the man was nicked just once on the left elbow). Although Tait's revisions to the canvas were relatively minor, they significantly altered the emotional tenor of the painting. The hunter remained in a "tight fix," but the bear's bleeding wounds indicated clearly that the woodsman's peril was much less critical than it may have been originally.[6]

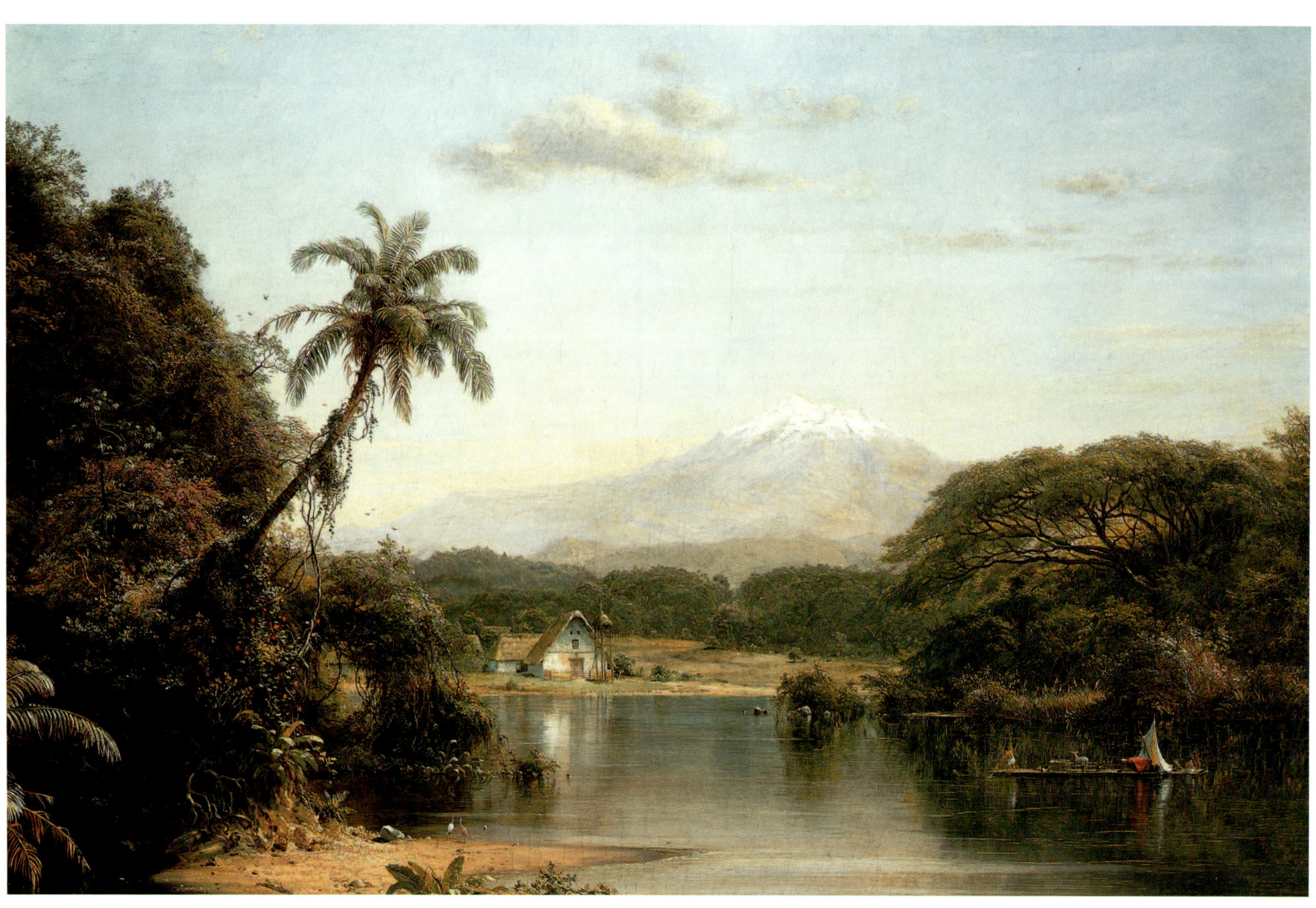

1857 (painted when the artist
was 30 years old)
Oil on canvas
24 x 36 in. (61 x 91.4 cm)
Unsigned

Early exhibition history: *Thirty-second
Annual Exhibition of the National Academy
of Design,* New York, spring 1857, no. 522.
Early publications: "Tropics Astir.
National Academy of Design," *The Home
Journal,* 13 June 1857, p. 2.
References: Manoogian, 1989, no. 19,
pp. 56–57.

When Thomas Cole died unexpectedly in February 1848, his long-time friend, Asher B. Durand, assumed the mantel of elder statesman among the growing community of New York landscape painters. But it was Cole's precocious student, Frederic Church, who most observers assumed would become the heir to the Catskill landscapist's legacy.[1] In many respects, they were right; Church was virtually born to greatness. He was intelligent, talented, and innately curious, but he was also well educated, well mannered and rich. As the painter Worthington Whittredge wrote in his autobiography with perhaps more than a touch of envy, Church "was fortune's favorite from the very beginning."[2]

And Church did not disappoint. Over the next thirty years, he became even more widely celebrated than his teacher had been, as he traveled the western hemisphere and erected a distinctive pan-American landscape aesthetic on Cole's sturdy foundation. His grand manner canvases depicting the volcanoes of Ecuador, the falls at Niagara, the icebergs of Labrador, and the poetic vistas of upstate New York and New England were at once Romantic in spirit, scientifically and topographically legitimate, and as rich in detail as they were epic in sweep. The private and public exhibitions of his great pictures were landmark events that thrilled audiences from New York, London, and Paris, and wealthy collectors paid then-staggering sums for the privilege of hanging a painting by Church in their opulent Victorian homes.[3]

Although destined for greatness, Church struggled slightly after the death of Cole, the weight of so much public expectation proving a difficult burden for one still in his early twenties. He had made a dazzling debut at the National Academy of Design in 1846, and at the 1847 exhibition he had again impressed critics with his utter mastery of the Cole idiom. But Church had difficulty developing a vision of his own invention, and his canvases of 1849, 1850, and 1851 were eloquent and at times brilliant variations on the Cole aesthetic, even as they remained trapped in the manner of the much regretted master. It was not for lack of trying to stake out some new territory of his own (see cat. 3), but regardless of where Church traveled in New York or New England – the Catskills, the White Mountains, or Mount Desert Island – the aura of his legendary teacher always awaited him.[4]

In 1851, Church sought new terrain in Virginia and across Kentucky all the way to the Mississippi River, and while one or two significant works came out of the journey, the painting of geologic curiosities and tourist amusements hardly suited his temperament and his taste for grandeur. Church's decision in 1852 to make an excursion to New Granada (now Colombia) and Ecuador may have been stirred by his reading of Alexander von Humboldt, the German naturalist, who had traveled in South America from 1796 until 1804.[5] But Church's plan also may have been motivated by a need to separate himself from Cole, and to find landscape scenery that not only interested him, but upon which he could inscribe his own vision, talent, and values.

Delayed for a year by political unrest in South America, Church and his friend Cyrus West Field finally sailed from New York in early April 1853 for New Granada, landing at the town of Barranquilla near the mouth of the Magdalena River. For miles and miles south up the great Magdalena, Church and Field wound their way by steamer and canoe through New Granada's marshy tropical lowlands and past impenetrably dense vegetation. Still on the Magdalena River in early June, Church and Field finally caught glimpses of a snow-peaked Cordillera mountain peak, probably the dormant volcano then known as Mount Puresé (now Mount Puracé). It was only as they neared the city of Bogotá that the two travelers finally abandoned the Magdalena, visiting Tequendama Falls, before turning south by southwest for the town of Popayán at the base of the Andes.[6]

Church and Field crossed into Ecuador in late August. After stopping in the city of Quito, they began their investigation of the great Ecuadorian volcanoes, Cotopaxi, Pichinchu, and Chimborazo, following the route that Humboldt had recommended. On his last trip to Europe, Thomas Cole had peered into the crater of Mount Etna in 1842, and captured the peak's impressive profile from the Sicilian village of Taormina. It was, however, Church, not Cole, who recognized the scale, heat, and fire of volcanic subject matter. For Church, the peak of Chimbrazo, which he climbed on 19 September, was more than a scenic device, it was a scientific marvel that spoke to the origins of the earth, and it was a sulfurous icon that suggested the sometimes angry power of God. Church's grand manner canvases of Ecuadorian volcanoes would brilliantly reconcile those seemingly antithetical forces as Cole never attempted in his handsome but tepid views of Mount Etna, and its narrow wisps of smoke.[7]

By late September 1853, Church and Field had reached the Pacific Ocean at Guayaquil, Ecuador, and began the long trip back to New York by way of Panama and its difficult land crossing to the Caribbean Sea. Church's experience of the tropics, the high Andean plains, the snow-peaked mountains, and the simmering volcanoes had fueled his imagination and inspired dozens and dozens of drawings and oil sketches. The magnificent scenery, the lush flora, the distinctive people, the animal life, and the vernacular architecture would provide Church with compelling subject matter for the next quarter century. But more importantly and more urgently, Church's 1853 journey to South America clearly distinguished his objectives and ambitions from those of his late teacher. Church would indulge certain affinities to Cole for the rest of his career, and at times even invite comparison, but with the public presentation of his first South American views, no one would ever again confuse the two painters.[8]

Cole believed in allowing subjects to percolate for a time before committing them to canvas, and Church may have chosen to exercise similar deliberation before producing his first, much anticipated paintings of South American subject matter.[9] It was not until the spring of 1855, eighteen months after his return, that he rather cautiously submitted four pictures to the National Academy of Design — a Magdalena River scene, a vertical composition of Tequendama Falls, the Cordilleras at sunrise, and a horizontal view of Cotopaxi. The selection was a coherent survey and almost a travelogue of Church's journey to New Granada and Ecuador, but the ensemble hardly satisfied the excited expectations of his impatient public. Moreover, Church's traveling companion, Cyrus West Field, already owned the views of Tequendama Falls and Cotopaxi.[10] Church may have been trying to suggest desirability by exhibiting paintings that were already sold, and to avoid any prospect of unpleasant collector apathy. But by showing works that already belonged to Field, Church drained the considerable enthusiasm the marketplace and collectors brought to the Academy's annual exhibitions.

In 1856, Church showed only one painting publicly all year, an Ecuadorian mountain scene. But his lack of exposure was largely the result of another important sketching tour, albeit one to a far less distant locale. Church made three separate trips in 1856 to Niagara Falls, and by early the following year, he had completed his most ambitious painting to date, the panoramic *Niagara* of 1857. *Niagara* fulfilled Church's early promise of greatness in the public imagination, as it simultaneously ratcheted the expectations that would greet all of his future canvases. More importantly, it achieved its lofty distinction on territory Cole himself had covered.[11]

As *Niagara* went on view at the New York gallery of Williams, Stevens and Williams in early 1857, Church was simultaneously plotting his return to Ecuador. The repeated reconnaissance necessary to complete *Niagara* made him realize that further and more focused scrutiny of the tropics and Andean volcanoes was necessary if he was to produce a South American subject of that same scale and majesty. Just weeks before departing for Ecuador, Church completed his most recent South American scene, *View on the Magdalena River*, and submitted it to the 1857 exhibition of the National Academy of Design. The painting may have been a reminiscence of Church's first sighting of the snow-capped Cordilleras from the Magdalena River, a moment that must have held some anticipation and delight after a month on the turbid waterway. From Church's vantage point on the sandy left bank, the river is a calm and wide expanse that leads to a chapel planted firmly in the middle ground. Its gabled roof rhymes with Mount Puracé, an airy peak that just emerges from the cool haze of the altitudinal distance.[12]

View on the Magdalena River, like most of Church's South American subjects, and indeed much of his work regardless of subject, bears the latent sense of having been painted by a traveler, which, of course, it was. But nearly all of Church's contemporaries also traveled in service of their landscape art, and their paintings somehow do not communicate the same arc of the journey. In his South American subjects, Church generally framed his views of the Magdalena River, of Cotopaxi, and even his masterful *Heart of the Andes* so they encompassed both the murky tropical lowlands and the thin crisp air of lofty mountain peaks, and more importantly yet, an effective sense of the distance in between. To experience his paintings was to embrace not so much the illusion of space, but the illusion of distance that had to be traversed.

Church's critics suggested that he traveled to find interesting
subjects more than inspiration, but that characterization was not
entirely fair. In Church's most successful pictures, he conveyed just
as much about the feeling of being a traveler as he did particular
information about the places he went. His paintings were sometimes
criticized for their excessive detail, for their documentary aspect,
and their indifference to the poetry, atmosphere, and charm of any
given locale. But as engaged as Church's paintings may have been
in pseudoscientific inquiry, the quality that they most effectively
communicated was the artist's own wonderment at the thrilling
experience of the utterly unfamiliar. Church successfully induced
that same feeling in his collectors, and much of his tremendous popularity derived from a shared sense of awe between the artist and
his adoring public.

By the time he produced *View on the Magdalena River*, it had
been nearly four years since Church's first journey to South America,
but he did not lack for inspiration. As he painted the murky waterway, the tropical foliage, and the distant volcano, he may have drawn
upon the anticipation of his upcoming second excursion to convey the
memory of his earlier sense of anticipation before seeing Cordillera
peaks from the Magdalena River. Anticipation fed anticipation, and
although he was still in his studio in lower Manhattan, Church once
again effectively expressed the wonderment of a traveler.

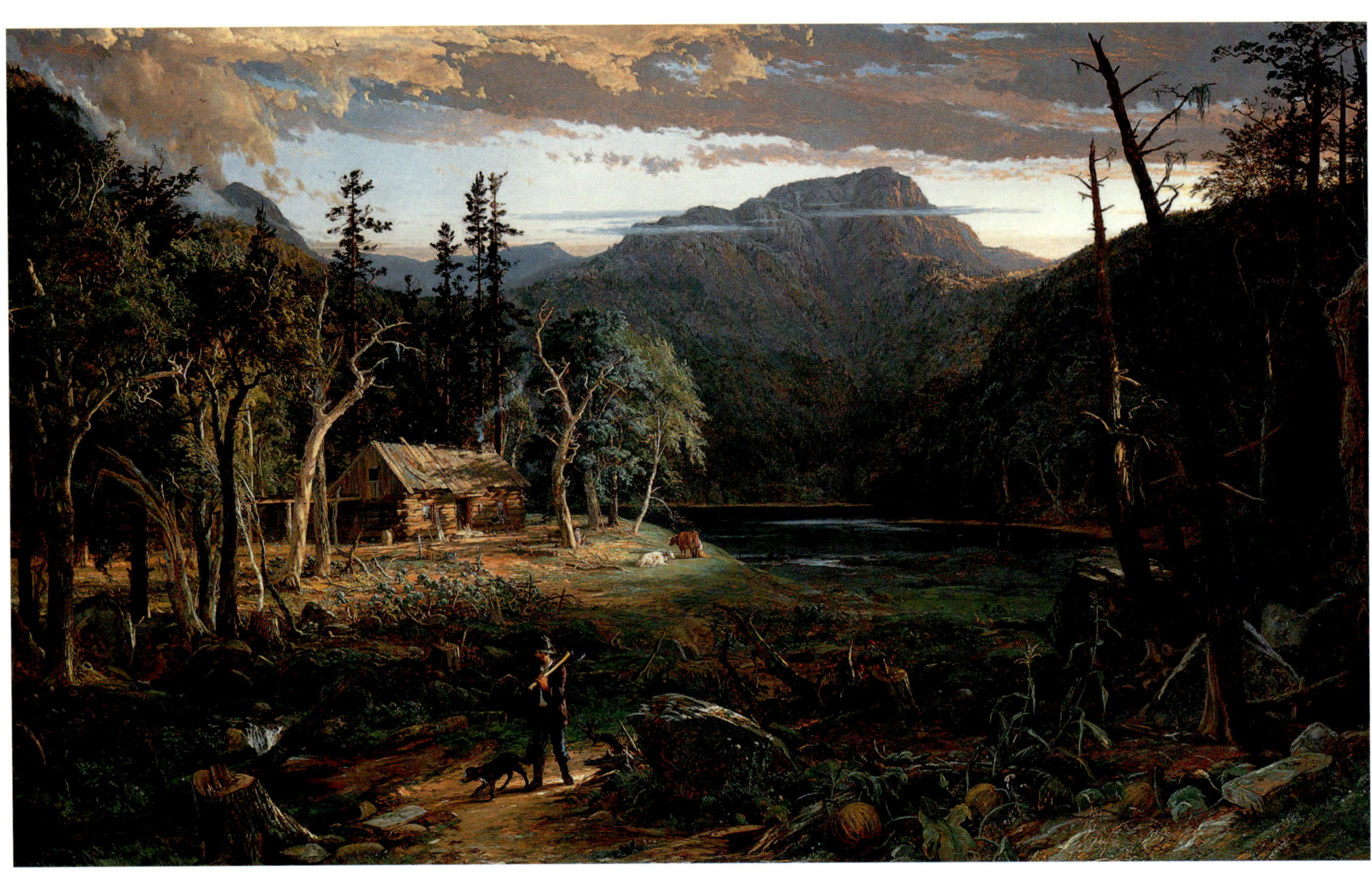

Early provenance: From the artist,
London, 1858; (sold by W. B. Huggins,
Glasgow) to a private collector, Glasgow,
Scotland, c. 10 March 1859.

Early exhibition history: *Annual
Exhibition of the Royal Academy of Arts,
London,* spring 1858, no. 741.

Early publications: Tuckerman,
1867, p. 536.

References: Manoogian, 1989,
no. 1, pp. 12–15. Manoogian, 1997, no. 4,
pp. 34–35 and 187.

1858 (painted when the artist
was 34–35 years old)
Oil on canvas
42 x 70 ¼ in. (106.7 x 178.4 cm)
Signed and dated at lower right:
J. P. Cropsey/1858

Jasper Cropsey was something of an artistic prodigy, but he became an accomplished draftsman during a five-year apprenticeship with the New York architect Joseph Trench. The supportive Trench not only taught Cropsey the principles of architecture, but he also encouraged his young colleague's talent for drawing and even financed his training in watercolor and oil painting. Cropsey proved an adept student, and by 1843, just after his twentieth birthday, his first canvas was accepted for the annual exhibition of the National Academy of Design. He contributed five paintings to the Academy show the following year, and on the strength of those pictures, he was elected an associate member.[1]

In 1845, Cropsey abandoned his fledgling architectural practice to devote himself exclusively to landscape painting. In August of that year, he went to the town of Catskill to pay his respects to Thomas Cole, and to learn what he could from the artist whose work had so deeply influenced his own early efforts. But most of Cropsey's days in Catskill were spent sketching the local landmarks with Cole's gifted young pupil Frederic Church. Perhaps Cropsey could not afford the tuition that Church's wealthy father paid to Cole, or having already labored through one long apprenticeship, he may have been unwilling to begin another. But in either case, Cropsey never became even an unofficial student of the great landscapist. And despite the unmistakable affinities between their two bodies of work, Cropsey never quite positioned himself in the legitimate line of promising Cole acolytes.[2]

Cropsey did, however, continue along Cole's well traveled path. His landscapes of the 1840s owed much to the older painter's example, he wrote a discourse on the art of landscape that borrowed heavily from Cole's famous "Essay on American Scenery," and in 1847, he traveled to Europe, just as Cole had done at a similar juncture in his own early career. Cropsey visited London, Paris, and the Swiss Alps, before settling in Rome, where he rented a studio that Cole had once occupied. He may well have been working there by February 1848, when Cole died unexpectedly at his home in Catskill.[3] The death of Cole was nothing less than the loss of a national treasure. William Cullen Bryant offered a funeral oration that moved America deeply, and Cole's closest colleagues Asher B. Durand and Church painted stirring tributes to their fallen friend and mentor. Cropsey remained in Rome and missed it entirely.

Cropsey's European sojourn lasted for two years and it flavored his subsequent work just as Cole's tour of the early 1830s had magnified his own ambitions. In July 1849, Cropsey finally returned to the United States, and after a trip to the White Mountains, he opened a studio in lower Manhattan. There, he produced ambitious allegorical landscapes that drew in roughly equal parts from his experiences in Europe and from Cole's literary and religious landscapes. Cropsey's allegories attracted largely favorable notices, as did his far more engaging autumn scenes (another staple of Cole) based upon drawings made at Greenwood Lake, in the Catskills, and in the White Mountains. But for all his efforts to emulate the great landscapist, Cropsey could never quite duplicate Cole's success.[4]

After seven years of struggle in New York, Cropsey was determined to make a change. In 1856, he auctioned all of the work that remained in his studio and moved to London to test the English market for American landscape paintings.[5] It proved a fairly sound career move, but Cropsey remained dissatisfied. He attracted collectors and more frequent sales in England, but the middling prices his canvases fetched and his generally unimproved livelihood continued to be a disappointment. The following year, when his Catskills sketching partner Frederic Church exhibited his majestic *Niagara* in London to an onslaught of gushing praise, Cropsey realized that he too must elevate the ambition of his American scenes and the size in which he painted them.[6]

Church had impressed English critics with a subject they believed to be emblematically American in scale and force. But Cropsey knew that Niagara Falls, for all its grandeur, was a tourist attraction more than a genuine expression of the American spirit. He was determined to respond to Church's play for an English audience, and to make the issue of authenticity the foundation of his contribution. Based on drawings he had made in the White Mountains in 1849, Cropsey produced a convincing view of a rustic pioneer homestead, *Eagle Cliff, Franconia Notch, New Hampshire* (fig. 1). By the spring of 1858, he had transformed that scene (or the idea behind it) into *The Backwoods of America*, his first attempt to present the American wilderness on a monumental scale.[7]

In *Eagle Cliff, Franconia Notch, New Hampshire,* and *The Backwoods of America*, the two makeshift cabins are nearly identical,

Figure 1:
Jasper Cropsey (1823–1900)
Eagle Cliff, Franconia Notch, New Hampshire
1858
Oil on canvas
North Carolina Museum of Art, Raleigh,
Purchased with funds from the State
of North Carolina, 1952 (52.9.9)

Figure 2:
Jasper Cropsey (1823–1900)
The Backwoods of America (detail)
1858
Oil on canvas
Manoogian Collection

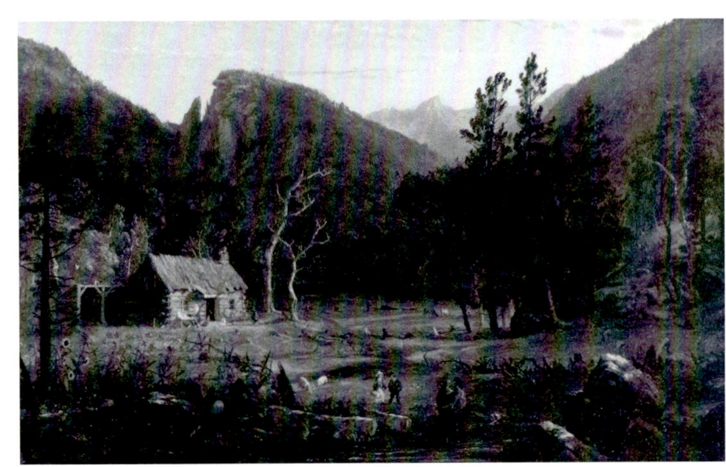

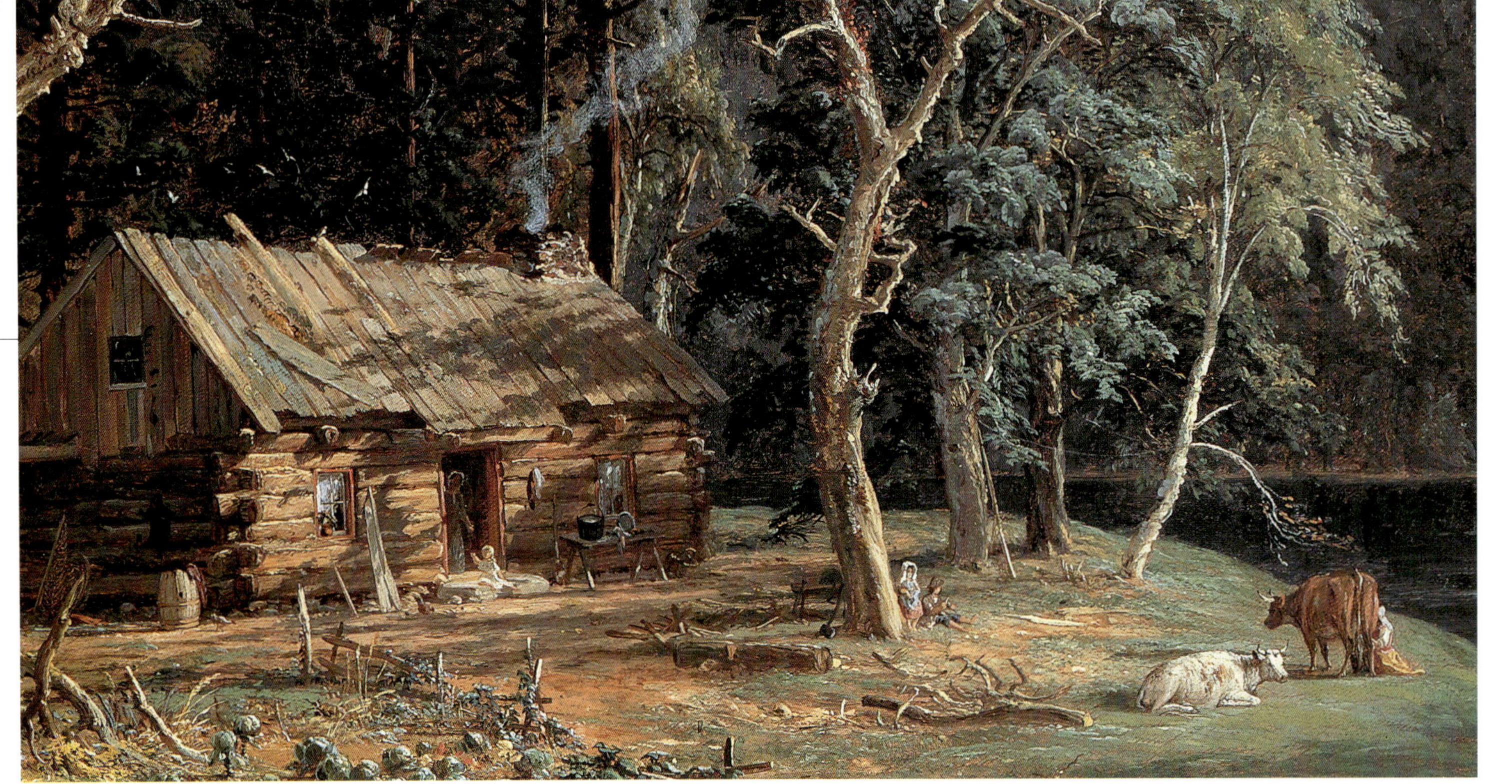

and so too are the frontier families that Cropsey positioned in and
around them. The two wilderness clans share tools and resources,
from benches to buckets and axes to fences, and from their garden
plot to their woodlot. It is not unusual that the artist would
borrow elements from a smaller painting to expand into a grander
scheme, but Cropsey was far from literal in his translation.
In moving his wilderness family from the homestead he had
witnessed at Franconia Notch to the mythic "backwoods of
America," Cropsey subtly shaded each family member's activity
to suggest the unfinished business at the heart of an authentic
pioneer experience.[8]

In *The Backwoods of America*, the pioneer patriarch is just
heading to the woods rather than standing alongside the product of
his axe, the giant birches he had felled in Franconia Notch. The man
with whom he conversed in the smaller picture launches a canoe
in *The Backwoods of America*, beginning a journey of his own (fig. 2).
The older daughter no longer carries a full pail of milk, but is still in
the process of milking. And the young son, moved from the foreground into the larger canvas's middle distance, carves a piece of
wood, prefiguring his father's labors and the woodsman's life he may
one day embrace. Each figure in *The Backwoods of America* labors at
some unfinished chore, and the detritus of pioneer life that litters
the farmyard, from the half-chopped log to the drying beaver pelt to
the unpicked crops similarly speaks to work yet to be done.

Cropsey exhibited *The Backwoods of America* at the 1858
annual exhibition of the Royal Academy of Arts, no doubt hoping it
would create something of the enthusism that Church's *Niagara*
had generated. But if the painting was noticed by critics and
admired by the public, as Cropsey later claimed, it remained unsold
when the exhibition closed.[9] Just weeks after the Royal Academy
show, he was despondent to the point of despair about his lack of
success and his perpetual shortages of money. He had been turning
out smaller and more marketable views of American and English
scenery to earn his living, but Cropsey understood that it took
paintings of scale and importance, like Church's *Niagara*, to establish an artistic reputation. During the summer of 1858, he wrote
to his wife, "if some good luck would come along that I could go on.
I should be so happy."[10]

Cropsey would go on, and he enjoyed some considerable
success in England, including a famous presentation to Queen Victoria,
but good fortune as he must have imagined it in the summer of 1858
would never be completely his. *The Backwoods of America* finally
found a buyer the following spring, when W. B. Huggins sold it to a
collector in Glasgow, but the transaction only netted Cropsey the
equivalent of $725. While it was his third most lucrative sale to
date, he had parted with his early masterpiece for a fraction of what
Church's major canvases were already attracting in New York. It
was an unfortunate pattern that would continue for much of
Cropsey's career.[11]

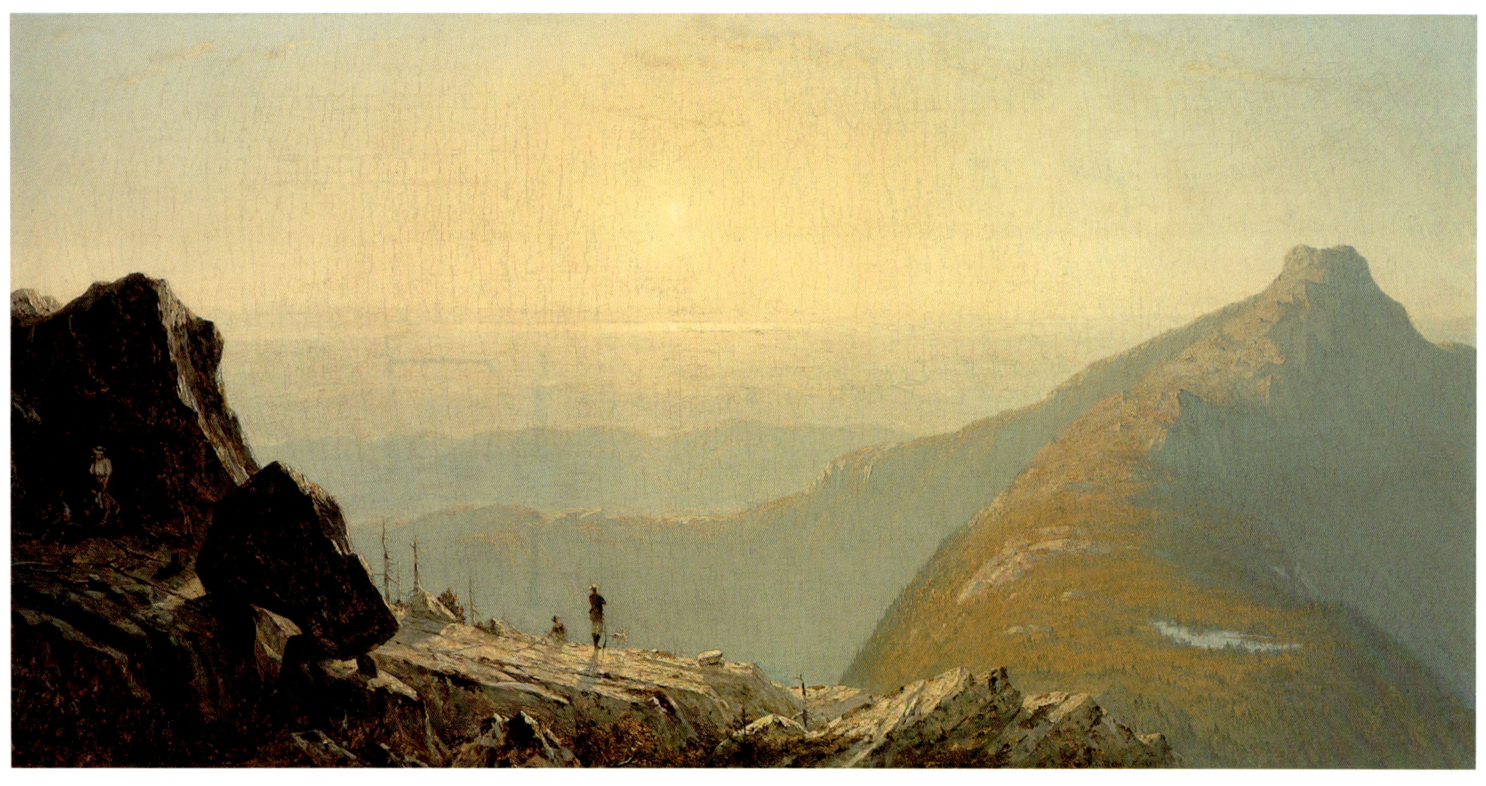

1859 (painted when the artist
was 35 years old)[1]
Oil on canvas
30 1/2 x 60 1/4 in. (77.5 x 153 cm)
Signed and dated at lower right:
S. R. Gifford 1859

Early provenance: From the artist,
New York, 1859; (sold) to Joseph Harrison
Jr., Philadelphia, 1859.

Early exhibition history: *Thirty-fourth
Annual Exhibition of the National Academy
of Design*, New York, spring 1859, no. 791.

Early publications: *The Crayon*, vol. 6,
March 1859, p. 91. "Exhibition at the
Academy of Design," *New York Semi-
Weekly Tribune*, 17 May 1859. Tuckerman,
1867, p. 527.

References: Manoogian, 1989, no. 15,
pp. 44–47. Wilton and Barringer, 2002,
no. 31, pp. 144–45.

In the summer of 1858, Sanford Gifford made his first American sketching trip after nearly two years of traveling in Europe. With the painter Richard Hubbard, Gifford trekked to western Pennsylvania, working in the hills and forests near the towns of Erie and Meadville. In July, they made their way back across New York State to the Green Mountains of Vermont, arriving at Mount Mansfield in August. The impressive views from the peaks of Mount Mansfield – the White Mountains of New Hampshire to the east, and Lake Champlain, just twenty miles to the west – were spectacular, but before the 1850s they were rarely seen by anyone but Native Americans (until they were driven away), hunters, and woodsmen. Although land speculators, hotel owners, and other concessionaires in the Catskills, the Adirondacks, and the White Mountains had labored tirelessly to make their frontier scenery more accessible to tourists, the Green Mountains of Vermont had remained largely untouched by developers, unrecorded by painters, and untrammeled by most tourists until the summer that Gifford and Hubbard arrived.[2]

In the 1850s, railroad lines had expanded significantly in Vermont, and the once difficult climb to the top of Mount Mansfield had been simplified by the narrow paths and the rock roads that were recently graded into its impressive slopes.[3] There may have been any number of reasons that Gifford and Hubbard chose to visit the Green Mountains in 1858, not the least of which was their increasing accessibility, but it was not their own convenience that the painters were considering. Gifford and Hubbard believed that if they did not travel to Mount Mansfield that summer, they would soon see it overrun with picnickers and leisure travelers, and indeed they were a year late at that. The same summer that Gifford and Hubbard journeyed to Mount Mansfield, the painter Jerome Thompson found his way there as well, and produced a genre tableau of attractive and well-dressed men and women enjoying an idle afternoon in the spectacular landscape that surrounded them.[4]

In Gifford's *Mount Mansfield* of 1859, four hunters and their dogs have climbed to a peak and set up camp for the night. At left, one man builds a fire as his companion looks on with a white clay pipe stuck in his teeth. Another figure emerges from a path below the peak, while yet a fourth man, wearing white britches, leans on his rifle and watches the sun gradually set beyond Lake Champlain and the

Adirondacks. There is no evidence of tourists or guides or mountaintop concessionaires in Gifford's painting, even though they were certainly there by the time he and Hubbard arrived. Beginning in 1858, travelers who climbed to the top of Mount Mansfield were rewarded with a comfortable bed for the night at the newly built Summit House, a soon-to-be popular inn. In his painting of 1859, Gifford rendered the so-called 'nose' and 'chin' of Mount Mansfield, the two peaks that bracketed Summit House. But he adroitly edited any evidence of the hotel and its guests from his luminous panorama. Only the man in white britches and his faithful dog are in a position to see the hotel, which would begin the process of civilizing yet another once remote section of the American wilderness.

Gifford had returned from Europe surprisingly little changed by his exposure to England and the continent. Although he had met John Ruskin, J. M. W. Turner, Jean-Francois Millet, and Thomas Couture, and seen landmarks of Europe's recent and ancient past from Stratford-on-Avon to the Roman Coliseum, his subsequent work bore little the effects of his remarkable journey. It may be that Gifford's trip to Mount Mansfield in 1858 played some role in purging that potential influence. Gifford produced at least twenty-one oil sketches and paintings of Mount Mansfield between 1858 and 1863, and in none of the works that survive does the Summit House or any trace of mass leisure tourism appear. In Europe, there was no escaping the profound physical and cultural influence that humanity had exerted over the landscape. Centuries of cultivation and civilization had assured that no corner of the continent was left unmarked or left free of human occupation. Gifford would increasingly seek American landscape subjects that were largely unspoiled, and where it was still possible to commune with nature unmediated by man, culture, and commerce, even if that were no longer possible at Mount Mansfield.[5]

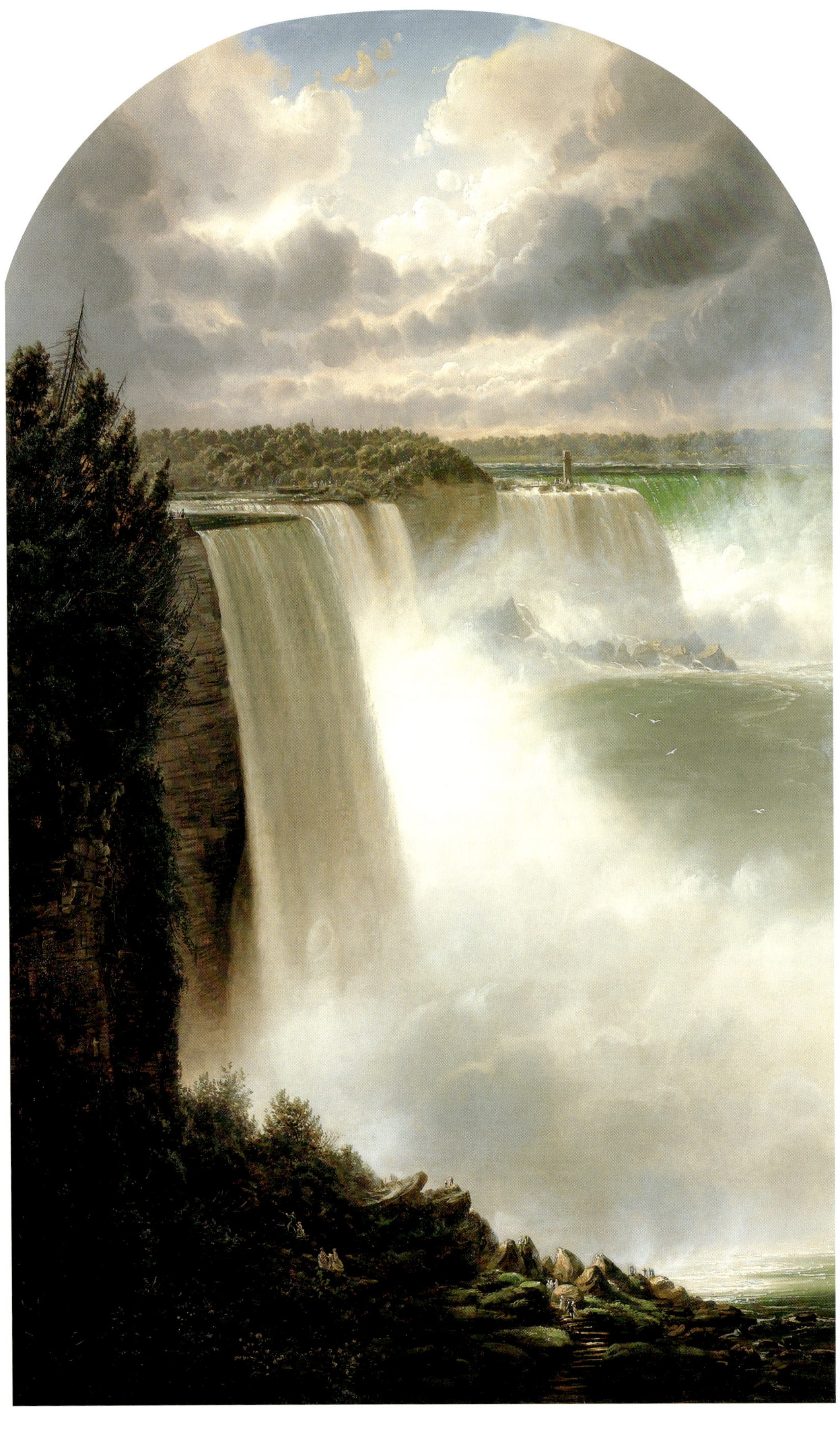

c.1860 (painted when the artist
was about 40 years old)
Oil on canvas
56 x 35 ⅛ in. (142.3 x 89.2 cm)
Signed at lower left: *Ferd Richardt*

Like so many other European artists who immigrated to the United States in the nineteenth century, Ferdinand Richardt was inspired by the scale and grandeur of the American landscape. A native of Denmark, and like Joshua Shaw (see cat. 2), already a well trained artist before he left Europe, Richardt eventually painted American scenery from the Adirondacks to Yosemite. But during his first decade in the United States, beginning in about 1855, no subject captivated him more than the monumental falls at Niagara.

It was impossible not to be overwhelmed by the awesome power of Niagara Falls. Native Americans had described the giant cataracts to the region's first European explorer, Jacques Cartier, as early as 1535, and a later traveler, Samuel de Champlain, marked the spot on his map in 1603, although he never saw the falls in person. It is generally agreed that Etienne Brûlé was the first European to visit Niagara Falls, in 1633, but the native Hurons killed him before he could describe the spectacle to his compatriots at home. It would be another fifty years before Father Louis Hennepin published the first eyewitness account of Niagara Falls, and it instantly became a best-seller.[1]

Stalwart American painters such as John Vanderlyn, Thomas Wentworth, and Alvan Fisher had made the difficult trek to the remote region in the early nineteenth century, but it was only with the completion of the Erie Canal in 1825 that Niagara Falls became a popular destination for leisure travelers.[2] Thomas Cole dashed to the falls in May 1829, less than a month before making his first trip to Europe. He wrote to his friend and patron Robert Gilmor in Baltimore, "Next Wednesday I intend setting off for the Falls of Niagara. I cannot think of going to Europe without having seen them. I wish to take a 'last lingering look' at our wild scenery." Cole hoped to fortify his American spirit with a gaze across Niagara, but that was only part of his reason for making the trip. Cole could not imagine presenting himself in Europe as America's most important landscape painter having never witnessed Niagara Falls, arguably his continent's greatest natural wonder.[3]

Cole would return to Niagara Falls in 1847, and Frederick Kensett, and more famously, Frederic Church made significant paintings of the falls in the 1850s. Richardt may have first traveled there within a year or two of his arrival in New York, and between 1855 and 1860, he apparently painted the cataract dozens of times from above and below and from both the American and the Canadian sides. By then, Niagara Falls was a much different place than it had been in the early nineteenth century. Steam-powered railroads had connected the city of Buffalo to Niagara in the 1840s, allowing tourists from New York to reach the falls in less than forty-eight hours. By 1847, the scenic wonder was attracting 40,000 visitors per year, and three years later that figure would double. Commercial development around the falls was already lamented for its vulgarity, as hotels and restaurants sprung up on both sides of the river. Souvenir stands hawked popular photographs (a recent invention) of Niagara Falls, and hosts of painters, not all whom were so gifted as Cole, Kensett, Church, or even Richardt, produced lively pot-boilers for the tourists.[4]

Richardt's *Niagara Falls* of about 1860 is perhaps his largest and most important interpretation of the landmark. Painted from the American side and most likely from Prospect Point, the American Falls pound downward at left, and Canada's Horseshoe Falls curl off to the right above clouds of spray and mist. They are separated by Goat Island and by Terrapin Point, where a stone tower stood during Richardt's era, and where a few brave tourists have crossed the rickety bridge to watch the rushing water from a perilously close position. Niagara Falls was more than impressive landscape scenery; it was a symbol of America's youthful vitality and potential for greatness. Richardt captured all of its grandeur and its awesome power, but without overly romanticizing the falls as even Cole, Kensett, and Church could not resist doing. Richardt's picture is teaming with tiny tourists, who clamor on the low rocks and take in the view from the bluff. They line the American side of Goat Island and cross over to have a look at Terrapin Point. While America's most important artists, Cole, Kensett, and Church, described Niagara Falls as the brilliant handiwork of an all powerful God, it took a somewhat more modest painter, newly arrived from Denmark, to render Niagara Falls as it actually appeared in the middle of the nineteenth century.

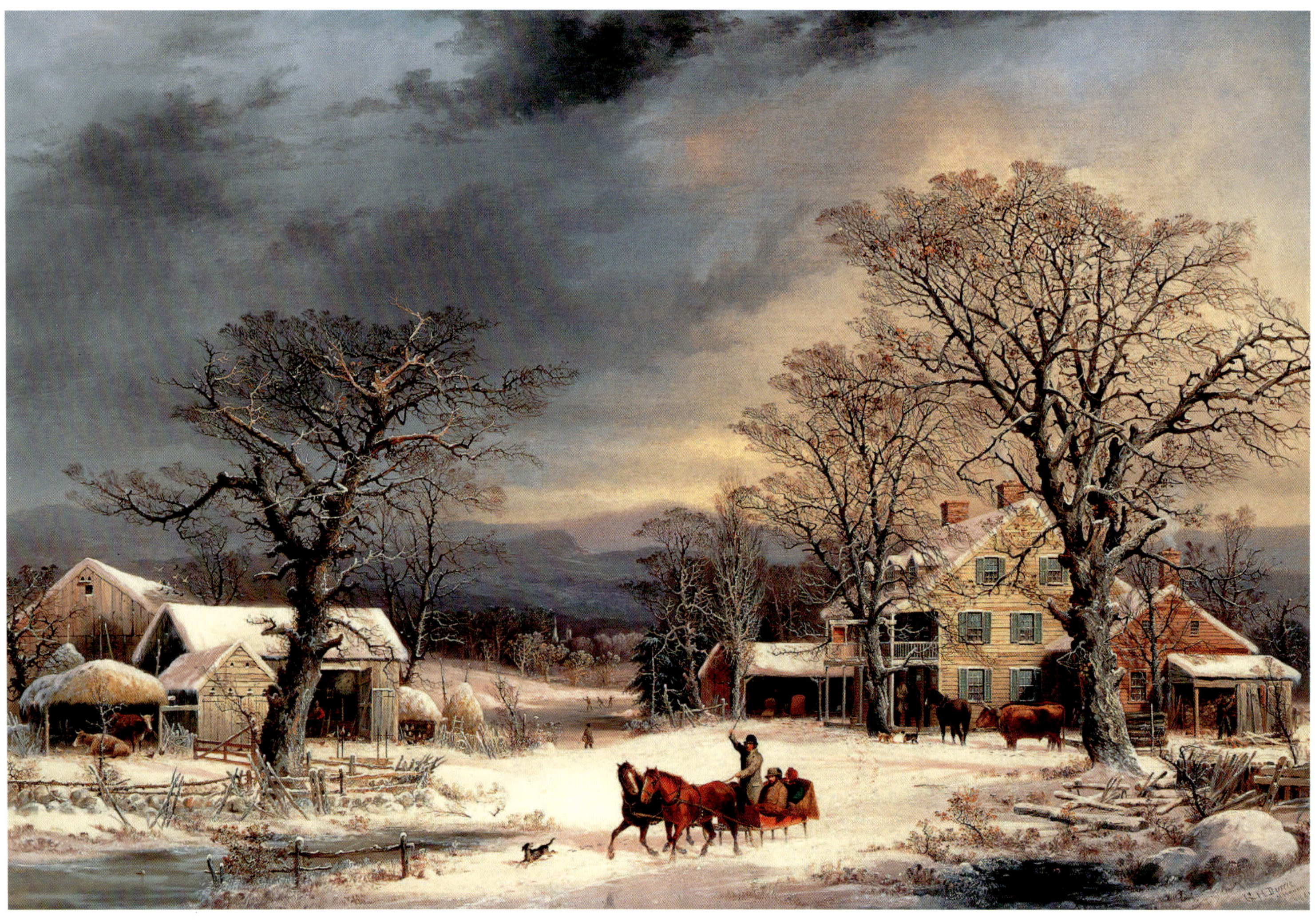

1861 (painted when the artist
was 40–41 years old)
Oil on canvas
36 x 53 ¾ in. (91.4 x 136.5 cm)
Signed, inscribed, and dated at lower
right: *G. H. Durrie/N Haven/1861*

Early exhibition history: *Thirty-
seventh Annual Exhibition of the National
Academy of Design,* New York, spring
1862, no. 478.
References: Manoogian, 1989, no. 25,
pp. 70–71. Manoogian, 1997, no. 30,
pp. 100–101 and 194.

George Henry Durrie worked much of his career in a New Haven, Connecticut studio, well separated from lower Manhattan, the commercial and intellectual center of the American visual arts. Despite his remove, Durrie became one of America's most popular painters of the mid-nineteenth century. There were artists of comparable ability even in New Haven, but the relationship Durrie forged in the early 1850s with Nathaniel Currier and James Merritt Ives, partners in a New York printing firm, would dramatically alter the course of his career. The enormous ambition and staggering success of Currier & Ives assured that Durrie's work would always be in demand and on the walls of thousands of homes across the country.[1]

Durrie's engaging vistas of the 1850s and early 1860s captured the ordinary charms of rural New England life under sanitizing blankets of pure white snow. His skillful placement of tiny genre scenes within sparkling landscape settings added the crucial element of human interest that Currier & Ives insisted was essential to truly popular art. But even though Durrie worked on a small scale to accommodate Currier & Ives artisans, much of the animating detail in his work was obscured by the vagaries of the chromolithography process. In the early 1860s, Durrie may have become frustrated by the frequently coarse reproduction of his finely wrought canvases, and considered shifting his professional ambitions away from the populist methods of Currier & Ives.[2]

Although ensconced in New Haven, Durrie would have been aware of the growing fashion for landscape painting in New York and the ballooning reputations of his native-Connecticut colleagues, Frederic Church and Frederick Kensett. In 1861, Durrie painted *The Half-Way House*, a rural inn and adjacent outbuildings set in the snowy Connecticut landscape under a gray winter sky. The scene brooked no new thematic territory, but in scale and in its elaborately embroidered detail, the canvas was by far Durrie's most ambitious work. In the spring of 1862, he sent *The Half-Way House* to the annual exhibition of the National Academy of Design, hoping to attract positive notices in the press, the respect of his colleagues, and perhaps the eye of an art collector.[3]

In *The Half-Way House*, Durrie rendered the Connecticut landscape with more care and textural fluency than he typically achieved in his small panels for Currier & Ives. The bare trees and scruffy brush, the rail fences and snow-packed roofs were picturesque but relatively uncontrived in their simple arrangement. The frozen snow was no expedient to cover acres of canvas with flat white paint, but a symphony of carefully modulated creams and grays. And the distant hills and sky were infused with a convincing sense of winter atmosphere. But for all of this expansive ambition, Durrie could not resist filling his newly opened landscape with the genre elements that made his work for Currier & Ives so popular. *The Half-Way House* included no fewer than six separate figural groupings, and even the animals bore the familiar attitudes of narrative painting.

In part because of artists like Durrie, snow scenes became increasingly popular in the 1860s, not just in commercial arenas such as Currier & Ives, but in the annual exhibitions of the National Academy of Design. As the Civil War altered the course of American life and ravaged the American landscape, the nation endowed familiar regional traditions with new poignancy, and even local weather patterns took on ideological significance. Blankets of snow, so common in the North, so rare in the South, were transformed by artists and poets into persuasive symbols of Northern continuity and the solidity of the Union.[4]

Unfortunately, Durrie did not benefit from the growing popularity of snow scenes in the Union north, and was unable to transform the perception of his art. *The Half-Way House* does not seem to have found a buyer at the National Academy of Design in 1862, and may have been among the works that Durrie sold in December of that year at Snedicor and Company, a New York auction house. Sadly, there would be only limited second opportunities for Durrie; he died after a brief illness in 1863.[5]

13   AUTUMN, LAKE GEORGE   Louis Rémy Mignot (1831–1870)

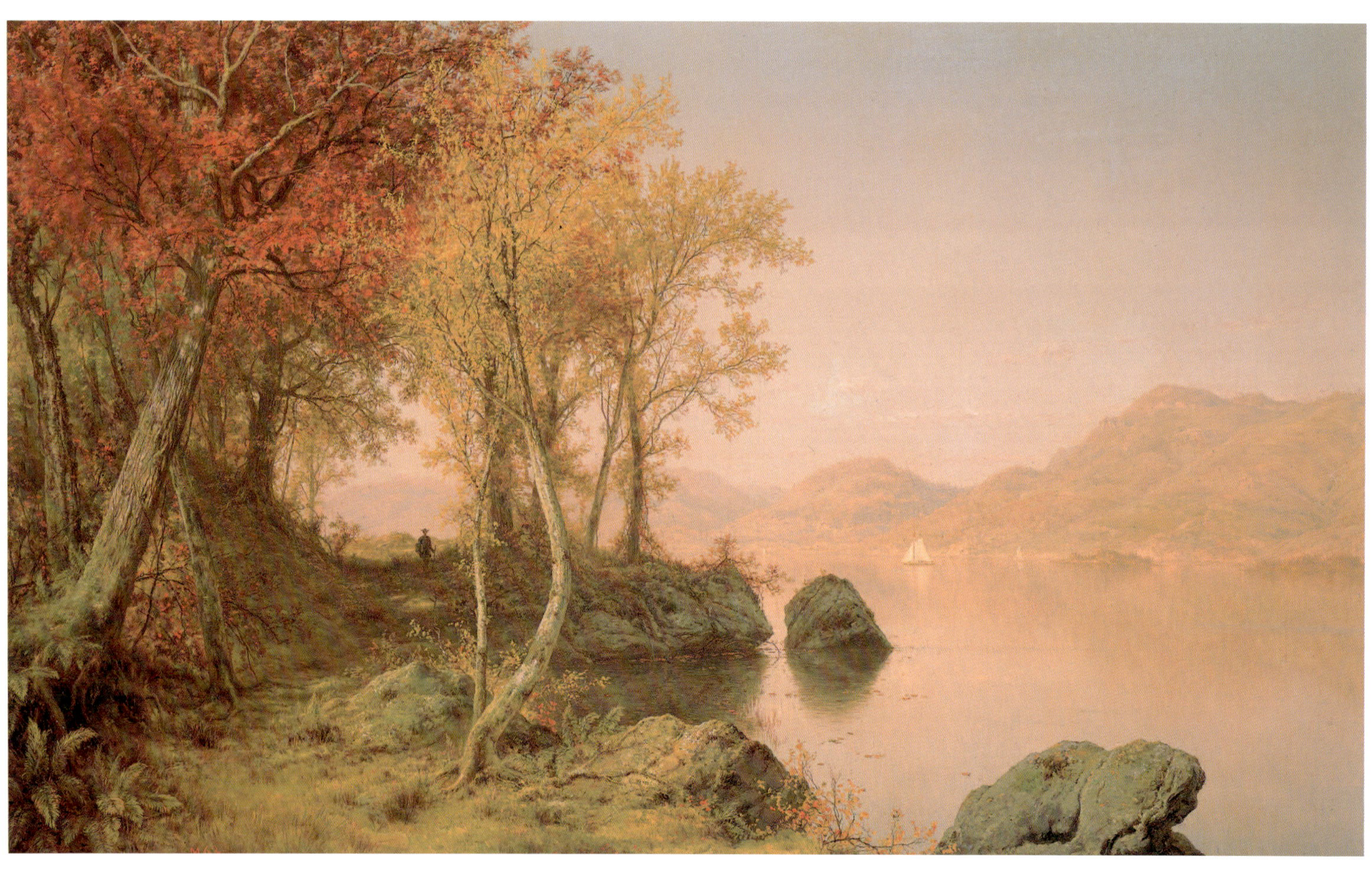

1862 (painted when the artist
was 30–31 years old)
Oil on canvas
24 ¼ x 40 in. (61.6 x 101.6 cm)
Initialed and dated at
lower left: *M. 62*

Early provenance: From the artist,
New York, 1862; (consigned) to Henry H.
Leeds & Co., New York, 2 June 1862; (sold)
to Mr. Egerton, Baltimore, 2 June 1862.
Early exhibition history: *A Choice
Collection of Paintings, and Studies from
Nature, Painted by Louis R. Mignot…*,
Henry H. Leeds & Co., New York, 2 June
1862, no. 19 as *Indian Summer, Lake
George.*

Early publications: *Catalogue of a
Choice Collection of Paintings, and
Studies from Nature, Painted by Louis R.
Mignot…*, New York: Henry H. Leeds &
Co., 2 June 1862, no. 19 as *Indian Summer,
Lake George.*
References: Manoogian, 1997, no. 9,
pp. 44–45 and 188. Manoogian, 1999, no. 30,
pp. 78–79.

By the spring of 1862, the Civil War had been skirmishing for a year. None of its most devastating battles had yet been fought, and many Americans in both the Union North and the Confederate South clung to the spare possibility that some swift resolution would stop the fighting. But even as a divided nation hoped for peace, regional antagonisms persevered, and hostility was not limited to the battlefields.

Louis Rémy Mignot was one of the few artists associated with the school of New York landscape painters to be a native of the American South. Born in Charleston, South Carolina, to parents of French extraction, Mignot experienced the death of his mother before his fourth birthday and virtual desertion by his father.[1] The loss of a caring mother and the absence of a dutiful father fotered a difficult upbringing in tradition-bound Charleston, and contributed to Mignot's lifelong feelings of dislocation and abandonment.

Mignot would form some of his most meaningful relationships with fellow artists in New York. In 1857, he accompanied Frederic Church on his second journey to South America, and the following year, he was among the first tenants of the Tenth Street Studio Building, a close community of American painters. Mignot was also willing to collaborate with other artists, most notably with Eastman Johnson and with Thomas P. Rossiter. Completing his absorption into the New York art world, Mignot was elected an Associate of the National Academy of Design in 1858, and a full Academician the following year.[2]

But everything changed with the start of the Civil War in 1861. Mignot found it difficult to remain in New York as a Southerner, even though his connections to Charleston and to the American South were tenuous at best. Mignot's withdrawal to the peaceful solace of Lake George in the fall of 1861 may have been in part to escape news of the war, but he also used the time to consider a plan to relocate to London.[3] Early the following year, Mignot completed *Autumn, Lake George*, a view of the upstate retreat in the splendor of its orange and yellow foliage. Under normal circumstances, Mignot would have submitted the painting to the National Academy of Design or to some other venue, but instead it joined the June 1862 sale of his studio contents held to finance his travel to London. But although it was consigned to commerce, *Autumn, Lake George* remained a poignant expression of Mignot's affectionate, if brief, embrace of the American North.[4]

In *Autumn, Lake George*, distant sailboats in soft, diffused light glide over a smooth sheet of water, while an artist, wearing a smock and carrying a pad of paper, ambles along a woodland path in search of an inspiring view. Although less rare to the region than most New Englanders believed, the brilliant displays of red, orange, and yellow autumn leaves had been associated with the American North since the colonial era. During the Civil War, paintings of Northern forests, especially in autumn, proliferated greatly, and were considered patriotic expressions of sympathy for America and the Union. All of this was well known to Mignot.[5]

In his 1867 *Book of the Artists*, Henry Tuckerman assumed that Mignot's Southern "nativity, temperament and taste" informed the vaguely generalizing quality of the artist's landscapes, whether tropical river scenes or snowy winter vistas. It has been argued more recently that it was not Mignot's Southern birth, but his rootless existence, his lack of any deep connection to anywhere, that informed his suggestive and atmospheric landscapes and enabled him to conjure the essence of most locales, if not their crisp outlines. Unlike Church, who was deeply connected to his native Connecticut, and who rendered each place he visited with almost scientific accuracy and a buyer's eye for detail, Mignot had never been more than an acquaintance of anywhere, including Charleston and, much to his disappointment, New York. Lacking a sense of place, Mignot offered hazy but attractive generalizations about any location he chose to paint.[6]

There may be some basis in both points of view. But in 1862, Mignot was neither Southern nor was he without roots. He had become profoundly and profitably connected to New York, and he may have resented that the sheer accident of his Southern birth was forcing him to leave. When he placed the figure of an artist in the encoded milieu of a northern forest in autumn, Mignot left behind his Southern origins and even his psychological neutrality. At that one time and in that one place, *Autumn, Lake George*, Mignot indicated his sympathy for his adopted home in the North, and elegantly protested the circumstances that were driving him away.

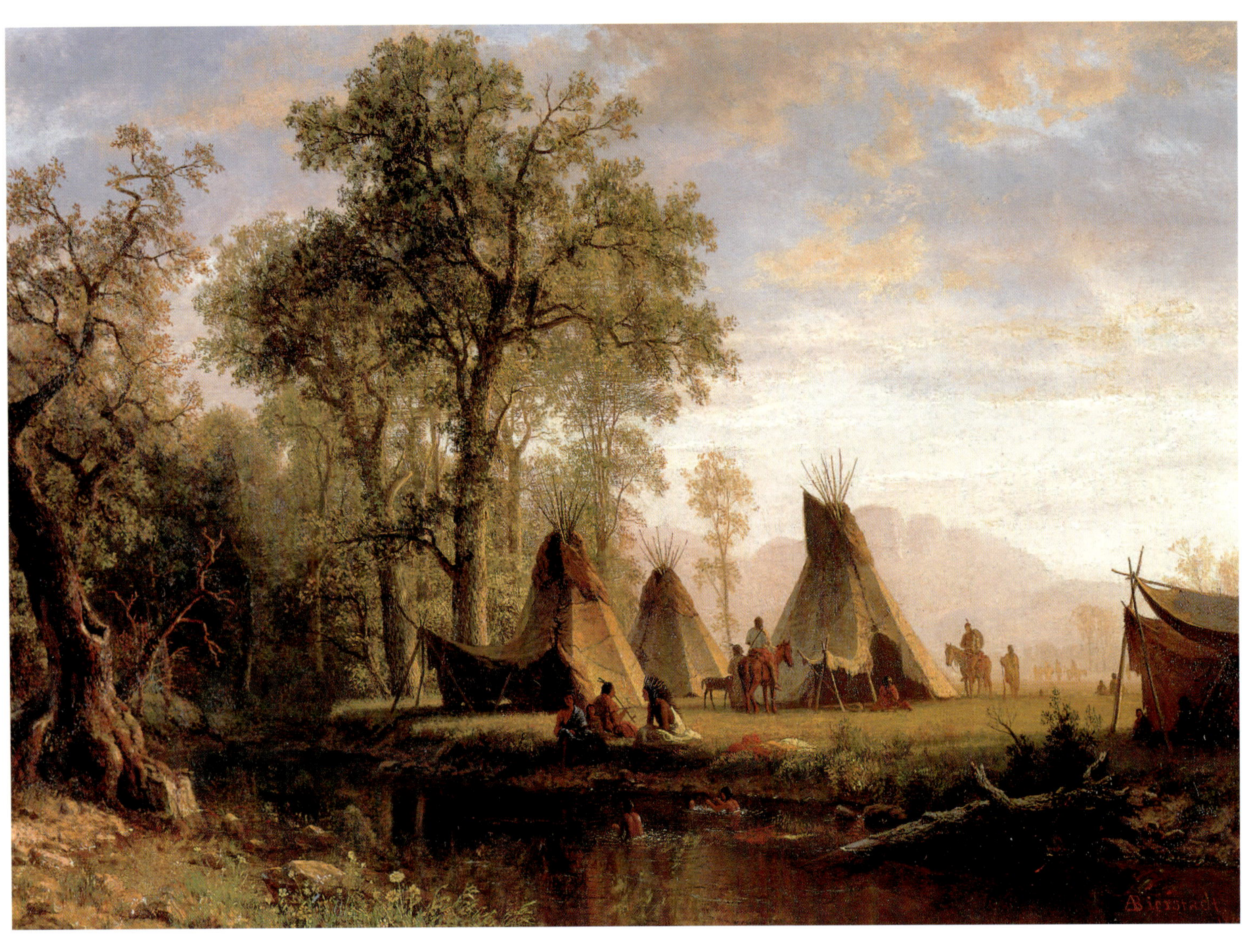

1862 (painted when the artist
was 32 years old)
Oil on canvas
20 x 28 in. (50.8 x 71.1 cm)
Signed and dated at lower right:
ABierstadt/1862

Early provenance: From the artist,
New York, 1862; (sold) to Hugh Nesbitt
Camp, Morris Heights, N.J.
References: *American Paintings,
Drawings and Sculpture Including
Property from the John F. Eulich
Collection,* Sotheby's, New York, 20 May
1998, no. 46.

Albert Bierstadt was the son of German immigrants who settled in the whaling port of New Bedford, Massachusetts, in the early 1830s. After achieving some success as a young drawing teacher in New Bedford, Bierstadt began his own formal education in earnest. In 1853, he traveled to Düsseldorf, Germany, to study with Johann Peter Hasenclever, a cousin of his mother and a leader of the realistic yet poetic painting style of the Rhineland region. But when Bierstadt arrived in Düsseldorf, he learned that Hasenclever had died unexpectedly, and his education was left largely to secondhand tutoring from fellow Americans Worthington Whittredge and Emanuel Leutze and occasional study with Hasenclever's Düsseldorf School colleagues Carl Friedrich Lessing and Andreas Achenbach.

During his four years in Europe, Bierstadt traveled widely in Germany, Switzerland, and Italy with Leutze, Whittredge, and William Stanley Haseltine. He developed a number of friendships in Europe with America's leading young landscape painters, including Sanford Gifford, with whom he visited the Alps in 1857. But due in part to Bierstadt's formidable ambition and competitive nature, few of his relationships with artists lasted for long or evolved into more than courteous professional acquaintanceships. At the end of the summer of 1857, having mastered the style and techniques of the Düsseldorf School, Bierstadt returned to the United States, eager to assume his position among America's first painters.

Bierstadt may have been contemplating travel to America's western frontier even while still in Europe. Within a year of his return to New Bedford, he was already prodding his not inconsiderable contacts in Massachusetts for permission to join the spring 1859 expedition to the Overland Trail led by the famous Col. Frederick W. Lander. It was crucial that Bierstadt make the trip, and not just because the local newspapers were already trumpeting his departure as if the plan were secure. Bierstadt had made an unimpressive public debut in New York the previous spring, showing an Alpine view at the National Academy of Design to virtually unanimous critical ambivalence. He would make a more fulsome contribution to the 1859 exhibition, but his deeper ambition resided in the American West. Early in 1859, he was granted permission to join Lander's party, and by April, well before the Academy exhibition closed, Bierstadt and the artist Francis Seth Frost were on their way to

St. Joseph, Missouri. There, Bierstadt would begin an excursion that was by far the most important event of his professional life.[1]

Col. Lander's party left St. Joseph on 5 May 1859, crossed the Missouri River into Kansas, and after a brief delay, continued northwest along the Little Blue River to Fort Kearney in the Nebraska Territory. Traveling the Oregon Trail along the Platte River, Bierstadt encountered the native Sioux and Shoshone, watching in friendly bewilderment as "Pike's Peakers" and other travelers made their way west to the gold strikes in Colorado or to rich farmland in the Oregon Territory. By 24 June, Lander's company arrived in South Pass at the foot of the famous Wind River Mountains. Bierstadt, Frost, and a muleteer broke off from the rest of the expedition, and spent the next few weeks cautiously exploring the region, sketching its spectacular scenery and native people, and struggling with limited success to produce stereoscopic views for the eager photography market in the east.[2]

On 10 July, Bierstadt wrote to *The Crayon,* describing the mountainous landscape in alternately reportorial and jubilant terms, and flavoring his narrative with anecdotes about the mosquitoes and other hardships. But much of Bierstadt's letter was devoted to the Native Americans he encountered on the journey. He could not avoid repeating common prejudices and misconceptions, infantilizing the native people and their "superstitious and naturally distrustful" attitudes. And he noted with a mixture of amusement and utter sincerity that he was perceived as a "strange medicine man" for attempting to draw portraits or to secure likenesses with his camera. But Bierstadt's letter also reveals a germinating sympathy for Native Americans, as he urged figure painters to make their way west to record their "manners and customs," and quickly, "for they are rapidly passing away."[3]

At the beginning of September, Bierstadt and Frost had returned as far as the Wolf River region of northeast Kansas, where they made drawings of the nearby Sac and Fox Indian camps and reveled in the last days of their Western odyssey. They intended to remain for two weeks, but by 18 September, Bierstadt was already back on the east coast, visiting his family in New Bedford and enjoying a taste of local celebrity. Before the end of 1859, Bierstadt was settled in Manhattan's fashionable Tenth Street Studio Building, and

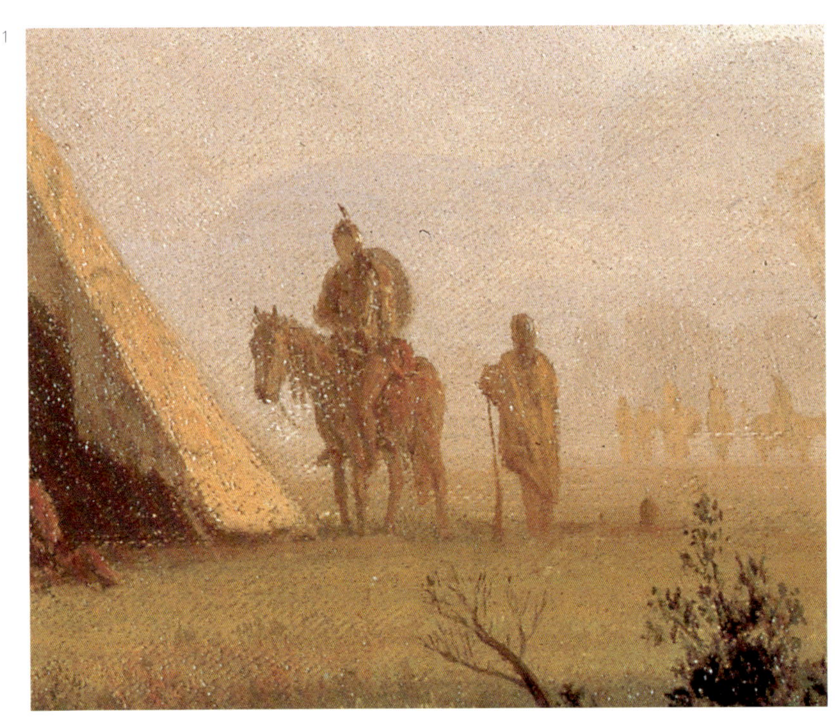

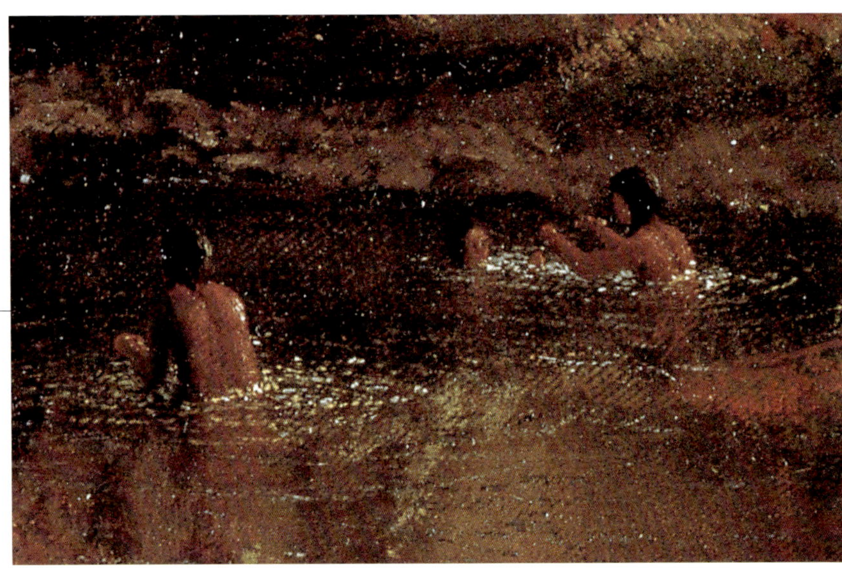

was hard at work on a Rocky Mountain scene for the spring exhibition of the National Academy of Design.[4]

Bierstadt no doubt had great expectations for his first great Western landscape, *The Base of the Rocky Mountains, Laramie Peak*, when it appeared at the Academy in 1860. His rival, Frederic Church, had enjoyed enormous success in the last few years with heroically scaled landscape paintings of such formidable vistas as Niagara Falls and the Andes Mountains of South America. But just as Church's initial paintings of Colombian and Ecuadorian scenery had failed to elicit the critical and popular response he had hoped for, Bierstadt's first view of the Rockies attracted encouraging notices in the local press, but hardly the unqualified raves he may have expected. More disappointing yet, the large canvas found no eager collectors to vie for its acquisition. Even so, Bierstadt's belief in grand manner Western landscape subjects and his confidence in his own abilities were not shaken by the muted response. He was already seeking another official escort to the Colorado frontier, and just as Church's second sojourn to South America had delivered masterpieces, Bierstadt was certain his return to the West would produce equally grand results. That trip, however, would be delayed for some time.[5]

Once the Civil War began in 1861, it became increasingly difficult for civilians to find noncombatant guides to the American West. As he awaited news from the Department of Interior, Bierstadt produced paintings of the Native American life he had witnessed along the Platte, Sweetwater, and Wolf Rivers in the Nebraska Territory and in Kansas. His *Indian Encampment* was one of at least a dozen pictures of small campsites and bands of traveling families that occupied him between 1860 and 1862. Although he had written glibly in his 1859 letter to *The Crayon* that native people were "appropriate adjuncts to the scenery," an opinion he was not the first to offer, the longer Bierstadt remained separated from the American West, the more thoughtfully he seems to have contemplated and the more sensitively he rendered Native American existence.[6] As he was eager to go west, but unable to, Bierstadt developed a greater than expected empathy for the Native Americans who so gracefully occupied the very country to which he wished to return.

In February 1863, just two months before he finally departed on his long-delayed second Western journey, Bierstadt unveiled the largest work he had produced to date, a ten-foot-wide painting called *The Rocky Mountains, Lander's Peak*. It was the aesthetic summation of all he had learned from his first trip to the American frontier, as well as from the many paintings he had produced since his return, including *Indian Encampment*. Bierstadt's *The Rocky Mountains, Lander's Peak* was epic and dramatic, and just as he had described in his letter to *The Crayon*, there were "jagged summits, covered with snow and mingling with the clouds … a scene which every lover of landscape would gaze upon with unqualified delight."[7] Although no peak in the Nebraska Territory was at that time named for Col. Lander, Bierstadt honored the man who had introduced him to the magnificence of the West, and whose death in Civil War battle the artist recently had mourned.

In *Lander's Peak*, Bierstadt acknowledged the fallen Colonel, but he also paid homage to the Native American cultures that had thrived for centuries in the shadow of that high mountain, regardless of what it was called. The entire foreground of *The Rocky Mountains, Lander's Peak* was a panoramic view of a living Shoshone village, and a carefully observed record of the "manners and customs of the Indians … still as they were hundreds of years ago." Bierstadt's 1862 *Indian Encampment* was in no way a study for *Lander's Peak*, nor were the other canvases of Native American life he produced between his first and second journeys to the West. But the scrutiny, documentation, and subsequent deliberation that led to *Indian Encampment* made the foreground of *Lander's Peak*, and indeed the entire composition, the rich expression that it was.[8]

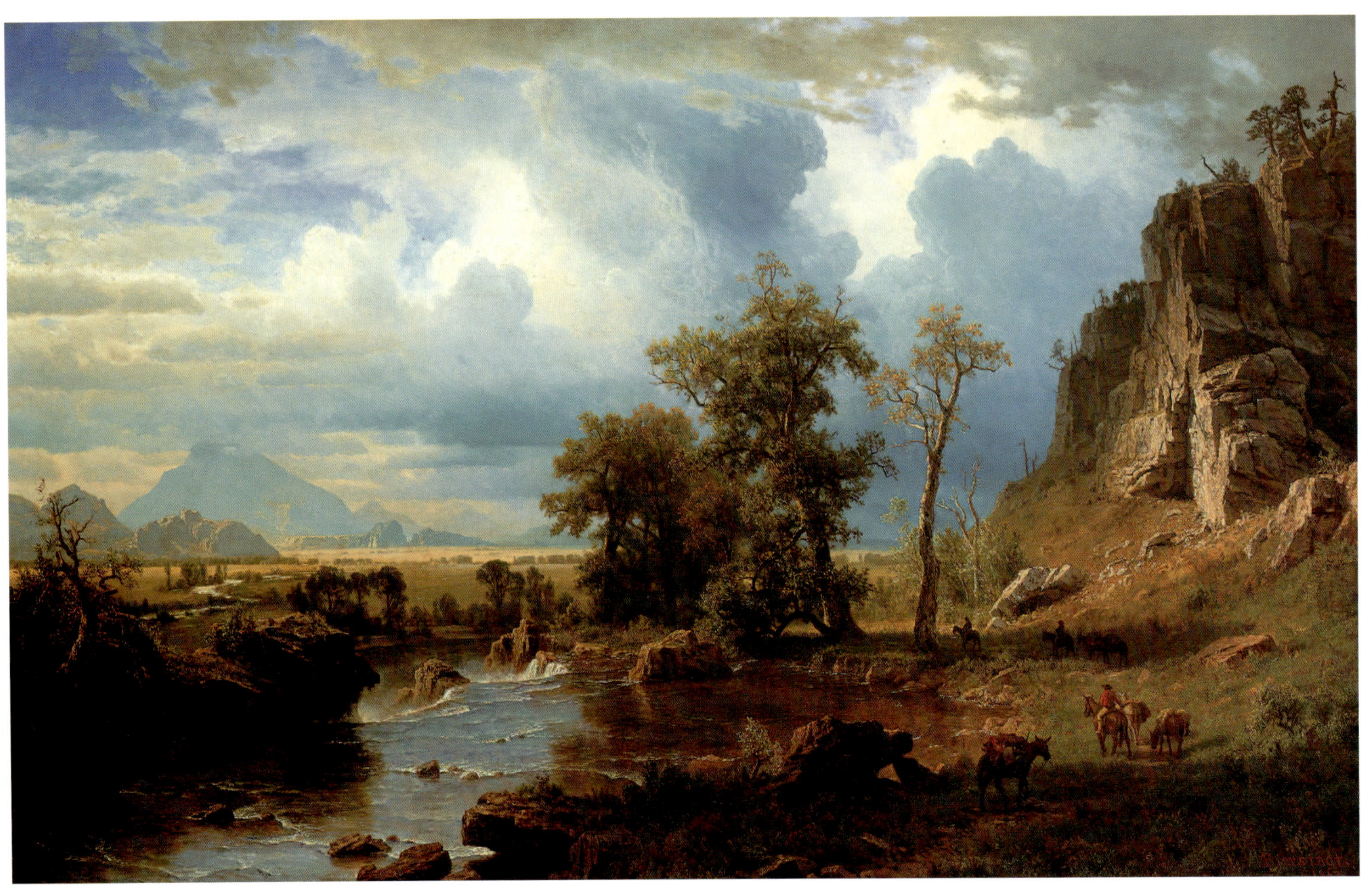

Early provenance: From the artist, New York, 1863; (sold) to Judge Hilton, New York, by 1867.

Early exhibition history: *Thirty-eighth Annual Exhibition of the National Academy of Design,* New York, spring 1863, no. 35 as *North Fork of the Platte, Nebraska.*

Early publications: [Fitz Hugh Ludlow], *New York Evening Post,* 22 May 1863. Tuckerman, 1867, p. 393.

1863 (painted when the artist was 33 years old)
Oil on canvas
36 x 57 ½ in. (91.4 x 146 cm)
Signed and dated at lower right: *ABierstadt/1863*

References: Manoogian, 1996, p. 29. Manoogian, 1997, no. 6, pp. 38–39 and 187. Manoogian, 1999, no. 3, pp. 24–25.

As his first trip to the American West was nearing an end in September 1859, Albert Bierstadt wrote to his hometown newspaper, the *New Bedford Daily Mercury,* describing one of the more arduous legs of the journey:

before we reached Laramie, we found ourselves suddenly out of provisions, and for several days were obliged to subsist on bread and water; the scenery being of so delightful a character, we found no time to hunt. I assure you, however, that it amply repaid us for the temporary deprivations in the sketches which we were enabled to add to our portfolios. [1]

Two months earlier, Bierstadt, another artist, Francis Seth Frost, and a muleteer had split off from Col. Frederick W. Lander's survey team that had guided them along the Platte River, deep into the Nebraska Territory. As Lander's expedition and protection continued west, Bierstadt, Frost, and their companion cautiously explored the area near South Pass and ventured into the fabled Wind River Mountains.

Bierstadt, Frost, and the muleteer began their journey home in August 1859, and had not gone far when they ran out of food. It is not difficult to imagine two painters so inspired by the landscape that they would rather draw than eat, but it is less plausible that a muleskinner would prefer to look for scenic views than to hunt for rabbits. Despite Bierstadt's colorful account, circumstances other than landscape painting convinced them to travel on empty stomachs. As a reporter for the *Boston Daily Evening Transcript* noted in March 1860, after a conversation with Bierstadt, the three men had not been so much distracted by the inspiring countryside, but had "lived on bread and water — not daring to fire a gun for fear of betraying their retreat to hostile Indians, tribes of whom had murdered three white travelers." [2]

Bierstadt completed *Platte River, Nebraska* early in 1863, as he prepared to make his second foray into the American West. Although the painting described the rugged Nebraska Territory, Bierstadt's inclusion of a stormy sky and three riders following the Platte River added an anecdotal element to the composition. As the Civil War raged in the Eastern states in 1863, many young men were taking their chances in the West rather than face increasingly certain death on the battlefield. Bierstadt himself had paid the $300 exemption to avoid conscription, and indeed his number was drawn in the draft

lottery. At the time, there was little shame in his decision, at least among his class and clientele. The war had become increasingly unpopular in New York, where the July 1863 draft riots plunged the city into a battle of its own. To New Yorkers, storm clouds on the horizon and even a short column of riders, regardless of where they traveled, would have been familiar symbols, and details that resonated deeply in 1863. [3]

But the three riders quietly skirting the Platte River probably represented a vivid memory for Bierstadt more than an allusion to the war. In 1863, as he considered his upcoming Western excursion, Bierstadt may have thought back to the summer of 1859 and the unsettling incident on the trail. Given how swift and narrow the Platte River appears in the painting, and the alternating plains and tall mountains, the three riders are probably still west of Fort Laramie. They are traveling downstream in an easterly direction, and could easily be in the area where Bierstadt, Frost, and the muleskinner found themselves riding in silent hunger to avoid betraying their position. The dramatic cloud formation creates an air of apprehension, as the riders remain strategically spaced, sticking to the shadows and eschewing conversation.

Bierstadt submitted *Platte River, Nebraska* to the 1863 exhibition of the National Academy of Design. [4] It was well regarded as a western landscape, but even Fitz Hugh Ludlow, who was about to accompany Bierstadt on his second trip West, had no sense of the work's latent meaning. Ludlow's review for the *New York Evening Post* described *Platte River, Nebraska* as:

a picture of broader lights and distances. Its breadth of light… is indeed admirable. Great tubular masses of limestone, upended and broken into successive ledges… are more picturesque than any remains of British abbeys… pure to the last degree. [5]

While the painting is all of those things, given that Ludlow was about to embark on his own journey West, a trip that would nearly kill him, he seems to have brought little insight or imagination to his reading of Bierstadt's picture. And since the hapless Ludlow was traveling at Bierstadt's urging, and had only the slimmest notion of the dangers that awaited him, perhaps his slender interpretation of *Platte River, Nebraska* suited the artist just fine. [6]

16   PEACE AND PLENTY, NORTH CONWAY, NEW HAMPSHIRE

Albert Bierstadt (1830–1902)

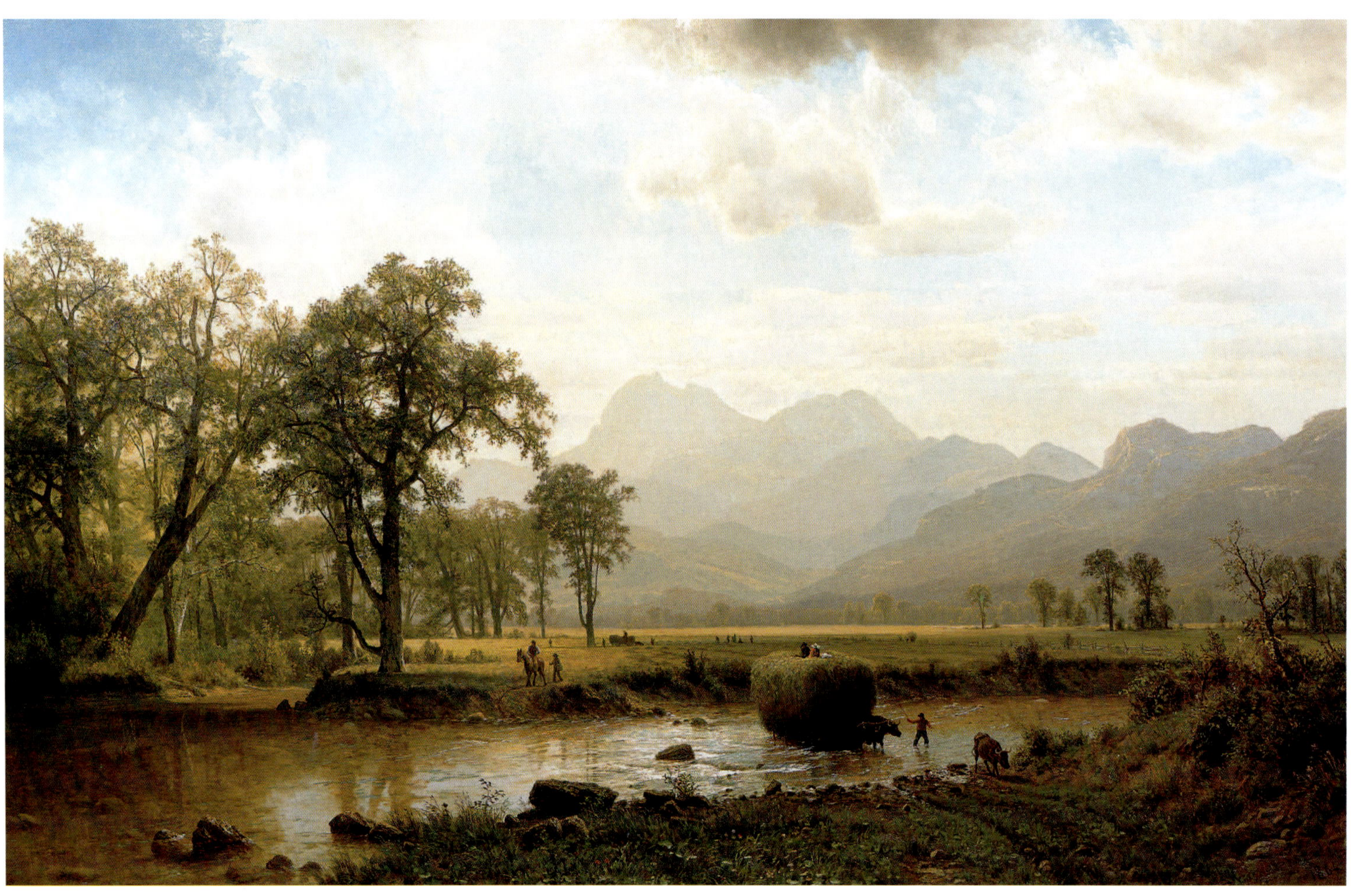

1864 (painted when the artist
was 34 years old)
Oil on canvas
36 x 58 in. (91.4 x 147.3 cm)
Signed and dated at lower right:
ABierstadt/1864

References: Anderson and Ferber,
1990, p. 191 as *Haying, Conway Meadows*.

Albert Bierstadt's second journey to the American West, in 1863, was far longer and more expansive than his first trip had been in 1859. He left New York in April with the writer Fitz Hugh Ludlow, and together they saw the Rocky Mountains of Colorado, the Great Salt Lake in Utah, Yosemite Valley in California, and Mount Hood in Oregon. It was not until 23 November that Bierstadt and Ludlow finally boarded a steamer in San Francisco bound for Panama, and it was three weeks later on 16 December that they arrived back in New York.[1]

During the eight months that Bierstadt was away, the masterwork of his first excursion, *The Rocky Mountains, Lander's Peak*, had been on display in Boston and in his hometown of New Bedford to enthusiastic public and critical response. Although *Lander's Peak* already had debuted in New York in early 1863, when the great picture returned to Manhattan in February 1864, it was as if New York writers were seeing it and Bierstadt himself for the very first time. The painting caused an even greater stir in April, when it was exhibited at the Metropolitan Fair organized by the United States Sanitary Commission to raise money for Civil War wounded. *Lander's Peak* was installed directly opposite Frederic Church's *Heart of Andes*, and a rivalry was begun.[2]

Before he produced even one major painting from his second excursion to the West, Bierstadt had emerged from a crowded field as the lone viable challenger to Church's lock on the public imagination. New York critics and the public alike seemed delighted that Church had acquired a competitor, and partisan writers did their best to stir controversy and debate over who was the superior artist. When Ludlow's first article about his travels in the West appeared in the April issue of *Atlantic Monthly*, Bierstadt still had not publicly presented a new painting from that journey, but it was, nonetheless, he who seemed to take the upper hand.[3]

Although his newly minted reputation depended upon his next major Western view, Bierstadt was unwilling to restrict himself exclusively to America's remote vistas. Even as he was leaving on his second Western excursion, he had exhibited a New Hampshire woodland scene as well as a view of the Platte River (see cat. 15).[4] Moreover, after eight months of sketching Western scenery, and then organizing a large exhibition for the Metropolitan Fair of Native American artifacts that included a wigwam and performing Indians, by the summer of 1864, Bierstadt may have been ready for some relief from Western themes. As he labored on large paintings of Mount Hood and the Golden Gate of California, Bierstadt also completed *Peace and Plenty: North Conway, New Hampshire*, a view of the relatively convenient wilderness of the White Mountains.[5]

For all of his professional investment in the American West, the enterprising Bierstadt had devoted as much time and effort to creating a market for views of the White Mountains. He had made his first trip to North Conway, New Hampshire in 1858, and returned there again in 1860, along with his brothers, the photographers Charles and Edward Bierstadt. In addition to Albert's paintings, the trip yielded a series of large-format photographs of White Mountain scenery that were later described in *The Crayon*: "The artistic taste of Mr. Albert Bierstadt, who selected the points of view, is apparent in them. No better photographs have been published in this country."[6] After spending the summer of 1862 in the White Mountains, the *New York Leader* noted that Bierstadt's New York studio was filled with studies and sketches of the region. One of the drawings may have eventually led to *Peace and Plenty: North Conway, New Hampshire*.

It is unknown precisely when in 1864 Bierstadt completed *Peace and Plenty: North Conway, New Hampshire*. It was certainly based on drawings of 1862 or earlier, given that he was in the West during the summer of 1863 and confined himself to his studio in 1864. In this haying scene, neighbors are helping neighbors harvest a field in the shadow of the White Mountains. An exaltation of community and cooperation that would have resonated deeply during the Civil War, the painting also offered solace from such weighty concerns in its charming foreground vignette. A farmer leads a heavily loaded wagon pulled by two straining oxen across a shallow stream. Just ahead of them is a cow, which the savvy farmer has no doubt brought to the fields to provide amorous enticement for the two weary oxen to pull harder. While the bovine romance may go unconsummated, that may not be true of the young couple, who steal a moment alone atop the loaded wagon.[7]

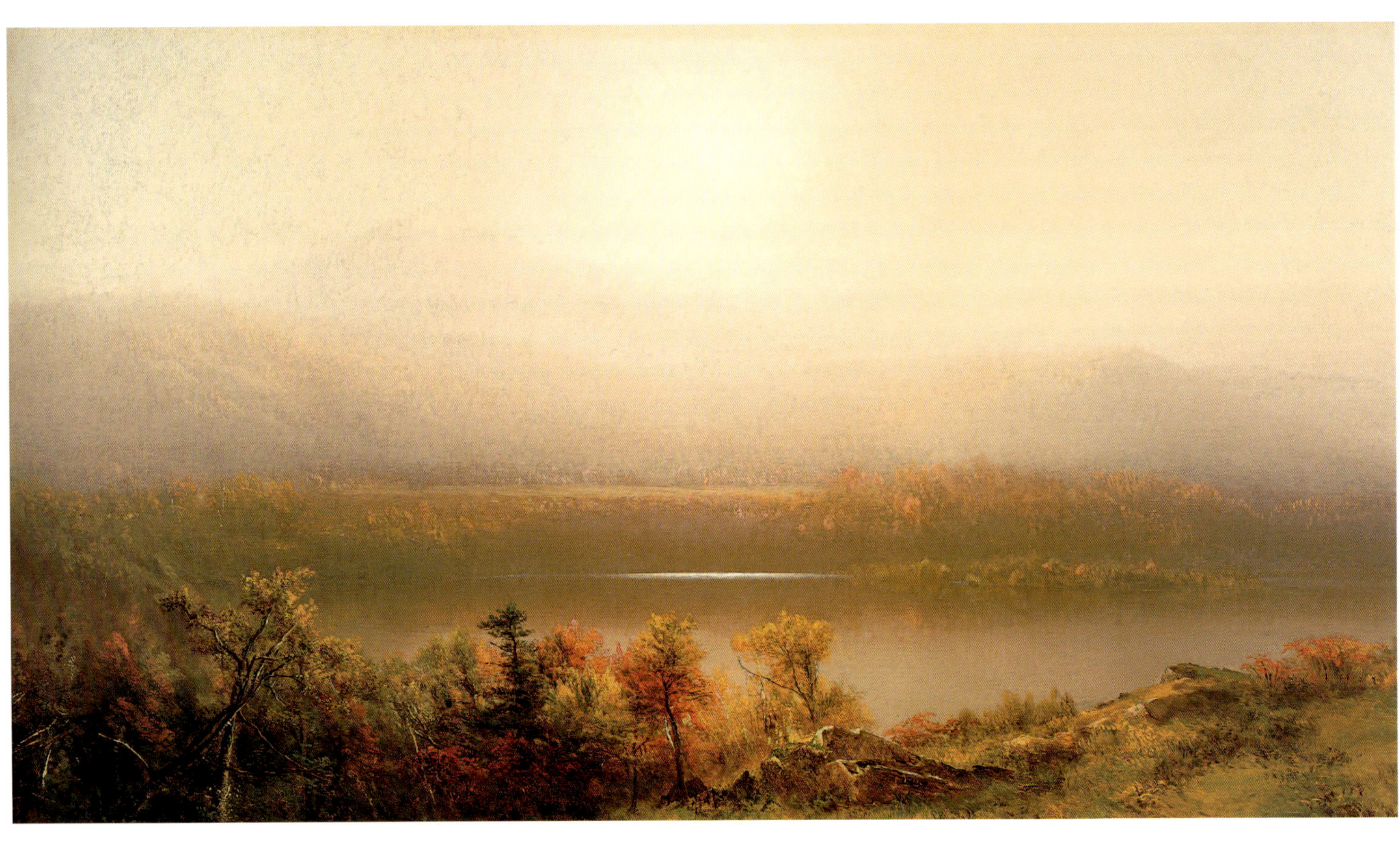

1863 (painted when the artist
was 27–28 years old)
Oil on canvas
27 x 48 in. (68.6 x 121.9 cm)
Signed and dated: *H Martin 1863*

A native of Albany, Homer Dodge Martin was rescued from an ill-suited existence as a mechanical draftsman by the thriving community of artists in the New York capital. In about 1852, the sculptor Erastus Dow Palmer apparently convinced Martin's father to allow his son to leave his apprenticeship and to pursue a career as a painter. Although Martin received almost no formal training, he was quickly taken under the wing of such notable Albany painters as George Boughton, Edward Gay, and the Hart brothers, William and James, and by 1857, the young painter had submitted his first canvas to the National Academy of Design.[1]

Situated on the Hudson River and within easy reach of the Catskills, the Adirondacks, and Lake George, Albany was a convenient stopping point for the many New York painters who journeyed to the wilderness for their inspiration and subject matter. Benefiting from this exposure, local Albany landscape painters quickly absorbed the lessons of Thomas Cole and his followers, and eagerly embraced the refinements and innovations that younger painters were introducing with each coming year. By 1863, when Martin left Albany and opened a studio in Manhattan, he was already well versed in the landscape style that Cole had invented, but he was aware of more recent developments as well.

In the late 1850s, American landscape painters such as Frederick Kensett and others began to move away from the strategies of Cole to achieve a more consciously organized and refined rendering of scenic subject matter. Their canvases became rigorously horizontal, not just in format, but in the expansiveness and openness of the landscape and increasingly the seascape subjects they chose to paint. Especially after his 1859 experiments on the Shrewsbury River in New Jersey, Kensett began to produce works that were carefully structured bands of horizontal sea and sky punctuated only by the occasional curling spit of land or the upright masts of sailing ships. The surfaces of his paintings eschewed impasto for an almost polished effect, and his canvases glowed with a luminous radiance constructed of an almost imperceptibly subtle modulation of color. Possibly inspired by the work of the Gloucester, Massachusetts, marine painter Fitz Hugh Lane, the paintings Kensett produced in the late 1850s and throughout the 1860s were revelations to his colleagues, and many of those painters, including Martin, tried their hand at this bracing new development.[2]

Martin's *Adirondack Lake* of 1863 was not a complete departure from the tradition of Cole, but it does bear a number of the innovations that Kensett introduced or perhaps borrowed from Lane. While Martin's foreground remains solid and agitated with protruding rocks and dense autumn foliage, the lake itself has already become a diffuse reflection and the far shore, the distant mountains, and the luminous sky have dissolved into nearly liquid panoramic bands of muted color. Martin's most direct application of the new idiom was in his treatment of the all but invisible sun, which radiates behind a screen of haze and is defined by only the slightest variation in the otherwise monochrome, yellow sky. A carefully placed streak of white horizontal reflection races across the surface of the lake, acknowledging the presence of the largely hidden orb and emphasizing the overall horizontality of the format and the subject.

Martin's early adaptation of Kensett's devices would prove indicative of the younger artist's not altogether desirable fluidity. Martin borrowed freely from Kensett's innovations, just as he would later adopt the principles of French Barbizon painting and eventually Impressionism. His openness to change left many of his experiments unresolved and some of his collectors uncertain of whom the real Martin was. But despite a career that was marked more by struggle than success, Martin found his share of admirers, especially among a younger generation of artists and writers who considered innovation the most supreme of virtues. Fifteen years after Martin died, one of his first biographers, the critic Frank Jewett Mather, wrote that Kensett "was the only one of the older artists who was worth imitating, and Homer Martin was about the only painter intelligent enough to grasp that fact. The fine Martins of the seventies are like glorified Kensetts."[3] Mather's comparison of Martin and Kensett was skewed by the moment in which it was written, but it does offer a sense of how utterly out of favor nineteenth-century landscape painting had become by 1912.

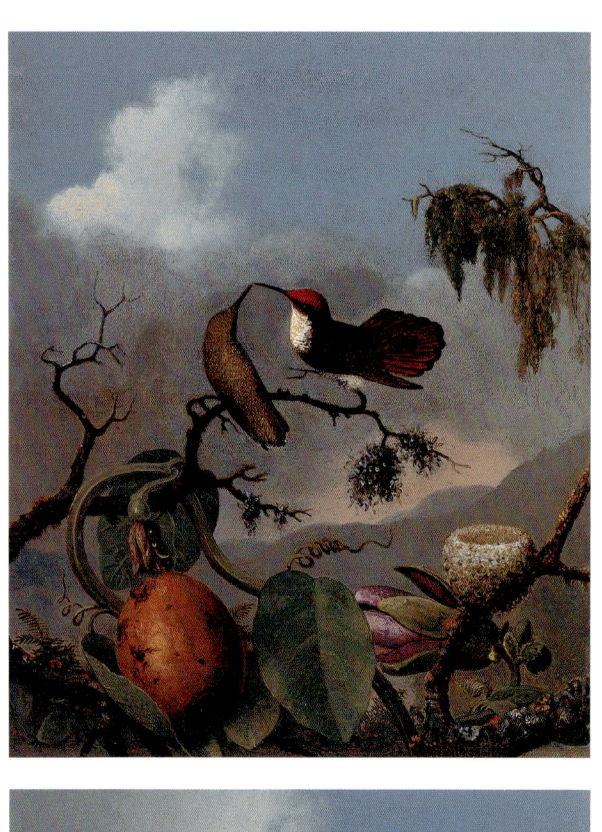

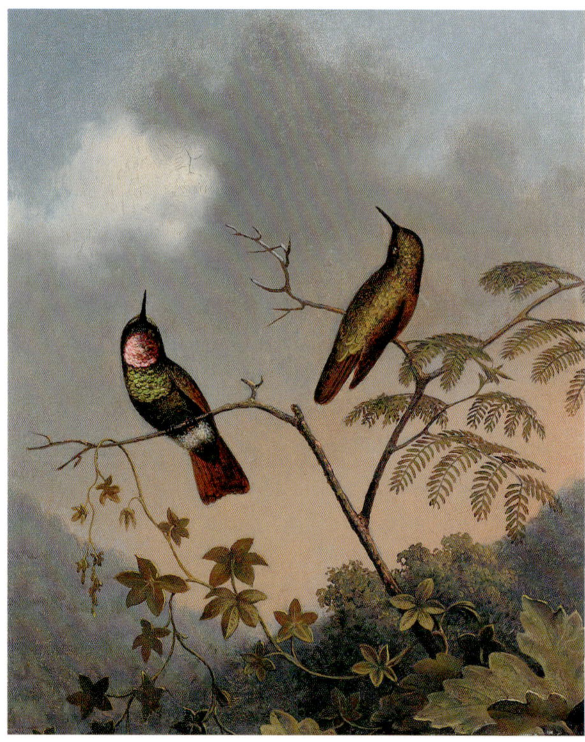

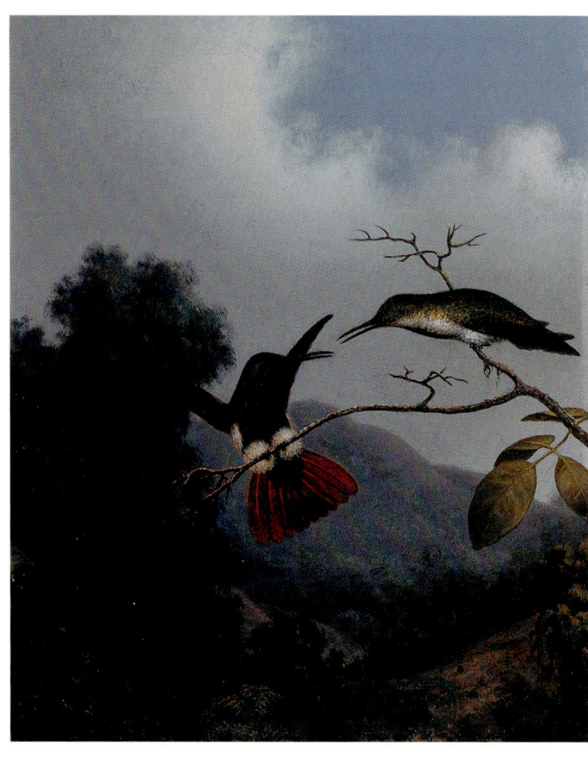

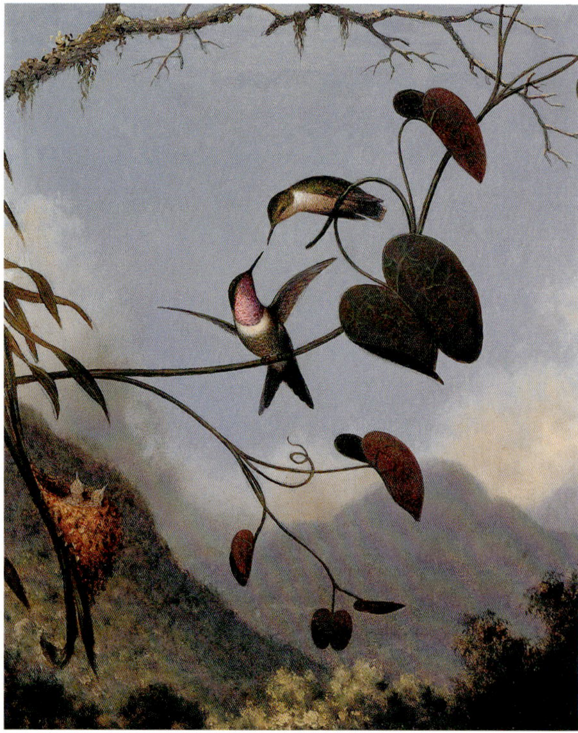

1863–64 or 1864–65 (painted when the artist was 44–45 years old)
Oil on canvas mounted on panel (16 paintings on four panels)
12 1/4 x 10 in. (31.1 x 25.4 cm) each
Unsigned

Early provenance: From the artist, London (possibly brought from Rio de Janeiro), 1864; (probably sold) to Sir Samuel Morton Peto, London, 1865.

Early exhibition history: (possibly 12 of the 16 paintings) *Exposicao Geral das Belles Artes de 1864,* Academy of Fine Arts, Rio de Janeiro, Brazil, February 1864, no. 75.

References: Manoogian, 1989, no. 44, pp. 116–123. Manoogian, 1993, pp. 39–44. Manoogian, 1997, no. 16, pp. 64–68 and 190. Stebbins, 2000, nos. 336, 344, 347, 349, 352, 357, 359, 361, 363–69, and 372, pp. 285 and 287–294.

Martin Johnson Heade made his first journey to South America in 1863, probably at the suggestion of his friend, Frederic Church. The famous excursions Church had made to New Granada (now Colombia) and Ecuador in 1853 and 1857 yielded some of the most widely discussed canvases yet to appear in New York, and catapulted the painter into the front rank of American artists. But unlike Church, whose paintings of the Magdalena River (see cat. 8) and the towering volcanoes of Ecuador could scarcely be separated from the wonderment and discovery of his epic journeys, Heade went to Brazil in search of a specific subject that he already knew well, and with clear intentions of what he would do once he had found it.[1]

In an article for *Field and Stream* written some thirty years after his Brazilian sojourn, Heade confessed that "from early boyhood I have been almost a monomaniac on hummingbirds." While perhaps exaggerating the affliction of his hummingbird affection, there is no question that Heade maintained a long and abiding interest in the various species, and transformed a youthful fascination into one of the most original artistic expressions of the nineteenth century. In September 1863, Heade left New York for Rio de Janeiro, where he intended to produce at least twenty painted studies of hummingbirds in their native habitats for an album of chromolithographs he would call *The Gems of Brazil.*[2]

Although most of the world's species of hummingbird were found within ten degrees of the Equator, Heade sailed further south to Brazil, in part because of the influential contacts who expected him there. Heade's friend from Newburyport, Massachusetts, the Reverend James Cooley Fletcher, had once been a missionary in Brazil. He was later part of the American legation in Rio de Janeiro, and before returning to New England, he had become a close friend of the emperor, Don Pedro II. Access to Reverend Fletcher's impressive social circle would have been appealing enough to Heade, but Rio de Janeiro was also a primary center for the growing commerce in hummingbird skins and feathers. Heade knew that if he could not find some species in the wild, and there were many that came nowhere near Brazil, he could in all likelihood acquire their skins in the Rio de Janeiro hummingbird marketplace.[3]

Heade initially grumbled about Brazil and Brazilians, but despite his early complaints, the journey proved a resounding success. By January 1864, he had already sent two of his hummingbird paintings to a lithographic firm in London for reproduction, and had completed no less than twelve others, which he brought to a private audience with Don Pedro that Reverend Fletcher had arranged. The emperor was much impressed with *The Gems of Brazil* and agreed to allow the artist to publish his folio of chromolithographs with the imprimatur of "his royal patronage."[4] A month later, Heade presented the same twelve paintings at an exhibition in Rio de Janeiro, where they were again admired by the emperor, by some of Brazil's leading citizens, and by the substantial community of American and English businessmen who were based in Rio. Before he left Brazil for London in early April 1864, Heade was presented the Order of the Rose by Don Pedro, and more importantly, he had acquired no less than sixty subscriptions for the published version of *The Gems of Brazil.*[5]

Heade's promising start in Rio de Janeiro did not translate into brilliant resolution in London, and the published version of *The Gems of Brazil* never materialized. Heade printed at least four separate chromolithographs of hummingbird subjects, each in more than a handful of impressions, but that was as far as he was able to advance the project. The lithographic process proved more cumbersome and time consuming than Heade had expected, it produced less than elegant results, and his limited resources did not go as far as he needed them to. Moreover, Heade had ambled into an already crowded marketplace, where handsome folio albums of ornithological prints already existed in considerable number. *The Gems of Brazil* would have been an original and inventive addition to the literature, but those virtues were not necessarily the qualities that most hummingbird aficionados were seeking. He was unable to interest enough London subscribers to keep the project afloat, and with his money exhausted, by late 1865, a disappointed Heade made his way back to the United States. He apparently brought with him the chromolithographs he had printed for *The Gems of Brazil,* but many of his hummingbird paintings seemingly remained in England. And there they would stay for more than a century.[6]

In 1981, sixteen of Heade's hummingbird paintings mounted on four panels appeared on the London and New York art markets after being hidden away for decades in an English private collection.

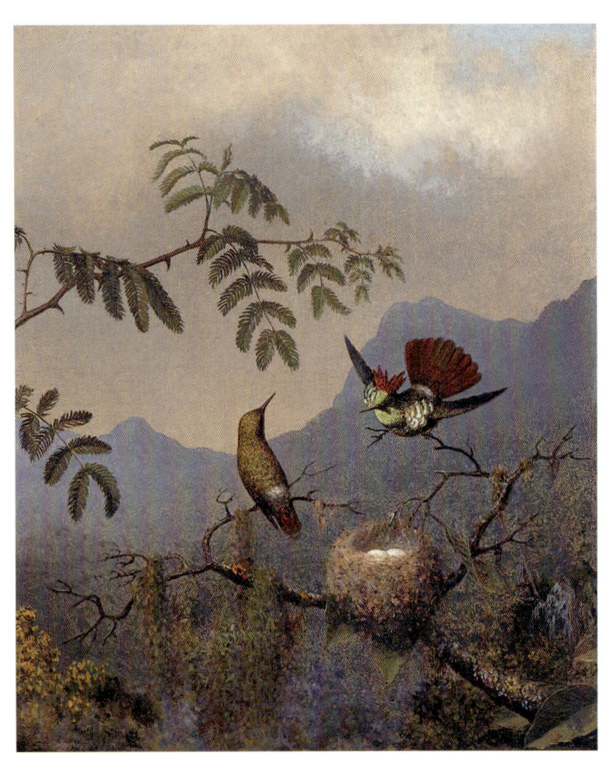
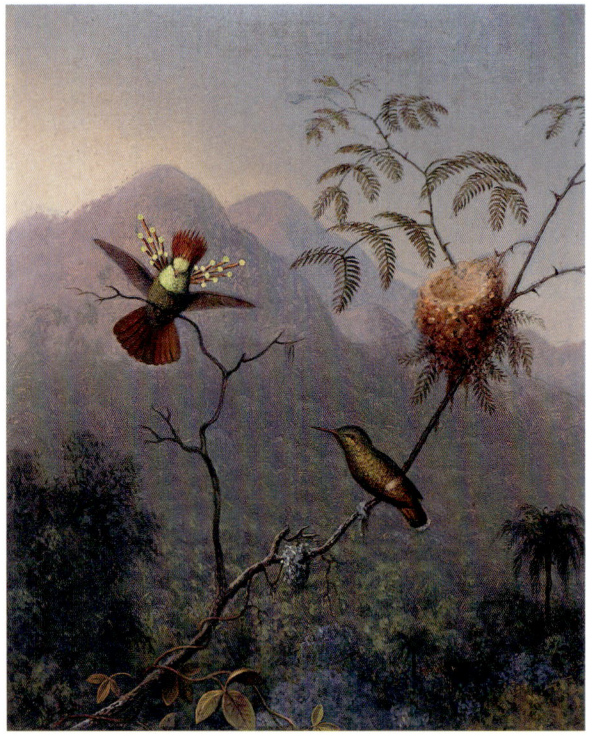
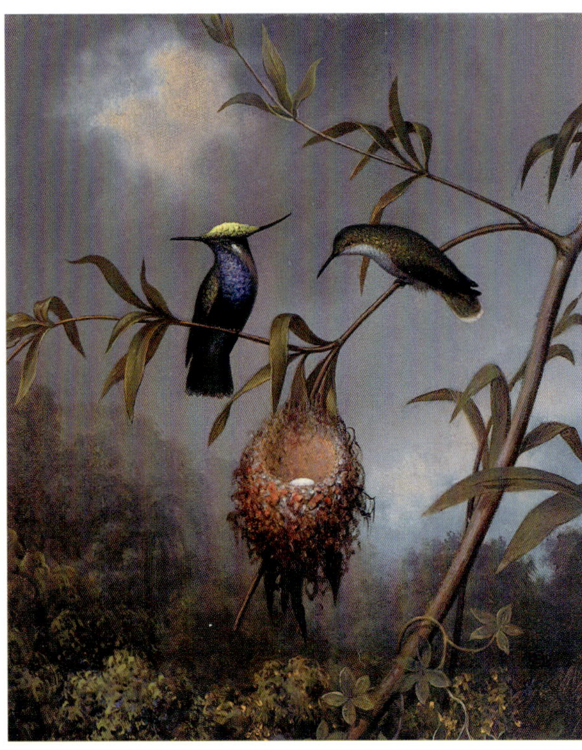
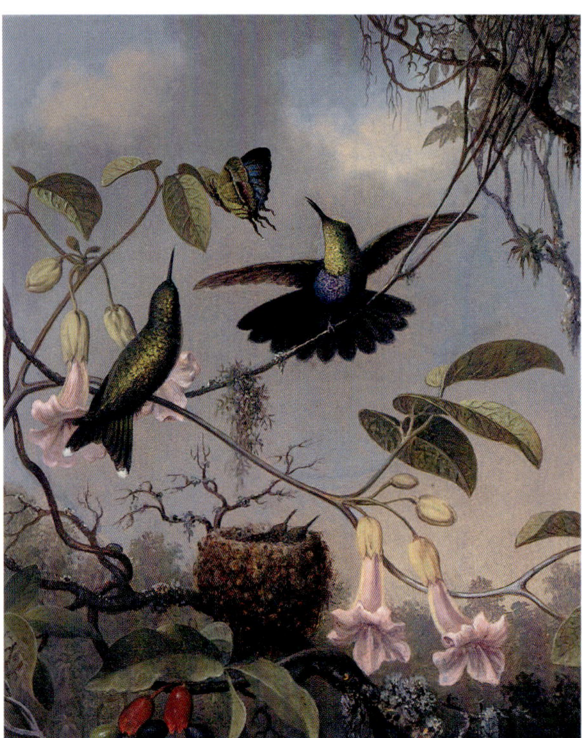

The canvases were instantly anointed *The Gems of Brazil*, and it appeared that one of the enduring mysteries of nineteenth-century American painting had been largely resolved. But as Theodore E. Stebbins Jr. has persuasively demonstrated in his most recent book on Martin Johnson Heade, the works that resurfaced in 1981 and are now in the Manoogian Collection are probably not *The Gems of Brazil* the artist painted and exhibited in Rio de Janeiro, and by extension, intended to publish in London.[7]

Stebbins rests his argument on three basic points. First, among the sixteen paintings that came on the market in 1981 was one that represented not a hummingbird, but a large Blue Morpho butterfly. Although beautifully realized, the butterfly was probably painted in London in September 1864, when Heade wrote to his friend, John Russell Bartlett, "I am working on birds & other insects now." Stebbins's second point is that none of the sixteen paintings in the Manoogian Collection served as the basis for any of the four surviving chromolithographs, which remains the only means of positive identification. Indeed, only one painting survives that relates directly to a chromolithograph and it is not among the pictures in the Manoogian Collection. Finally, Stebbins suggests that the sixteen paintings now known as *The Gems of Brazil* are simply too accomplished to have been among the original works Heade painted in Rio de Janeiro. His *Two Green-Breasted Hummingbirds*, the one surviving painting that corresponds directly to a chromolithograph, bears the tentative hand and compositional changes that one would expect from an initial effort. The paintings in the Manoogian Collection are not only beautiful, they are, in Stebbins's words, "confidently painted."[8]

If Stebbins is correct, then it still remains a mystery what became of the fourteen or sixteen or twenty paintings that Heade designated *The Gems of Brazil*, assuming that designation remained fixed in the artist's mind and linked exclusively to the canvases he produced in Rio de Janeiro. As interesting as it would be to know precisely which twelve paintings Heade exhibited in Rio, it could be that defining *The Gems of Brazil* in that way is narrowing his vision of the project unnecessarily. Just as Heade painted hummingbirds in Brazil that were not native to that country, and just as he continued to produce hummingbird subjects in London, and even as he hired,

fired, and rehired English lithographers, perhaps the artist's conception of the project was more mutable and fluid than the surviving historical record would suggest.

In 1879, Clara Erskine Clement and Laurence Hutton wrote that the "original designs" for Heade's *The Gems of Brazil* had been acquired by the British railroad magnate Sir Morton Peto. And in fact, a number of the hummingbird paintings in the Manoogian Collection bear the inscription, "Peto," and are assumed to have come from that collection. Since Sir Morton spent the autumn of 1865 in the United States and then went bankrupt in 1866, Stebbins has suggested that he probably bought his hummingbird paintings during the summer of 1865 or before.[9] But during the first half of 1865, Heade had not yet given up on his publication project and most certainly would not have sold the paintings he needed for translation into chromolithography.

In the strictest sense, the paintings that belonged to Sir Morton Peto, which resurfaced in 1981, and are now in the Manoogian Collection, were probably not *The Gems of Brazil* the artist intended to reproduce. But Clement and Hutton would not have made the link between the title, *The Gems of Brazil*, which was hardly common knowledge, and the collector, Sir Morton Peto, arbitrarily, and must have either discussed the project or the purchase with Heade or with Sir Morton. One of two things must have happened. Heade either described to Clement and Hutton the hummingbird paintings he sold to Sir Morton as *The Gems of Brazil*. Or Heade sold them to Sir Morton as *The Gems of Brazil*, and the railroad tycoon passed that title along to Clement and Hutton. In either case, as Heade reluctantly accepted in 1865 that his publication plans would not be realized, he may have already considered the entire corpus of hummingbird paintings, whether produced in Rio or in London, as worthy of the designation *The Gems of Brazil*.

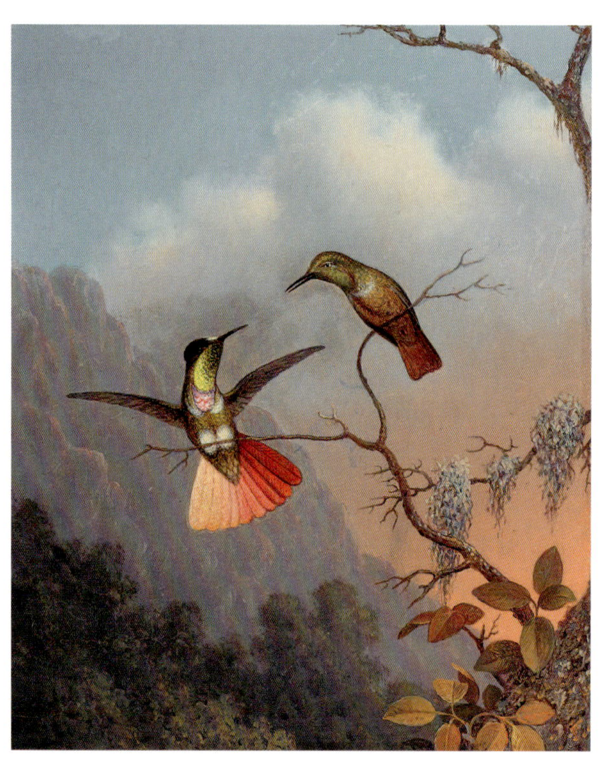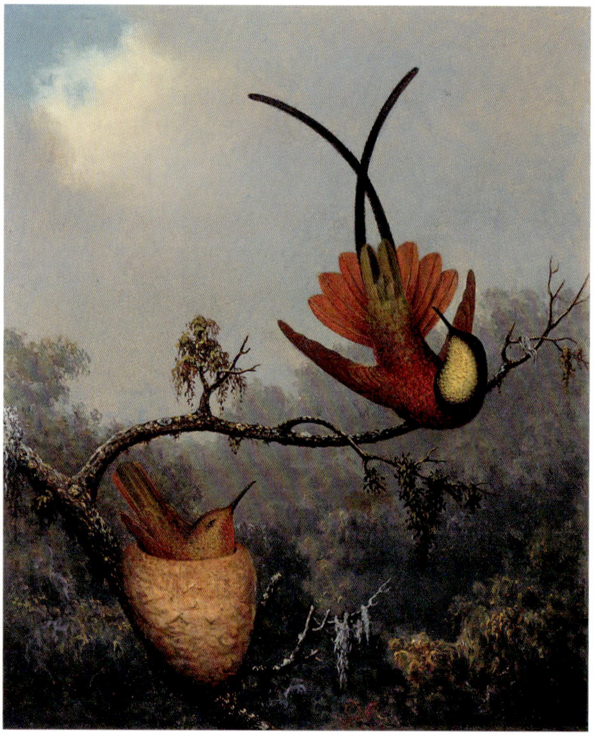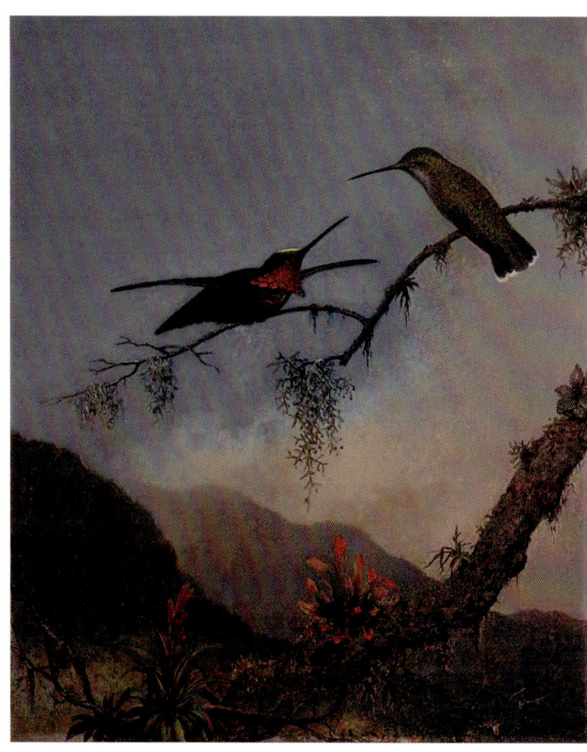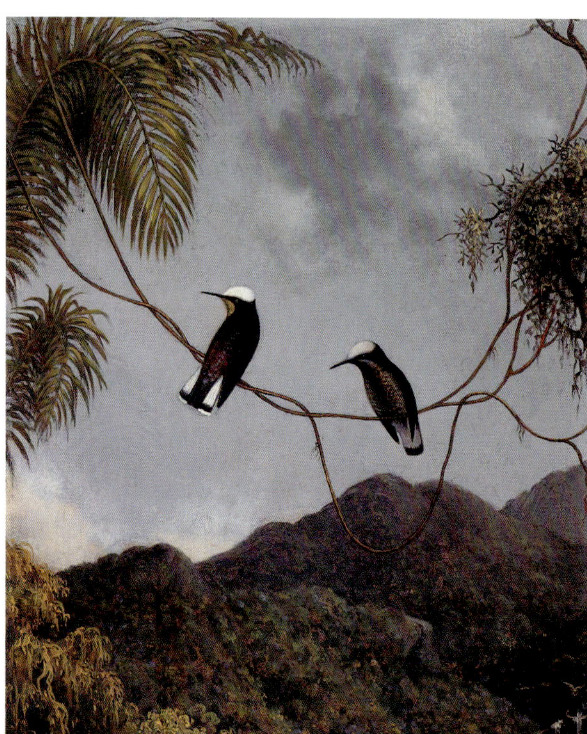

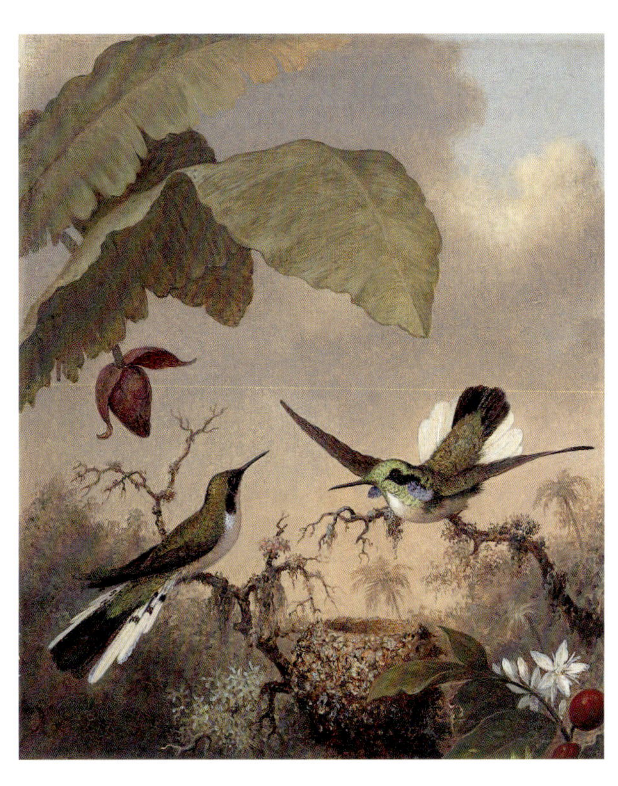

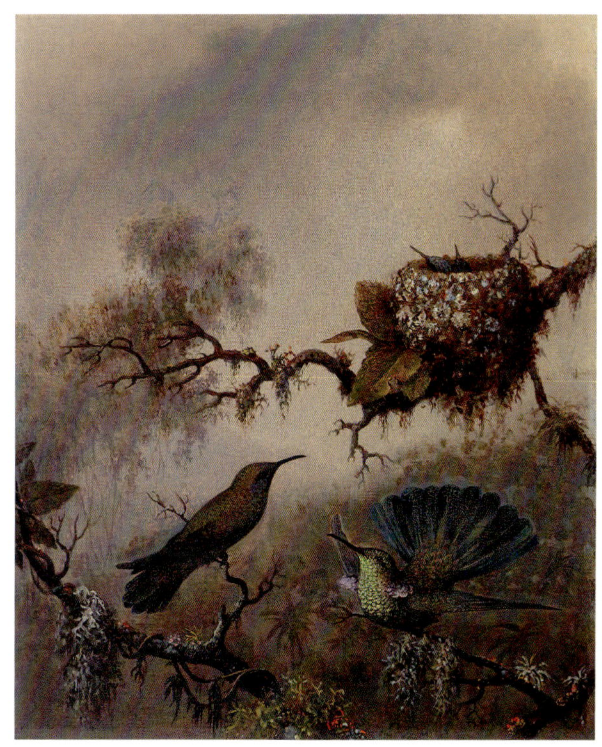

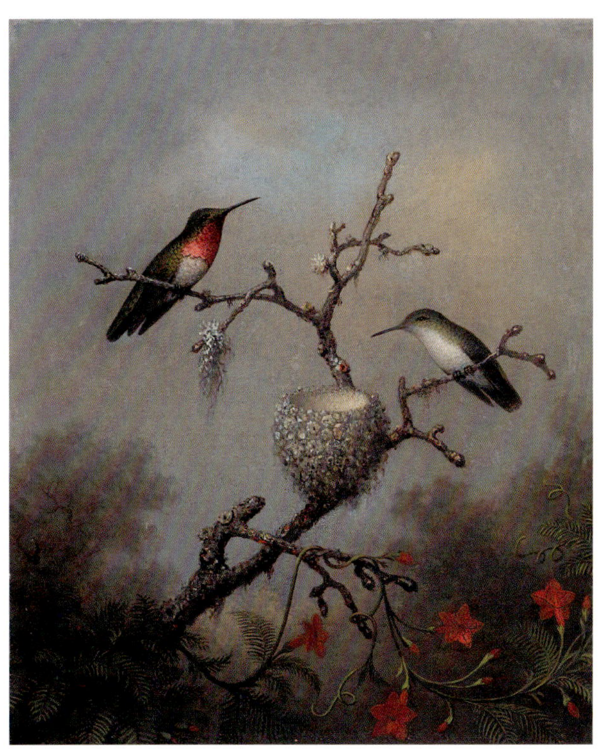

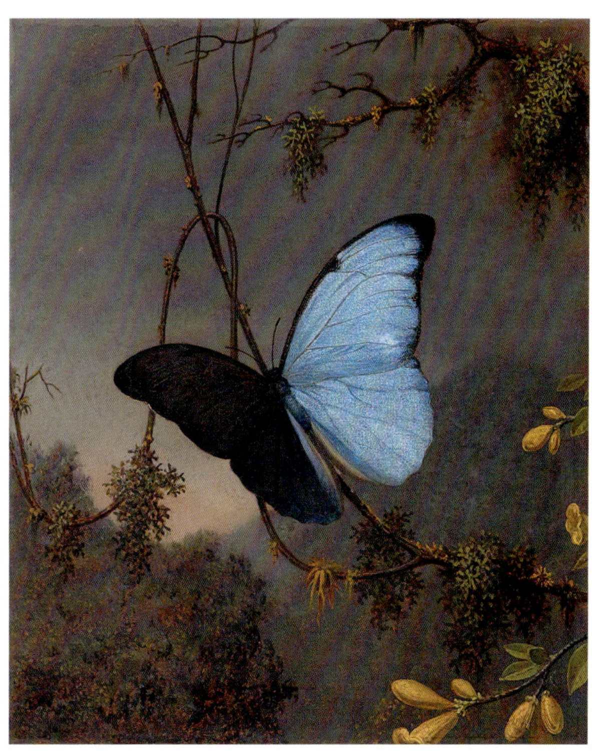

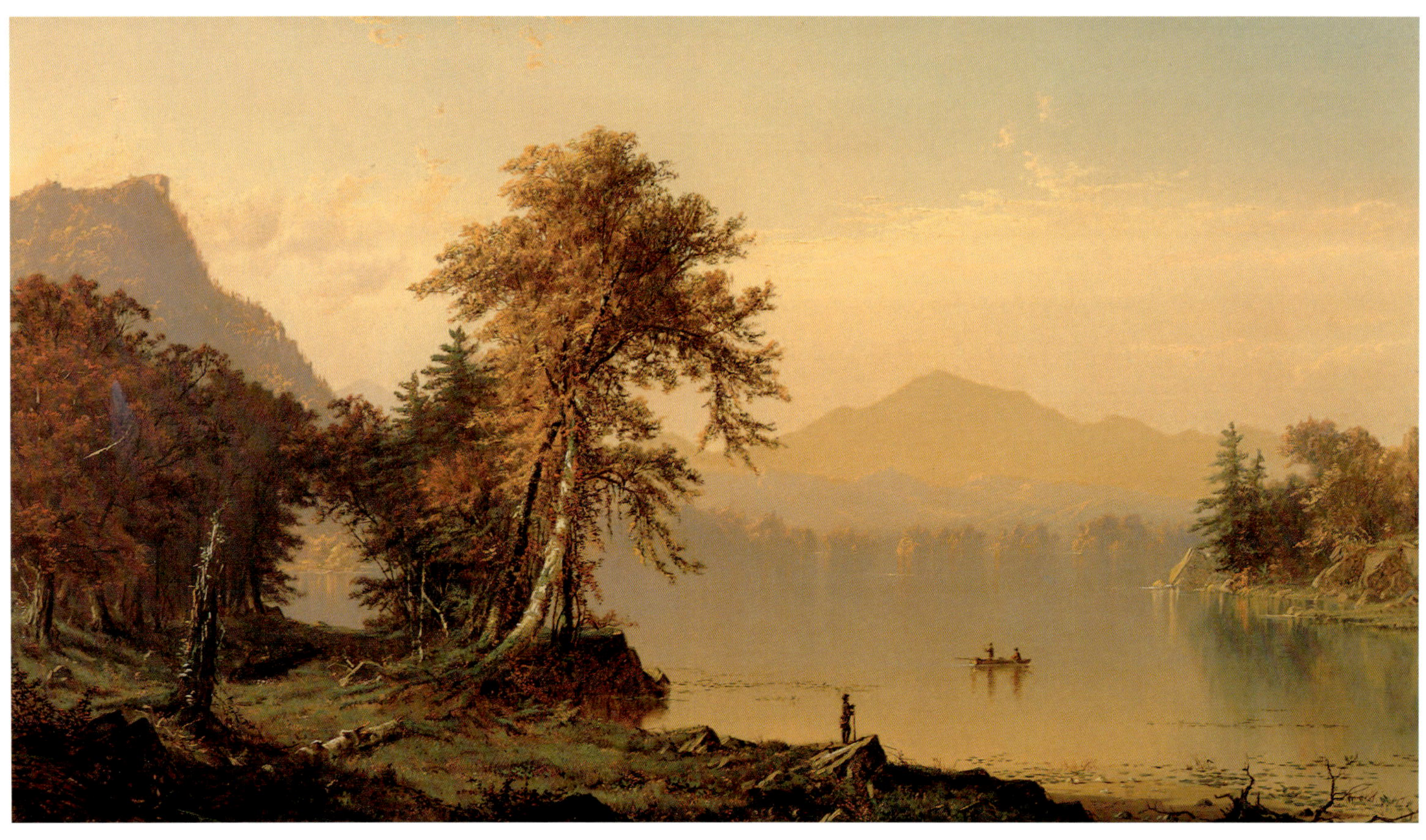

1864 (painted when the artist
was 26–27 years old)
Oil on canvas
34 x 60 in. (86.4 x 152.4 cm)
Signed and dated at lower center:
A.T.Bricher/1864

A native of Portsmouth, New Hampshire, Alfred T. Bricher spent his youth in the northern Massachusetts coastal town of Newburyport. By 1851, he was working in Boston as a dry goods clerk or perhaps as a bookseller, and possibly taking art classes at the Lowell Institute, although he would later claim to be entirely self-taught. Bricher gave up dry goods (or books) in 1858 to become an artist, and returned to Newburyport to launch his new career. He spent much of the following year in Boston, and in 1860, he opened a studio in the Merchants' Bank at 28 State Street.[1]

It is tempting to imagine young Bricher crossing paths with the forty-year-old Martin Johnson Heade in the salt marshes of Newburyport in 1859. Heade made his first trip to the village that year, and would eventually immortalize its marshes in scores of luminous landscapes (see cat. 23). There is no evidence that the two painters met at that time, but during the late summer of 1859, Bricher found himself in the company of the New York artists William Stanley Haseltine and Charles Temple Dix, sketching at Mount Desert Island off the coast of Maine. It is not entirely clear how Bricher, a professional artist for less than a year, came to join the better trained, the more experienced, and the far more worldly Haseltine. They could have met coincidentally on such a relatively small island, but perhaps it was the grateful Heade, pleased by his visit to Newburyport, who introduced his two younger colleagues.[2]

Bricher possessed a good deal of ambition, and most of it was directed toward becoming a successful landscape painter in the manner of the late Thomas Cole, Frederic Church, or even Albert Bierstadt, who was a native of New Bedford, Massachusetts, and was beginning to make a name for himself in New York. It may have been at Haseltine's (or Heade's) urging that Bricher traveled to New York in October 1860, and on that same trip made the essential pilgrimage to the Catskills to see for himself where Cole had reinvented American landscape painting. The trip yielded at least five canvases that Bricher deemed significant, including views of such famous Cole landmarks as Catskill Creek, Kaaterskill Clove, and Kaaterskill Falls. The following summer, in August 1861, Bricher traveled to North Conway, New Hampshire, which Cole had similarly pioneered, and where such important artists as Asher B. Durand and Frederick Kensett had also set their easels before the majestic White Mountains.

Had Bricher stayed longer, he might have encountered Bierstadt, who arrived in early September with his sister and his nephew.[3]

If Bricher and Heade did not encounter one another in Newburyport in 1859, they must have met in 1862, when they independently but almost simultaneously moved into Boston's Studio Building at Tremont and Bromfield Streets. No documents survive to suggest a close friendship or a significant relationship of any kind, but the affinities between their work, their ambitions, and their travels are tantalizing. It could have been Heade, for example, who introduced Bricher to Grand Manan Island off the coast of New Brunswick. The older artist visited Passamaquoddy Bay during the summer of 1862, and nearby Grand Manan Island would later become one of Bricher's favorite sketching destinations. In August of the following year, Heade worked at Rye Beach on the New Hampshire shore halfway between Bricher's two hometowns of Portsmouth and Newburyport. There is no evidence that Heade and Bricher made either of these excursions together, indeed it is virtually certain that they did not. But the trips may have been spawned by conversations in the Studio Building in Boston, or certainly would have been discussed there once Heade had returned.[4]

Bricher became most widely known in America for the chromolithographs of his work that, beginning in 1866, the Boston printing firm Louis Prang and Co. published and distributed. Few subjects interested Heade more in the early 1860s than chromolithography, which he planned to use for his proposed 1864 album of hummingbird prints, *The Gems of Brazil* (see cat. 18). It is difficult to imagine that Heade did not discuss the subject of chromolithography at some length before setting sail for Rio de Janeiro, given his great ambition for the project. The circumstances that later brought Bricher together with the firm of Louis Prang are unknown, but the young painter may have been emboldened by Heade's enthusiastic expectations for the medium of lithography.[5]

In 1864, while Heade was in Rio de Janeiro or on his way to London, Bricher was in Boston, completing his most important painting of White Mountain scenery, the impressive *View of Mount Washington*.[6] The work was a summary of Bricher's early infatuation with Cole and Church, and the strategies they had developed for recording the rugged American landscape. In *View of Mount*

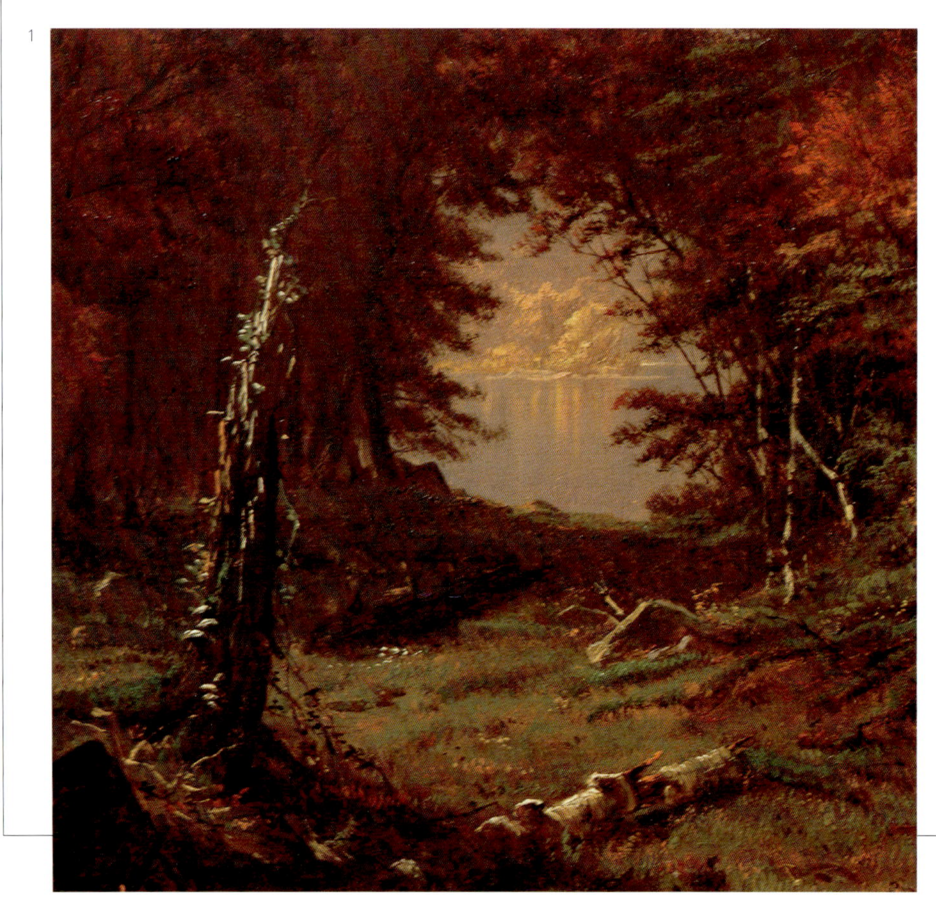

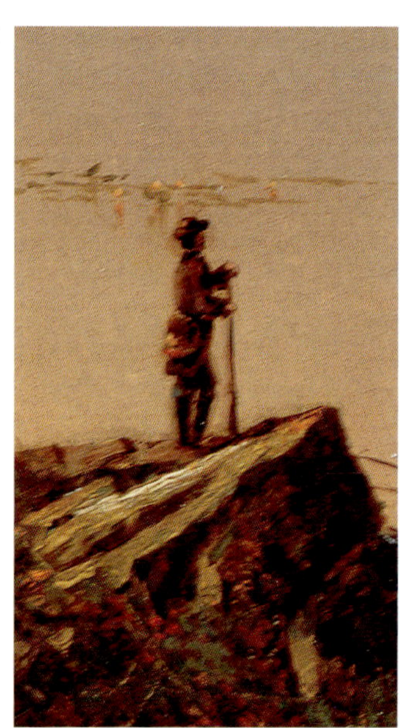

Washington, Bricher placed a lone romantic figure on the banks of what may be the Saco River, and as he leans on his long rifle, he gazes across its expanse to Mount Washington rising majestically in the distance. His view is interrupted only by a spit of land on the right and a small rowboat slipping silently across the still water. The foreground birch and oak trees are covered in autumn foliage, except for one staggered trunk *(fig. 1)* that has been struck by lightening, a common device in the work of Cole that spoke to the mortality of all living things.

By the time Bricher painted *View of Mount Washington* in 1864, New England's autumn spectacle had long been a favorite subject of American landscape painters. Cole could not resist the brilliance of fall color, such younger artists as Jasper Cropsey and Louis Rémy Mignot (see cat. 13) specialized in the annual scenic wonder, and the landscapist Jervis McEntee (see cat. 25) would paint almost nothing else. Before the Civil War, the magnificence of autumn in New England appealed to the public for its uniquely American quality. The dazzling red, orange, and yellow foliage flamed nowhere so astonishingly as in the United States, and that arboreal phenomenon quickly became a source of national pride. Once the Civil War began, autumn scenery – more familiar in the North than in the South – became a convincing symbol of the Union cause. But by the armistice at Appomattox, autumn's fleeting radiance was most frequently equated with so many abbreviated lives that had been lost on the battlefield.

Bricher may have painted *View of Mount Washington* in the autumn season to commemorate his own family's contribution to the roster of war dead. In 1864, Alfred's younger brother, William Bricher, was killed in Virginia at the Battle of Spotsylvania Court House, a bloody encounter that resulted in nearly 30,000 casualties on both sides during a two-week period. William Bricher's death may in part explain the elegiac quality that filters through *View of Mount Washington,* as the solitary figure, possibly a surrogate for the painter himself, watches a boat glide across peaceful waters to another shore *(fig. 2)*. One man rows while another looks back, a last glimpse, perhaps, at a short life ended far too soon and far too abruptly.[7]

For all its debt to Cole and Church, *View of Mount Washington* also marks the first subtle shift in Bricher's thinking about the American landscape that may suggest the influence of Heade. Although the work remains firmly grounded in the format and the compositional strategies of the New York landscape painters that Bricher so admired, his treatment of the soft evening light indicates a movement toward the luminance that was so crucial to Heade's landscape canvases of the early 1860s. Bricher may have been equating the dimming of his brother's life with the dimming of the day, or perhaps he had been moved by the twilight subjects of Church or Sanford Gifford (see cat. 10). But the almost palpable atmosphere of *View of Mount Washington,* the careful cadence of receding compositional elements, and the elegantly simplified background are consistent with Heade's views of Newburyport marshes from 1862 and 1863. And despite the lack of tangible evidence to connect the two, with each passing year, Bricher's paintings came to resemble the work of no artist so much as Martin Johnson Heade.

William Stanley Haseltine (1835–1900)

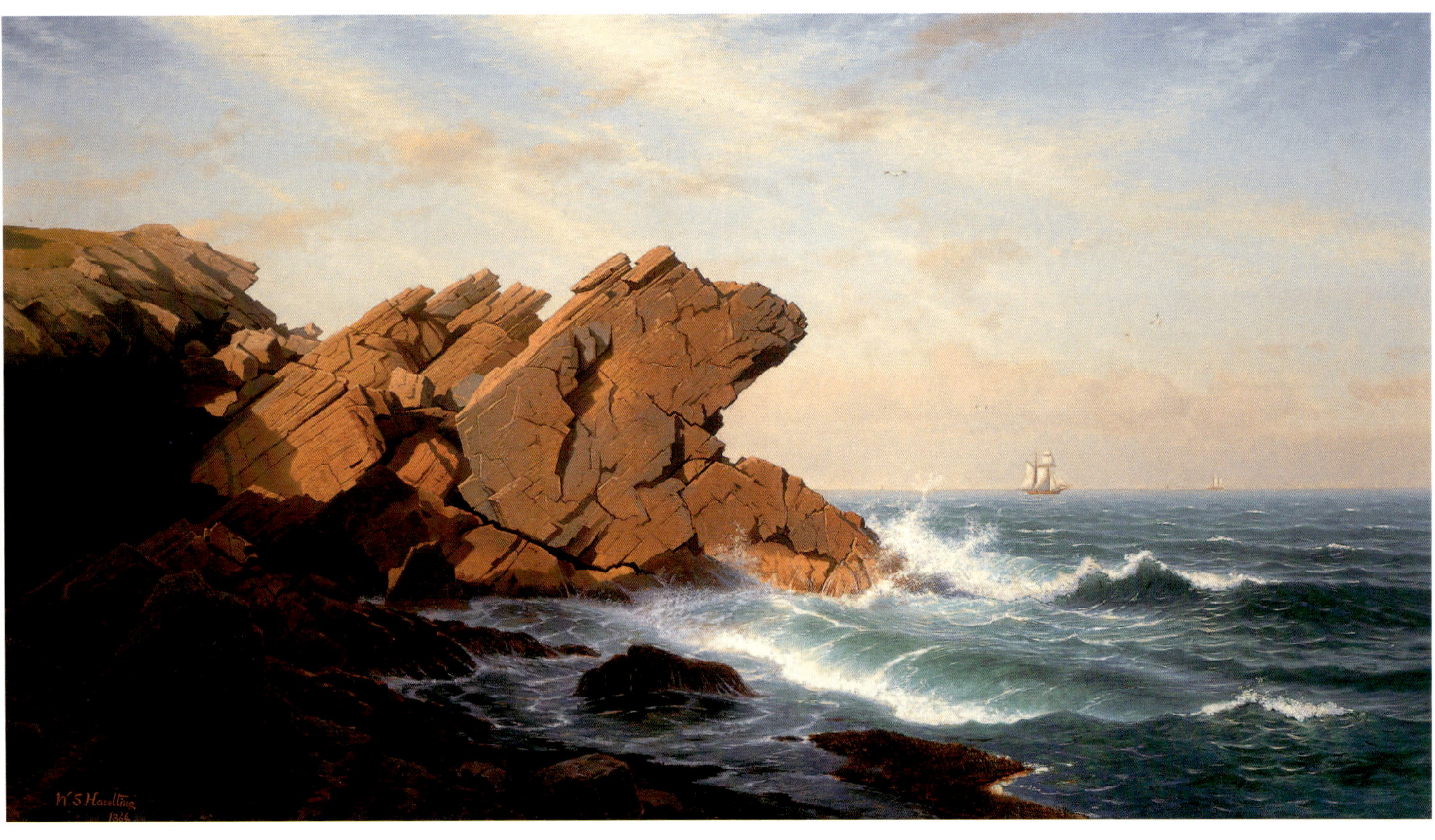

1864 (painted when the artist was 29 years old)
Oil on canvas
31 1/4 x 56 1/2 in. (79.4 x 143.5 cm)
Signed and dated lower left: *W. S. Haseltine/1864*

Early provenance: From the artist, New York, 1865; (sold) to Rutherford Stuyvesant, New York, by April 1865.
Early exhibition history: *Fortieth Annual Exhibition of the National Academy of Design,* New York, spring 1865, no. 212 as *Pulpit Rock, Nahant.*
Early publications: "Among the Studios," *Watson's Weekly Art Journal,* vol. 2, no. 6, 3 December 1864, p. 83.

"Fine Art Gossip," *Watson's Weekly Art Journal,* vol. 2, no. 10, 31 December 1864, p. 147. "Among the Studios," *Watson's Weekly Art Journal,* vol. 2, no. 13, 21 January 1865, p. 195. "National Academy of Design. North Room," *New York Times,* 29 May 1865.
References: Manoogian, 1996, p. 24. Manoogian, 1999, no. 23, pp. 64–65.

William Stanley Haseltine came from a prominent Philadelphia family, and attended boarding school in Princeton and the University of Pennsylvania before graduating from Harvard in 1854. But Haseltine's ambitions resided in the arts, and after months of pleading, he finally persuaded his father to allow him to study in Europe. By the autumn of 1855, Haseltine was in Düsseldorf, training at the Academy and traveling through Germany, Switzerland, and Italy. He was back in the United States in 1858, and like his fellow students, Worthington Whittredge and Albert Bierstadt, he returned accomplished in the realistic style taught by the Düsseldorf School.[1]

Haseltine settled in New York in 1859, renting quarters in the Tenth Street Studio Building, the aesthetic and commercial nexus of American landscape painting. Although he continued to exhibit views of the Italian coast near Naples, Amalfi, and Capri, he gradually developed a reputation as a capable painter of American subjects as well. He had gravitated to seascape subjects in Europe, but that interest blossomed along the shores of Mount Desert Island in Maine and Narragansett Bay in Rhode Island. After the spending the summers of 1862 and 1863 sketching the New England coast, and exhibiting the meticulous shoreline views that resulted from those drawings, Haseltine came to be regarded among America's best marine painters, frequently compared to the much admired Frederick Kensett.[2]

Haseltine's 1863 views of the rocky Rhode Island coast at Narragansett were popular with collectors, but there was also a critical backlash that suggested his work was too repetitive and that he should consider other subjects. Haseltine ignored the clamor of critics, and in early 1864, he was painting the Narragansett coast as he awaited the birth of his second child. But tragically, on 11 June 1864, Haseltine's twenty-ninth birthday, his wife, Helen, and his infant son died in childbirth. The artist consoled himself with work, and by the end of the summer, he was sketching near the town of Nahant, Massachusetts. He elected to forego Narragansett, but more for the fond memories he and Helen shared of Rhode Island than any chiding by New York critics.[3]

Haseltine was back in Manhattan by October, and writers quickly commented upon the extraordinary drawings he had produced at Nahant. One critic noted that "the rocks, water and sky being painted with such a closeness and fidelity to nature as to leave little for the artist to add when he comes to use them in large works."[4] During the fall and winter of 1864, Haseltine put those sketches to good use, and generated no less than eight significant views of the impressive rock formations at Nahant. On 3 December 1864, *Watson's Weekly Art Journal* reported that Haseltine was at work on a "view of the 'Preacher's [sic] Rock.' … The color of the rocks, with the sunlight falling full upon them, is warm and strong," and on the last day of 1864, the periodical offered an update and the prediction that the "large picture of 'Pulpit Rock' … promises to be a strong and effective work." By 21 January 1865, *Watson's Weekly* announced that the painting was finished, and was "a picture of great beauty and excellence."[5]

In late April 1865, Haseltine submitted *Summer Afternoon, Nahant, Massachusetts* to the spring exhibition of the National Academy of Design as *Pulpit Rock, Nahant.* The work was already sold to Rutherford Stuyvesant by the opening of the Academy show, as were at least two and perhaps three other Nahant subjects.[6] But the critics who complained about Haseltine's views of Narragansett believed he had simply moved his obsession with rocky shorelines north to Massachusetts:

> *This rock nuisance pursues us again in No. 212, by Mr. W. S. Haseltine, N.A., who gives us the peculiar formation of 'Pulpit Rock, Nahant.' The charm of such a hard transcript is unknown to us. We recognize the manual skill of the artist, and no more. It would be a relief if Mr. Haseltine would go to work at once and paint a quarry. He might in such wise get over it, and become as surfeited as the rest of the public.*[7]

In 1867, Henry Tuckerman, describing Haseltine's tireless analysis of rock formations, wrote that his "rock-portraits … speak to the eye of science of a volcanic birth and the antiquity of man." Scholars have since made interesting use of Hasletine's links to the Harvard scientist Louis Agassiz, to Darwinism, and to any number of contemporaneous ideas about geology and the origins of the world.[8] But as Haseltine sat on the rocks at Nahant during the summer of 1864, he may have been thinking more about their enduring permanence than their origins in the weeks after losing his wife and child.

Thomas Moran (1837–1926)

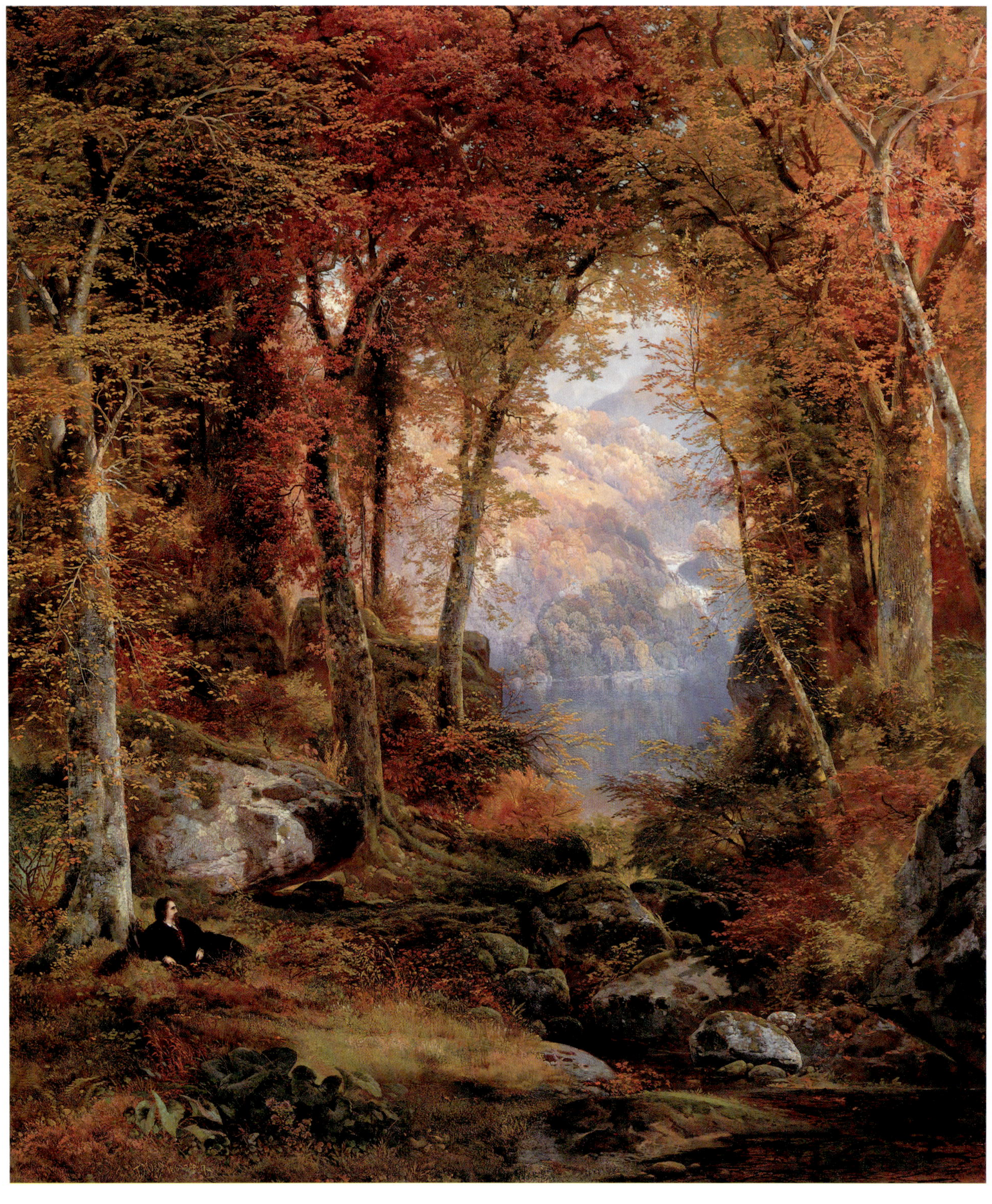

1865 (painted when the artist
was 28 years old)
Oil on canvas
40 x 34 ¼ in. (101.6 x 87 cm)
Signed, dated and inscribed at lower
left: *T. Moran/1865 – Op 17 –*

Early provenance: From the artist;
(possibly sold) to Mr. Baird, by 1866.[1]
Early exhibition history: *Forty-first
Annual Exhibition of the National Academy
of Design,* New York, spring 1866, no. 474.
References: Manoogian, 1989, no. 8,
pp. 30–31. Manoogian, 1996, p. 25.

Thomas Moran was from a family of English textile workers whose traditional cottage livelihoods were all but eliminated by the power looms and other industrial machinery developed in the 1830s. Seeking to escape the economic hardship that gripped Lancashire, England, the Moran family made their way to the United States, settling first in Baltimore before moving onto Philadelphia. But their days at American looms were not many. In one generation, Thomas Moran and three of his brothers shifted the family trade from textiles to the visual arts, and established this country's most important legacy of landscape painters.[2]

The oldest of the Moran sons, Edward, was the first to take up painting, the first to open a studio in Philadelphia, and his was the encouraging example that inspired his younger brothers. But it was the second son, Thomas, who became the most celebrated artist and far and away the most successful. His heroic views of Yellowstone and the Grand Canyon from the early 1870s onward were hailed masterworks, and became cultural icons that spurred among the first organized efforts to preserve America's unique natural monuments. Thomas Moran's dramatic images of Western landscape captured its awesome spectacle, but without compromising the individuality and integrity of each singular element in the composition.[3] That ability to overlay a rich general sweep with elegantly fitted detail was a skill Thomas Moran had learned years earlier in Philadelphia, working in Edward's studio.

By the time Thomas Moran abandoned his apprenticeship at a Philadelphia printing firm in 1856, and produced his first canvases and watercolors under the watchful eye of his older brother, American landscape painting was at the summit of its popularity and influence. After the death of Thomas Cole in 1848, Frederic Church and Asher B. Durand had assumed the leadership of a growing cast of New York landscapists that included such notable painters as Frederick Kensett, Jasper Cropsey, and Sanford Gifford. That circle enjoyed enormous critical, popular, and commercial success in the 1850s, and were encouraged by patrons and dealers to make ever bolder and more dramatic statements about the American landscape. In the somewhat naïve decade leading up to the American Civil War, these successful artists were barely aware that they had critics and rivals, and if they did know, they well underestimated their potency.

In 1847, the influential English writer and theorist John Ruskin brought out an American edition of his *Modern Painters*, which offered the first broad assault on the basic values that the New York landscape school held inviolable. Although it was in no sense aimed at American artists, Ruskin's critique struck a nerve in the United States. The English writer questioned the very compositional formulas and studio strategies that Americans since Cole had considered the basis of their own art and indisputably sound. He ridiculed Claude Lorraine, Salvatore Rosa, and their English descendants, who had provided the foundation upon which Cole and his followers had erected their aesthetic values. Ruskin argued that the work of Claude and Rosa was too contrived and too much the product of studio artifice to properly describe the reality or the truth, let alone the divinity or the moral majesty, of the natural world. Even the older New York landscapists were affected by the reasonableness of Ruskin's persuasive prose, and for a younger generation of artists and writers, it was like a call to arms.[4]

In 1857 and 1858, an exhibition of contemporary English painting was staged in New York and Philadelphia featuring the work of the Pre-Raphaelites, who Ruskin had championed for the last five years. A group or brotherhood of painters committed to Ruskin's more "truthful" representation of nature, the English Pre-Raphaelites inspired dozens of imitators in the United States. That the brotherhood also possessed a literary arm and was largely the product of one formidable critical voice attracted any number of young American writers to the Pre-Raphaelite cause, and insured that the movement and its local followers would receive more than ample press coverage.[5] For the young, English-born Thomas Moran, barely twenty-one years old, the opportunity to see the work of the Pre-Raphaelites, and to hear the excited voices that supported their revolutionary principles, would have suggested an appealing direction that his own early art might take.[6]

By 1865, when Moran painted *Under the Trees*, the short-lived Pre-Raphaelite movement in America was at its peak. A small group of artists, architects, scientists, and attorneys in New York had founded the Association for the Advancement of Truth in Art in 1863 and had set out to reform America's visual arts and architecture along the lines Ruskin had been calling for since the 1840s. They published a

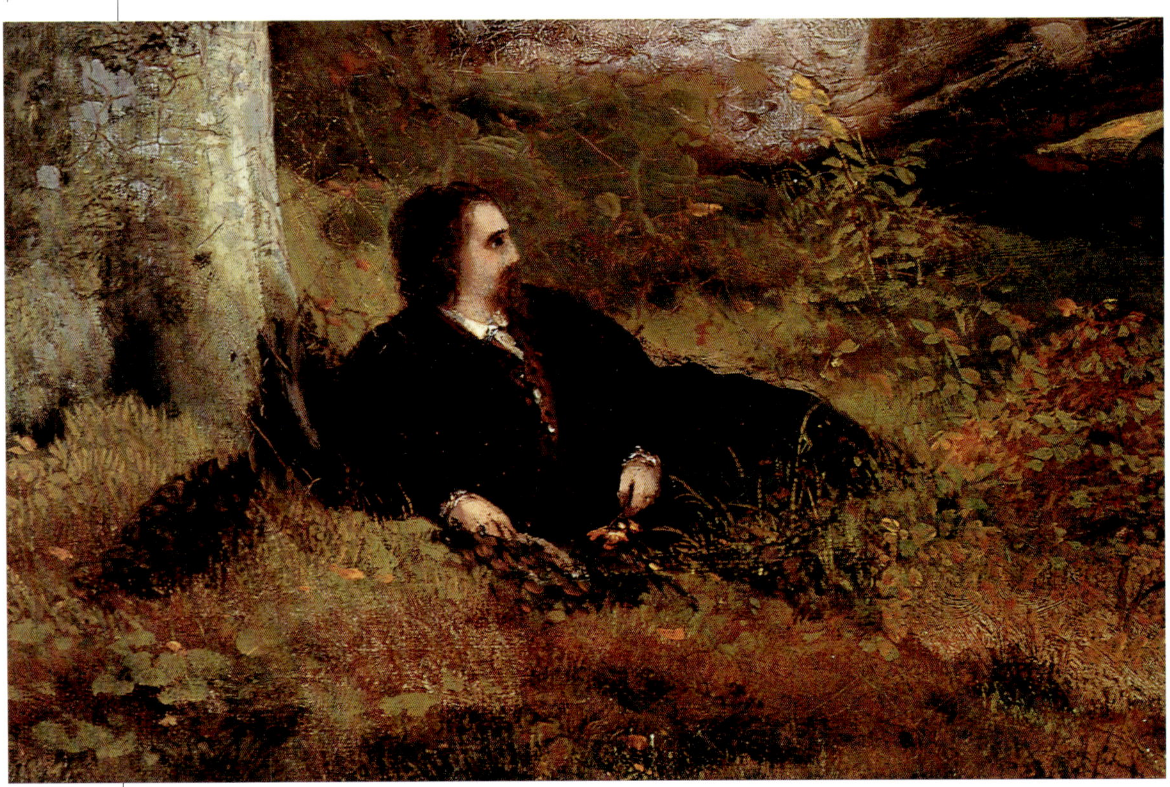

Figure 1:
Thomas Moran (1837–1926)
Under Trees (The Autumnal Woods)
(detail)
1865
Oil on canvas
Manoogian Collection

journal called *The New Path,* and their subscribers and membership rolls swelled with each passing month. Philadelphia even contributed a member, William Trost Richards, and while his relationship to Moran was tenuous, each would have been aware of the other's work, and the similarities between their two aesthetic ambitions.[7] Moran himself never joined the association, and he eventually abandoned Pre-Raphaelitism's "determined realism" for a style more indebted to another Ruskin favorite, the English master J. M. W. Turner, but for most of the 1860s, his work was very much in step with the brotherhood's beliefs.

Under the Trees was the product of Moran's exposure to Ruskin and the Pre-Raphaelites. Like many of his early paintings, it was a staggering labor of meticulous detail, so time consuming to manufacture that he assigned it and forty-two other early canvases an opus number. The commitment of time alone and the perfectly nil possibility that the artist would financially recoup his efforts once the work had sold probably did as much as anything to undermine Moran's continued use of Pre-Raphaelite aesthetic principles. Even such a devout member of the American movement as Charles Herbert Moore complained of painstaking toil and miniscule outcome, noting in a letter to Thomas Farrar that in three hours work he had painted "about as much canvass as I cover with the end of my thumb."[8] If Moran made that much progress on *Under the Trees* in three hours, no doubt he would have been satisfied.

In *Under the Trees,* his seventeenth opus, Moran produced a Pre-Raphaelite masterpiece. Capturing, as Ruskin would have urged, a more or less random view through a forest interior to a mountain lake and hillside beyond, "selecting nothing and rejecting nothing," Moran articulated each leaf in a forest of fall foliage, each twig and each blade of grass rendered with inscrutable care.[9] He was as committed to the lowliest lichens as he was to the sweeping canopy of the tallest trees. The distant vista is flattened into a decorative pattern by the pale but even sunlight that barely penetrates the forest floor, where a lone, half-reclining male figure takes in the view. The bearded man holds a sprig of leaves that he has snatched from a branch on the way to his repose, and in that simple, almost throwaway remark resides Moran's conception of Pre-Raphaelitism. The bearded man's appreciation of the forest depended upon his observation of both the overall beauty of his surroundings and in finding the distinctive loveliness of each constituent element. Moran would have hoped that *Under the Trees* would stimulate the same desire in the viewer, the same capacity to experience the painting in general terms, but also to admire the attractiveness of its extraordinary detail. As Ruskin suggested, "If you can paint one leaf, you can paint the world."[10]

Thomas Worthington Whittredge (1820–1910)

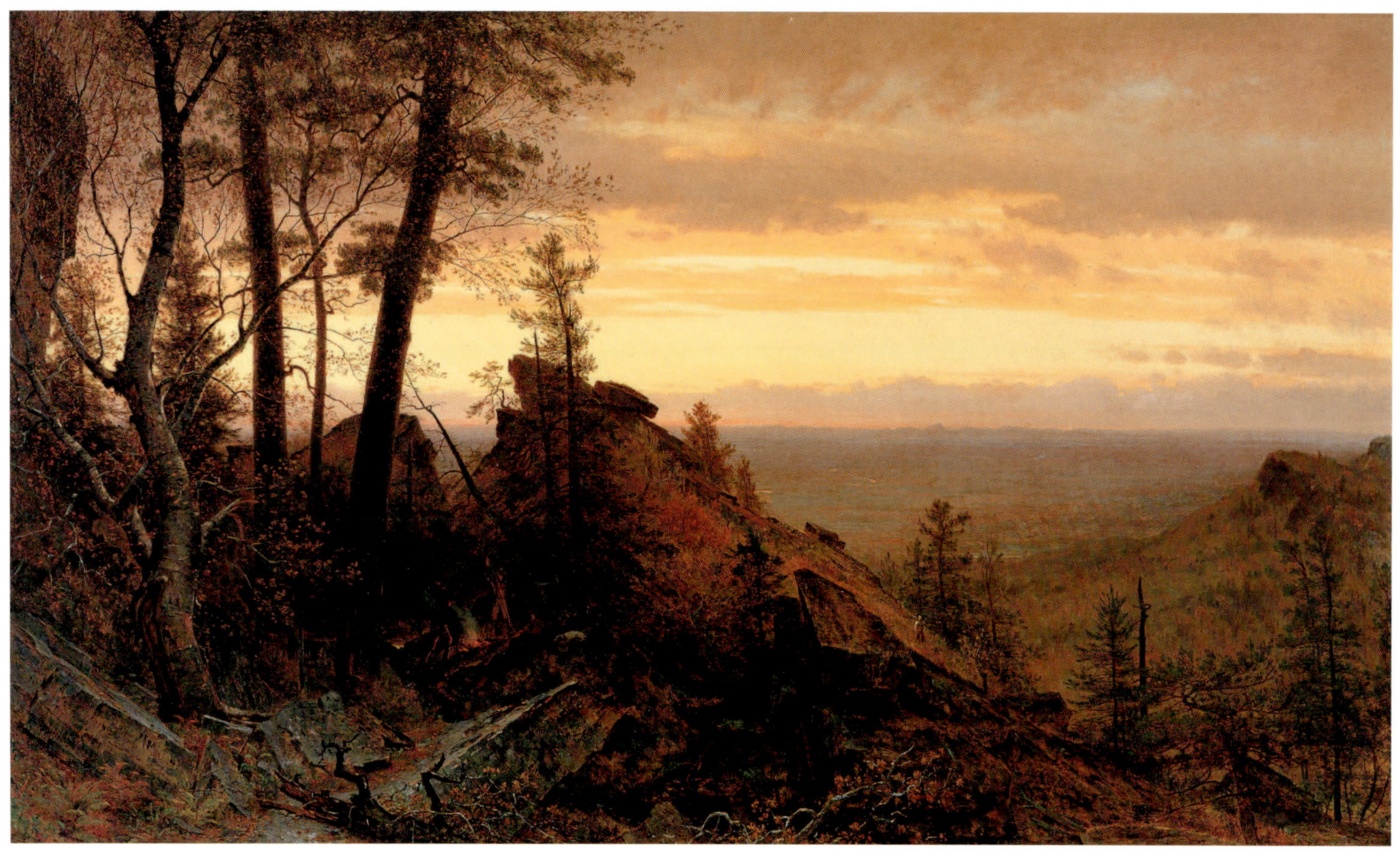

Early provenance: From the artist, New York, 1865; (sold) to S.P. Avery, New York, 1865; (sold) to Winthrop B. Smith, Philadelphia, by 1867.

Early exhibition history: *Fortieth Annual Exhibition of the National Academy of Design,* New York, spring 1865, no. 205. S.P. Avery Gallery, New York, January 1866.

Early publications: Sordello, "National Academy of Design. Fortieth Annual Exhibition; Third Article," *New York Evening Post,* 22 May 1865, p.1. "Fine Arts," *New York Evening Post,* 6 January 1866, p.2. "Avery's Gallery," *New York Evening Post,* 12 January 1866, p.2. "Art Notes," *The Round Table,* 27 January 1866, p.55. Tuckerman, 1867, pp.517–18.

References: Howat, 1987, pp.182–83. Manoogian, 1989, no.7, pp.26–29. Manoogian, 1997, no.11, pp.48–49 and 189.

1865 (painted when the artist was 44–45 years old)
Oil on canvas
45 x 68 in. (114.3 x 172.7 cm)
Signed and dated at lower left: *W. Whittredge 1865*

Worthington Whittredge returned to the United States in 1859, after a decade in Europe. His years in Düsseldorf, studying with Andreas Achenbach and working alongside the American sensation Emanuel Leutze, were well spent, as were his travels in Italy with Albert Bierstadt and William Stanley Haseltine.[1] But by remaining abroad for most of the 1850s, Whittredge missed a fertile period for landscape painting in America. His ambitious colleagues, Frederic Church, Sanford Gifford, and Bierstadt were younger than he was, but they were all much further along in their careers. Whittredge well understood in 1859 that he "must produce something new…inspired by my home surroundings."[2]

Although he had begun his career in Cincinnati, Whittredge settled in New York in 1859, renting quarters in the Tenth Street Studio Building. Richard Morris Hunt's Beaux-Arts structure was the first building erected in New York specifically for fine art studios, and from its opening in 1858, it was the center of American landscape painting. Church had a studio there, as did Gifford, Haseltine, and Bierstadt. The building contained an exhibition space and the tenants held regular open studios attended by throngs of collectors, journalists, and the curious public. Church debuted *Niagara* in the Studio Building in 1858 and *Heart of the Andes* in 1859, and Bierstadt followed suit with *The Rocky Mountains – Lander's Peak* in 1863. It was where Whittredge would establish himself, and although much of the light that found him on Tenth Street was reflected from Church and Bierstadt, it exceeded the exposure he would have received elsewhere.[3]

Unlike the artist-adventurers, Church and Bierstadt, Whittredge sought a convenient wilderness in which to work, and seemingly chose the nearest primitive region to his New York studio. The Shawangunk Mountains were less than eighty miles north of Manhattan, but they offered a rugged synopsis of frontier America. The picturesque area, studded with granite boulders and graced with views of the Hudson River to the east and the Catskills to the west, may have come recommended by Jervis McEntee, who also kept a studio on Tenth Street, and was a native of nearby Rondout. Whittredge worked in the Shawangunks with McEntee and Gifford in September 1861, and during the summer of 1864, he and Gifford returned there together.[4]

Whittredge may have felt pressure to bring something fresh to the landscape idiom, but he embraced themes that were already popular. At the National Academy of Design in 1860, Church's *Twilight in the Wilderness* had dazzled visitors with its spectacular light and color. The work created a vogue for crepuscular effects, and Gifford, Bierstadt, and others immediately followed Church's lead. Artists had been contemplating sunsets for centuries, and the subject was far from unknown to Americans. But in the late 1850s, improvements in the chemical dye processes added hot cadmium reds and yellows to artists' paint boxes. Whittredge took up the materials, seized the theme, and completed *Twilight on the Shawangunk Mountains* in early 1865. It appeared at the National Academy that same year.[5]

By the early 1860s, some American writers were already weary of the dimming of the day that took place each year on the walls of the National Academy. In 1864, James Jackson Jarves lamented the "overstrained atmospheric effects…intense gradations of skies and violent contrasts of positive color," as he accused artists of seeing "the landscape through stained glass."[6] Others disagreed, and took comfort in the exquisitely transitory red, pink, and yellow clouds draped over distant horizons. Writing about *Twilight on the Shawangunk Mountains* in 1867, Henry Tuckerman described it as "a memorable landscape – remarkable for its vivid and true effects of light – the deep but clear amber gleam of the horizon in contrast with the wild and shadowy hills."[7] Similarly, three of the woodsmen in Whittredge's painting eschew the glorious sky for the light of their own fire, while a fourth man returns along the escarpment trail, no doubt having watched the sun drop behind the Catskills. Even on canvas, there were some who admired sunsets and those who would not be bothered.

Winthrop B. Smith acquired *Twilight on the Shawangunk Mountains* perhaps in early 1866, when it went on display at the gallery of S.P. Avery. Smith had been a successful book publisher in Cincinnati, where he met Whittredge, and had made a fortune printing *The McGuffey Reader.* After thirty years in the publishing business, Smith retired in 1863 and moved to Philadelphia. He probably purchased *Twilight on the Shawangunk Mountains* to support a fellow Cincinnatian, and to decorate his new home with a magnificent landscape. But Whittredge's meditation on the fleeting and transitory nature of twilight may have spoken to the Cincinnati publisher, whose own life was in transition as well.[8]

23   SUNSET ON THE MARSHES   Martin Johnson Heade (1819–1904)

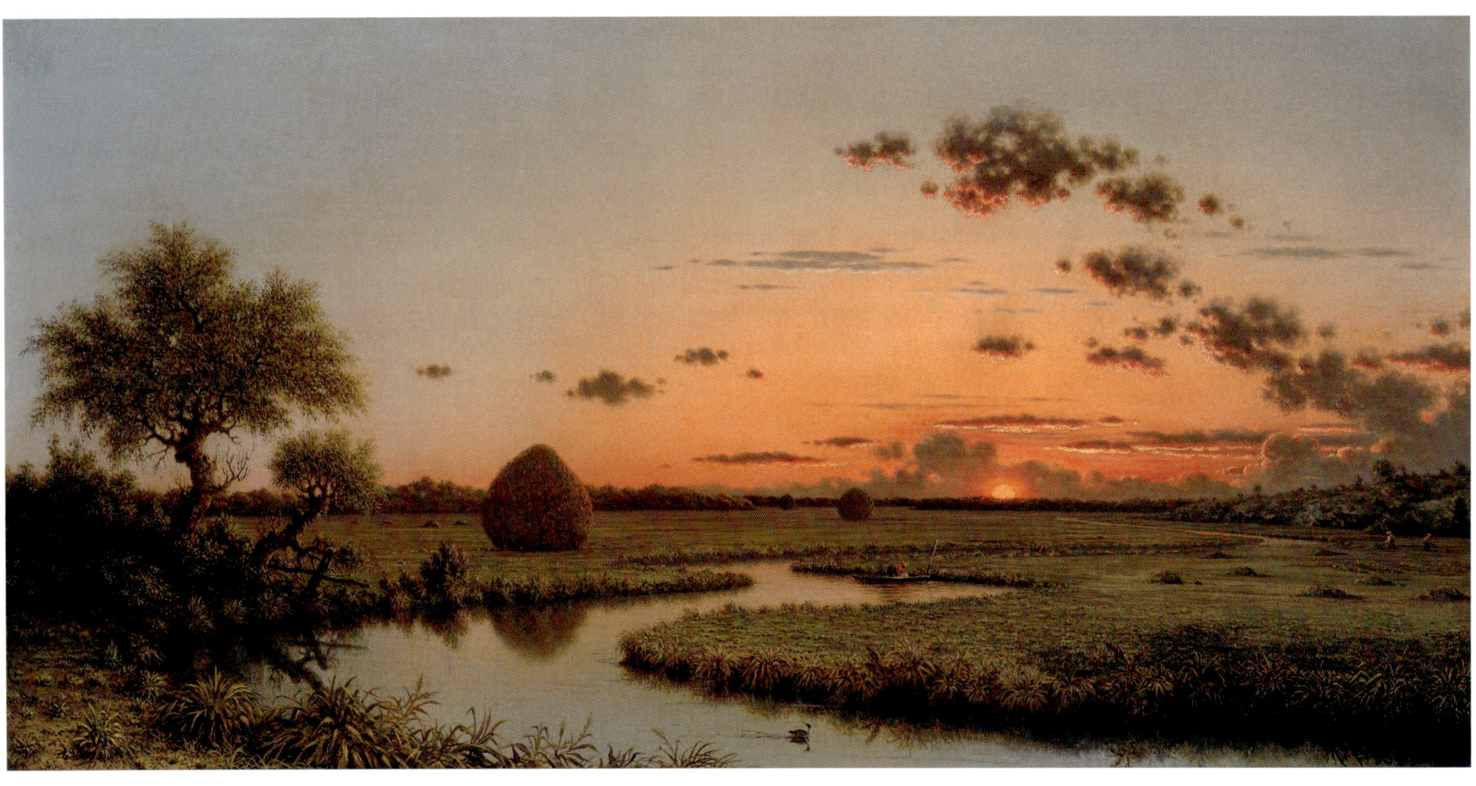

1867 (painted when the artist
was 47 years old)
Oil on canvas
27 x 53 in. (68.6 x 134.6 cm)
Signed and dated at lower right:
M. J. Heade 67

Early exhibition history: (Possibly)
Goupil Gallery, New York, April 1867 as
*Sunset View of the Marshes near
Newburyport.*[1]
References: Manoogian, 1989, no. 21,
pp 60–61. Manoogian, 1997, no. 8, pp. 42–43
and 188. Stebbins, 2000, no. 171, p. 244.

In late 1865, Martin Johnson Heade returned to America from London after his failed effort to produce *The Gems of Brazil,* the book of hummingbird prints (see cat. 18) upon which he had pinned such hope. He had been away from the United States for more than two years, and in that interval, the Civil War had finally ended, Lincoln had been re-elected and then assassinated, and Heade's friend, Frederic Church, had acquired a formidable rival in the painter of Western vistas, Albert Bierstadt. Whether it was the disappointment of his scuttled publishing project or the changing face of America, Heade had difficulty settling into a routine or even finding a studio. He flitted from Providence, Rhode Island, to New York, to Trenton, New Jersey, before simply leaving again in June 1866 on another excursion to the tropics. He stored his work in Church's studio and sailed for Nicaragua.[2]

As Heade wrote to his friend John Russell Bartlett, he went to Nicaragua "to get material for a good-sized picture," but the artist saw little to inspire him, and predictably, found the tropics less than desirable in July. By the second week of August, he was back in New York in search of a studio. He was about to lease quarters in the Somerville Gallery, when Church suggested that Heade sublease his room in the Tenth Street Studio Building. The precise nature of their arrangement is unclear, but by October 1866, Heade was settled in 51 Tenth Street at the center of New York's thriving milieu of landscape painters. His tenure in Church's studio would prove among the most successful years of his career.[3]

Heade did complete at least two paintings of Nicaraguan scenery, and perhaps the *Lagoon in Nicaragua* that he showed at the National Academy of Design in 1867 was the "good-sized picture" he had predicted to Bartlett. That canvas is now lost, and its dimensions are unknown, but if Heade had staked particular ambition on the painting, it was quickly dashed by caustic reviews. One critic, writing for *The Round Table,* suggested that "*Lagoon in Nicaragua* has miasma enough about it to induce low fevers in the gallery."[4] Heade struggled upon returning from England, struggled in Nicaragua, and struggled to produce agreeable paintings of its scenery. If there was some reason that compelled him to produce a large painting, he may have turned to the Newburyport, Massachusetts, salt marshes out of familiarity and sheer comfort with the subject matter. The

largest painting Heade completed in 1867 was his brilliant meditation on salt grass and twilight, *Sunset on the Marshes.* Unfortunately, almost nothing is known about the work once it left Heade's, or rather Church's, easel.

Heade began painting the salt marshes of northern Massachusetts in 1859, and after moving into Church's New York studio, he extended his territory to include Long Island and New Jersey. Heade's panoramic marshes were dense with atmosphere, punctuated by regular cadences of stacked hay, and capped by the glow of evening skies, evocative mist, or dramatic approaching storms. When Heade painted *Sunset on the Marshes* in 1867, he had been making regular excursions across the Hudson to Hoboken, but he probably intended the great canvas to suggest the area around Newburyport, where the marshes were frequently divided by meandering streams.[5]

Heade's reasons for working on a larger scale in 1867 are not altogether clear. He had produced sizable canvases in the early 1860s, but during his years in Rio de Janeiro and London, he had retreated to cabinet-sized or small easel pictures. It may have been Heade's deepening friendship with Church that encouraged him literally to expand his horizons. Certainly no artist had achieved as much success painting on a monumental scale, and even Church's smaller canvases communicated a persuasive sense of grandeur. During the more than ten years that they would share a studio on Tenth Street, Church frequently tried to aid his friend's career, and Heade listened as well as his eccentric nature would allow. It may have been at Church's urging that Heade painted *Sunset on the Marshes* on such an impressive scale.[6]

In April 1867, Heade exhibited a now unidentified but no doubt major canvas called *Sunset View of the Marshes near Newburyport* at the Goupil Gallery in New York. The gallery was owned by Michael Knoedler, a close friend of Church's, who had just commissioned him to paint a commanding view of Niagara Falls for the upcoming 1867 Exposition Universelle in Paris. It may be that Church, feeling at least partially responsible for the size of Heade's *Sunset on the Marshes,* also helped him find an important commercial venue at which to exhibit it.[7]

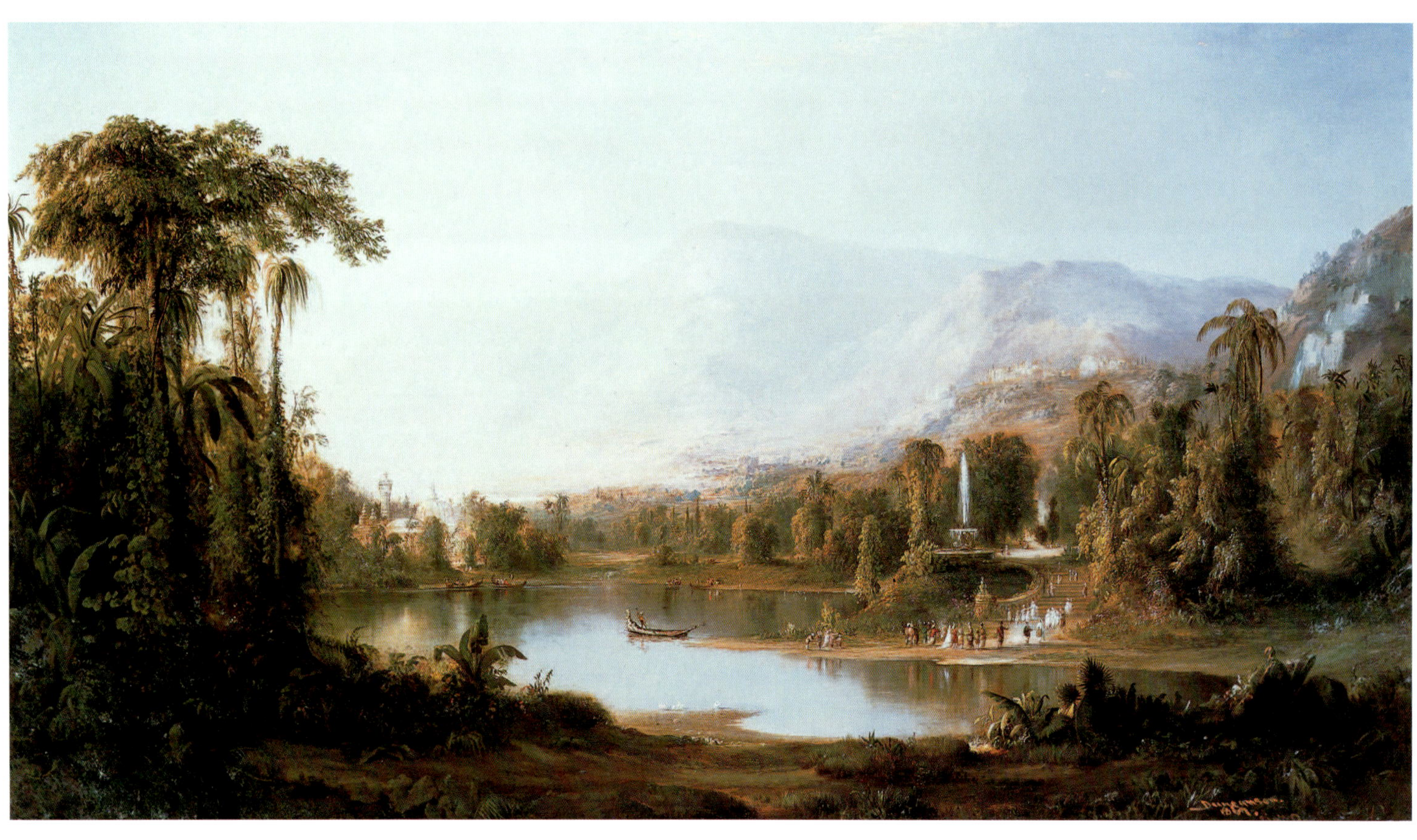

1867 (painted when the artist
was 45–46 years old)
Oil on canvas
28 5/8 x 52 1/8 in. (72.7 x 132.4 cm)
Signed, dated, and inscribed:
Duncanson/1867/Cin. O.

References: Manoogian, 1989, no. 6,
pp. 24–25. Ketner, 1993, no. 120, pp. 130–31
and 202 as *Vale of Kashmir.*

Trained as a house and carriage painter in the 1830s, Robert S. Duncanson transformed himself into a competent portrait artist in the 1840s, and by the end of the decade he had become a well regarded landscapist in Cincinnati, Ohio. The son of freed Virginia slaves, who eventually settled in the Michigan territory, Duncanson apparently received no formal education, but was intelligent and profoundly literate. He would have witnessed and experienced racial prejudice in Michigan, on his travels as an itinerant portraitist, and in antebellum Cincinnati, just across the Ohio River from slaveholding Kentucky. But in Cincinnati, Duncanson also found supportive fellow landscapists in Worthington Whittredge and William Sonntag, a thriving abolitionist culture led by the Beecher family of ministers, and enough liberal collectors of fine art to support his improbable ambition.[1]

Duncanson's roving career as portrait painter came to an end in 1848, when he was commissioned by the Reverend Charles Avery, a Pittsburgh abolitionist and speculator in Michigan copper, to produce a view of the Cliff Mine on the banks of Lake Superior. Duncanson's painting of the Upper Peninsula landscape was evocative, poetic, and far from the commemorative topographical document Reverend Avery may have been expecting. In the 1840s, Cincinnati had earned the nickname, "Athens of the West," through its support of the visual arts, including frequent exhibitions of American landscape paintings. Duncanson clearly had benefited from this exposure, and although his *Cliff Mine, Lake Superior, 1848* was a somewhat naïve in composition, it revealed an awareness and an understanding of the works of Thomas Cole and Asher B. Durand he had seen in Cincinnati.[2]

In the 1850s, Duncancson's mature paintings frequently described the American landscape in Arcadian terms. Nature's perfect order was a common theme in the Romantic poetry Duncanson admired, but it also percolated through the paintings and writings of Cole, Durand, and other New York artists. In such works as *The Voyage of Life,* which was acquired by a Cincinnati collector in 1846, and especially in his "Essay on American Scenery," Cole proffered that the pristine wilderness was the only place to experience true perfection, and by extension, to know God's divinity unmediated by the corruption of man. Duncanson was so taken with the great landscapist that, in 1852, he copied another of Cole's meditations on Arcadia, his *Garden of Eden* of 1828.[3]

As much as mainstream literary and artistic sources may have shaped Duncanson's taste for Arcadian subject matter, the idea of a perfect American Eden would have resonated with a good deal of topicality and poignancy to an African American and a descendant of southern slaves. Duncanson was not the only artist or writer to imagine the American landscape as a paradise rather than the site of chattel bondage it remained in the years leading up to the Civil War. But it would have been achingly evident to Duncanson's admirers that the artist's utopian vistas belied the cruelty and shame perpetrated on his race and on the American landscape by those who would profit from both.[4]

When the Civil War broke out in 1861, Duncanson remained in Cincinnati, even with its proximity to potential frontlines just across the Ohio River, and he produced two of the largest and most important paintings that year, *The Land of the Louts Eaters* and *Western Tornado.* During the summer of 1862, he made an expansive sketching tour, which took him down the Ohio to the Mississippi River, north to Minnesota, across Canada through Toronto and Montreal, and on to New Hampshire before circling home to Cincinnati in October. The trip led to some of Duncanson's most appealing studio landscapes, including views of Minnehaha Falls and Minnenopa Falls in Minnesota, but it also may have convinced him to resettle across the border in Canada.[5] He had shown *The Land of the Lotus Eaters* and *Western Tornado* at a jewelry store in Toronto in late 1861, the first stops on what Duncanson hoped would become an international tour. His return to Canada the following year may have been to investigate further opportunities while he worked out the logistics for bringing his pictures to England.[6]

But a year later, in the spring of 1863, Duncanson was still in Cincinnati. In March, a writer for the *Cincinnati Daily Enquirer* visited his studio and described a small oil sketch called the *Vale of Kashmir,* which Duncanson planned to develop into a larger painting. But as Civil War battlefields spread westward and the fighting intensified during the summer of 1863, Duncanson made no further progress on the larger *Vale of Kashmir.* By September, he had finally made his way to Montreal, but planning only to pass through Canada, he initially produced little work. Difficulties arose, however, in securing English venues for *The Land of the Lotus Eaters* and *Western Tornado*, and he would remain in Montreal for nearly two years. It was there in 1864 that he completed the expanded version of *Vale of Kashmir*, the first of three similar landscapes based upon Thomas Moore's 1817 book length poem, *Lalla Rookh*.[7]

Thomas Moore's popular poem describes the journey of Lalla, a princess sent from Delhi to Kashmir to join her betrothed, the King of Bucharia, whom she has never met. On the way, she encounters Feramorz, a poet, who enchants her with stories and verses that stir her imagination and her passion. The poet and the princess appear to be victims of a doomed romance, and Feramorz may suffer the repercussions of charming a king's intended bride. But in the end, Feramorz reveals to Lalla that he has only disguised himself as a poet, and is in fact the King of Bucharia, the man she is meant to marry. Duncanson's 1864 treatment of the subject captured the arrival of Lalla and Feramorz in Kashmir after the intrigue of the journey has been happily resolved. He presented the *Vale of Kashmir* at the spring 1865 exhibition of the Art Association of Montreal; it attracted little or no critical notice, but seemingly did find a buyer.

The Civil War ended in April 1865, and during the following summer, Duncanson at last made his long delayed tour of the British Isles. He may have brought several major canvases with him, including *Western Tornado*, *Prairie Fire*, *Niagara*, and *Oenone*, but the only paintings he is known to have exhibited were *The Land of the Lotus Eaters* and *Chaudiere Falls near Quebec*, which appeared in Dublin, Glasgow, and London to considerable acclaim. Even Alfred Tennyson, upon whose poem *The Land of the Lotus Eaters* was based, congratulated Duncanson for capturing "a land in which one loves to wander and linger."[8] Duncanson found enthusiastic supporters in England, and quite possibly collectors, and may have considered settling there permanently. But if so, the plan never materialized. Before the end of 1866, after a year and a half in England, and just over three years since he had left Ohio, Duncanson was back in Cincinnati, and had opened a studio on Fourth Street.[9]

The Montreal exhibition of Duncanson's 1864 *Vale of Kashmir* was the only public presentation of the work during the artist's lifetime. O. S. Wood of Montreal apparently purchased the painting directly from the 1865 show, and it was not seen again publicly for the rest of the nineteenth century and well after. Within a year of his return to Cincinnati, Duncanson began and completed an even larger version of *Vale of Kashmir*, which either immediately or at some later moment acquired the title *Arcadian Landscape*. His reasons for returning to the subject are unknown, but he had made copies of his paintings before. While in Montreal, he had produced a second version of *The Land of the Lotus Eaters*, knowing that he was taking the earlier canvas to England, and had every expectation of selling it there.

It would seem likely that a patron in Cincinnati commissioned the 1867 painting now known as *Arcadian Landscape*, but it is unclear how Duncanson would have induced the commission and produced such a close variant of a canvas he no longer owned. The 1864 *Vale of Kashmir* was in a Canadian private collection, and it is doubtful that anyone in Cincinnati had seen it exhibited in Montreal two years earlier. Duncason may have used the small 1863 oil sketch of *Vale of Kashmir* to solicit and complete the commission, but there is nothing to say that he still owned that sketch in 1867. It is possible that during his longer than expected stay in Montreal the resourceful Duncanson had *Vale of Kashmir* photographed as he had *The Land of the Lotus Eaters* and another painting, *City and Harbour of Quebec*. But if he attracted a commission for the 1867 *Arcadian Landscape* with a photograph of the 1864 *Vale of Kashmir*, no print of that image has survived.[10]

Not only are the origins of *Arcadian Landscape* unknown, the 1867 painting was seemingly never exhibited during Duncanson's lifetime, suggesting that it probably went directly to a patron. Unfortunately, it is not known who the original owner was, and by the time the canvas resurfaced in the twentieth century, it had lost all connection to Thomas Moore's poem, *Lalla Rookh*. With so little in the way of documentation, it is entirely possible that Duncanson himself eliminated the poetic allusion, and chose the more general title, *Arcadian Landscape*, allowing for a broader interpretation of the work. The only source and justification for calling *Arcadian Landscape* by the title *Vale of Kashmir* is that its composition is so similar to the earlier canvas of 1864.

Whether or not he chose it, Duncanson probably would not have objected to the title *Arcadian Landscape*. For early readers of

Thomas Moore's *Lalla Rookh,* and in all likelihood for Duncanson as
well, the appeal of the poem was in the sentimental and predictable
happy ending of Lalla and Feramorz, who overcome (admittedly
manufactured) obstacles before arriving safely in Kashmir, their own
Arcadia. The lovers' fortitude in the face of uncertainty was seen in
Moore's time as having parallels in the poet's support of Irish independence and his sympathy for Catholicism in Anglican England. For
Duncanson, Moore's poem of forced marriage, shifting identities,
confusion, betrayal, and Lalla's impending separation from the man
she loved would have resonated as a much romanticized variant of the
African Diaspora in America. Connecting *Lalla Rookh* to American
slavery would have required a great deal of optimism on Duncanson's
part, but it may have been no coincidence that he produced *Vale of
Kashmir* in the year after the Emancipation Proclamation took effect.
And it is perhaps perfectly reasonable that Duncanson would transform his *Vale of Kashmir* into an *Arcadian Landscape* upon returning
in 1867 to a United States that had finally been rid of slavery.

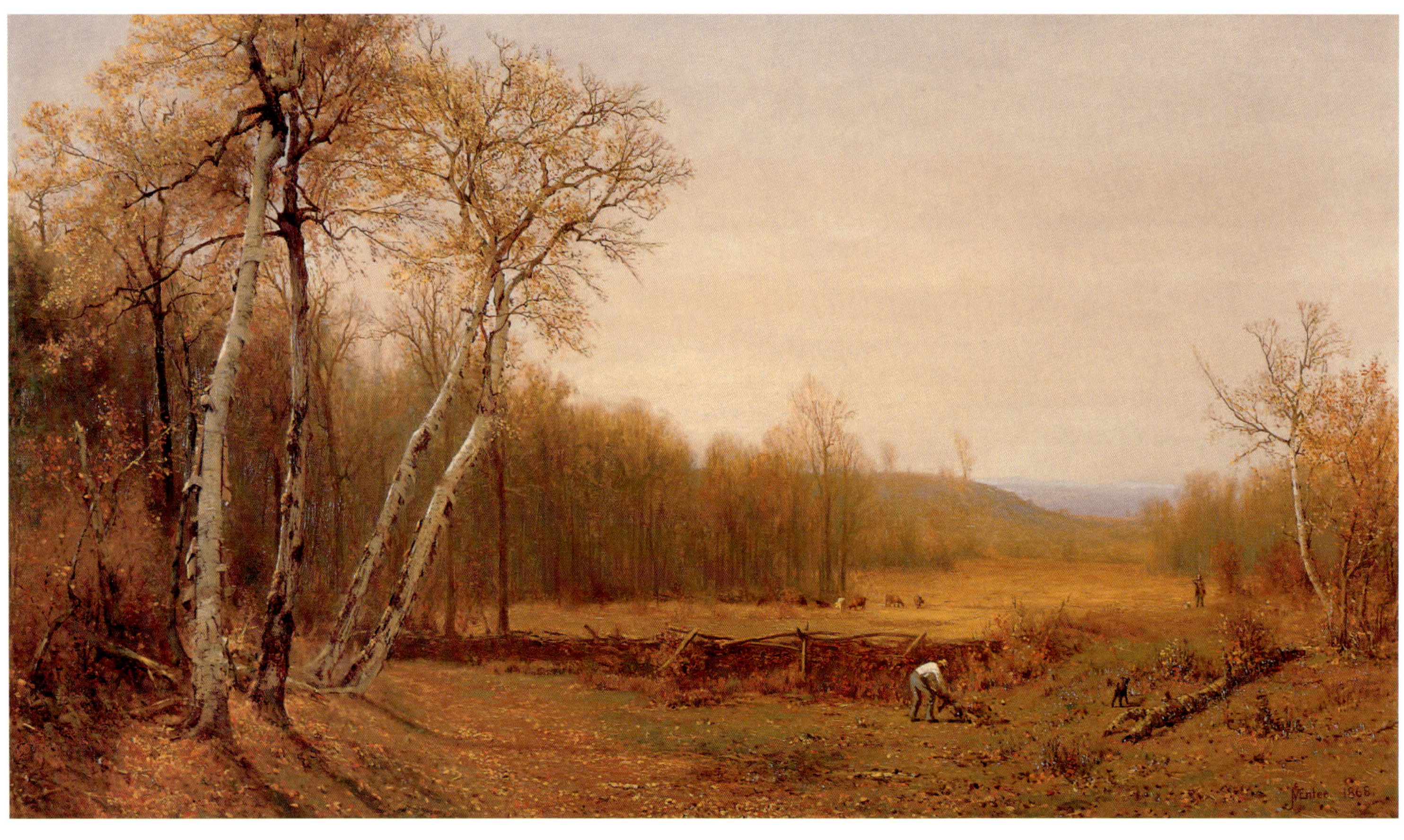

1868 (painted when the artist
was 39–40 years old)
Oil on canvas
24 x 42 in. (61 x 106.7 cm)
Signed and dated at lower right:
JMcEntee 1868

References: Howat, 1987, pp. 278–79
as *Autumn, Landscape.*

Jervis McEntee was at the heart of the American landscape movement of the mid-nineteenth century. He was a pupil of Frederic Church in 1851, he worked and lived in the Studio Building on Tenth Street in Manhattan, and in 1861 he was a made a full Academician at the National Academy of Design. McEntee was well liked by his colleagues, and was seemingly present at every cultural event held in New York during the 1860s and 1870s. But despite his important place among America's mid-century landscape painters, McEntee possessed a pessimistic nature that bordered on melancholic.[1]

For all his early promise, McEntee spent much of the 1850s in his hometown of Rondout, New York, working in a feed store. In 1859, he returned to Manhattan after an eight-year absence, and was quickly embraced by his old friends. His painting *Melancholy Days* was so well received at the 1860 National Academy of Design exhibition that largely on its strength he was elected an Associate of the Academy that year. During the 1860s, McEntee made autumn landscapes his trademark subject. While Jasper Cropsey and others reveled in the annual scenic mania that set October treetops aflame, McEntee devoted himself to the softer and dimmer November light that bathed the hills near Rondout in hushed monochromatic tones. His gentle golden browns spoke to the last days before winter rather than the chromatic explosion that marked the end of summer.[2]

In the late 1860s, the public, collectors, and dealers responded favorably to McEntee's reserved autumnal landscapes. Critics appreciated his restraint and discipline in comparison to the bombast of Albert Bierstadt and the grandiosity of Church. In the years immediately following the end of the Civil War, quietude was not an undesirable quality, and McEntee's "preference for the soberer phases of Nature" was rewarded with significant exposure in the press. In distinguishing McEntee from his more celebrated colleagues, and particularly from Church, one critic wrote that he was "educated in the studio of the most popular artist of the country, who sets him no example."[3] A review of McEntee's submission to the 1867 National Academy of Design exhibition aptly summarized the artist's intentions and probably his temperament as well:

The cheerless, chilly breath of late November is felt in every part of this admirable painting. Frost has touched all the leaves and dulled

the thousand hues of October into one monotonous brown. The gray clouds that overhang this sunless landscape seem ready to fall in snow... and makes one feel that the saddest and most melancholy days of all the year have come.[4]

The years 1867 and 1868 may have marked the pinnacle of McEntee's success or at least his sense of professional satisfaction. He was represented in the American section of the 1867 Exposition Universelle in Paris, the first World's Fair after the Civil War and an important international showcase for American painters. McEntee's participation speaks to his popularity at least among the members of the selection committee, which consisted of such notable figures as the art dealer Michael Knoedler, the collector John T. Johnston, and the writer Henry Tuckerman. The following year, McEntee joined Church, William Stanley Haseltine, and Sanford Gifford on an extended excursion to Rome, where they worked in neighboring studios and painted together in the Italian *campagne.*[5]

McEntee painted *Autumn Scene* in 1868, but it is unknown whether he completed it in New York or in his studio on the Via dei Greci in Rome.[6] The familar wooded landscape near Rondout was so indelibly inscribed upon McEntee's imagination that he could have painted it from memory and almost certainly did. McEntee later told the writer G. W. Sheldon, "What I do like to paint is my impression of a simple scene in Nature." It was an important distinction for the moody McEntee to try to make. Landscape painting had to be more about his perception of a place than the direct observation and documentation of it. That he preferred "simple" views like that of *Autumn Scene* to the spectacular subjects favored by his famous colleagues may also suggest an occasionally troubled mind searching for quiet and order.[7]

In *Autumn Scene*, McEntee painted a farmer at work in a high country meadow, building a rail fence and clearing his pasture. He pulls at a branch as his dog glares at a neighbor, who has emerged from the woods with a rifle and a hound of his own. Although the dogs eye each other alertly, there is nothing to suggest that the immanent encounter between the two canines or between the two men will be anything but cordial and calm, like the November landscape that surrounds them.

26   MISSISSIPPI RIVER (DUBUQUE, IOWA)   Alfred Thompson Bricher (1837–1908)

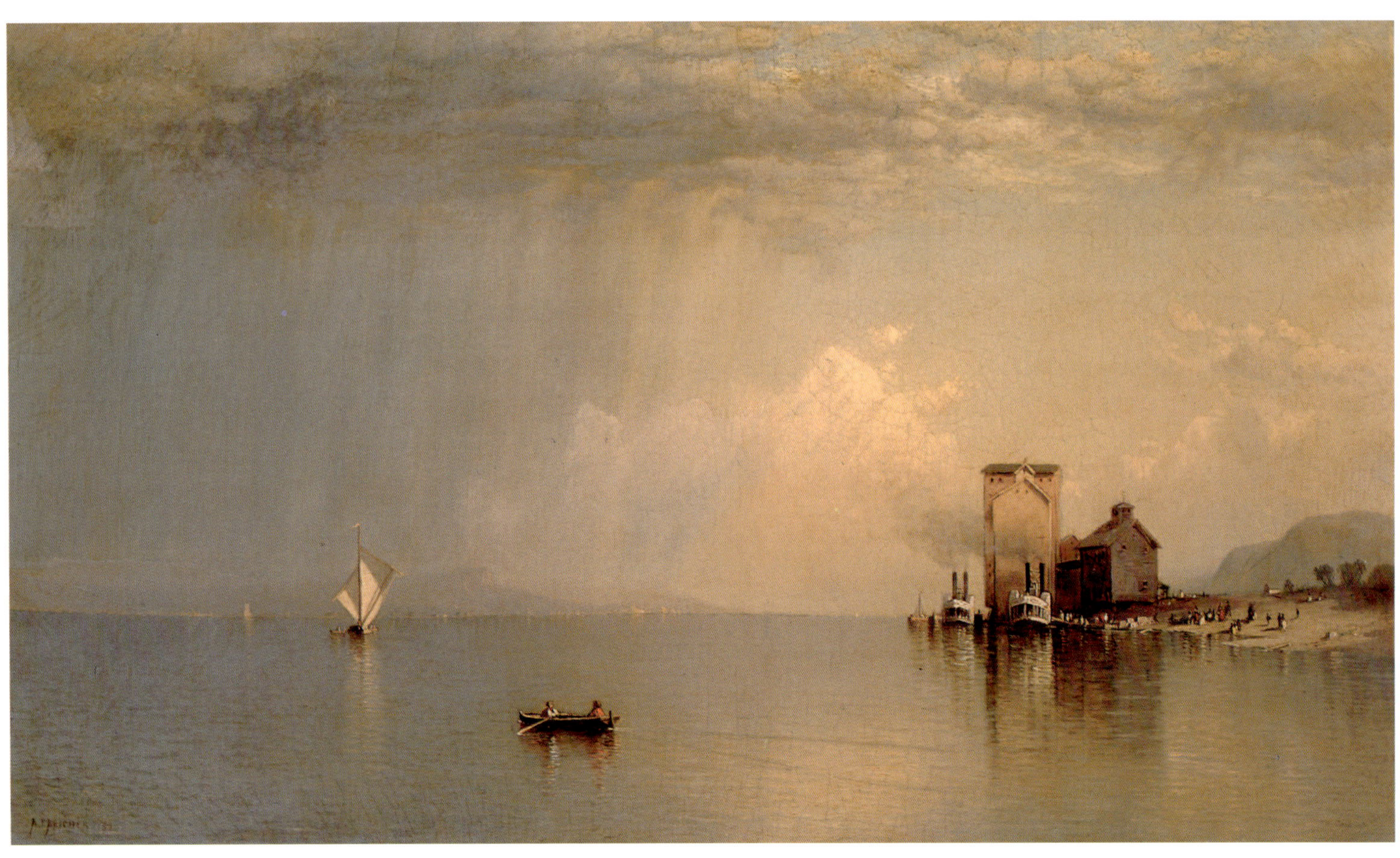

1870 (painted when the artist
was 32–33 years old)
Oil on canvas
23 x 41 in. (58.5 x 104.2 cm)
Signed and dated at lower left:
AT Bricher 1870

In 1866, the first full year after the end of the Civil War, many of America's young artists found themselves traveling widely and freely for the first time in their lives. With the Atlantic sea lanes once again safe, hundreds of prospective painters and sculptors made their way to Europe to further their educations in England, France, and Germany. Many more ventured into an American West that the landscape painter Albert Bierstadt had rendered so romantic and appealing. Alfred T. Bricher was among the young painters who left the comfort of Boston for a taste of adventure in America beyond New England. He did not journey as far as the spectacular scenery that Bierstadt immortalized. But Bricher's sketching excursion along the upper Mississippi River in Iowa, Wisconsin, and Minnesota would yield a significant body of work that made a unique statement about the American landscape.[1]

Bricher may have been sent to the Mississippi River on an assignment for the Boston lithography firm of Louis Prang and Co., for whom he had just begun to make drawings for reproduction.[2] But he was probably also lured there by Martin Johnson Heade, who had been a fellow tenant of Boston's Studio Building in 1862 and 1863. Heade had spent three years in St. Louis during the early 1850s, and surely described the great river to his young colleague as he regaled him with tales of his many and frequent voyages. But as Bricher gazed across the wide expanse of the Mississippi River in June 1866, and watched a Midwestern thunderstorm rolling in from the south, it was not Heade's travel advice that he appreciated. Despite having grown up in Newburyport, Massachusetts, the setting of Heade's broad and poetic salt marsh subjects (see cat. 23), it was only as Bricher contemplated the Mississippi River and the landscape of the upper Midwest that he finally understood the quietude, the atmosphere, and the horizontal grandeur of the older painter's canvases.[3]

Although Bricher left only the synoptic sketchbook record of his excursion along the upper Mississippi, he probably traveled by steamboat, like so many trappers, entrepreneurs, and salesmen, and so much merchandise and grain. Side- and Paddle-wheelers made regular stops at the lively river towns north of St. Louis, from Hannibal, Missouri, through Keokuk and Dubuque, Iowa, to La Crosse, Wisconsin, and St. Paul, Minnesota. In early June, Bricher disembarked at Dubuque, and remained in the area for nearly two weeks, sketching the great river and its picturesque tributaries as well as the nearby bluffs and hills.[4] He would later produce two major paintings of the Mississippi River at Dubuque. One was a view from below the village, and *Mississippi River (Dubuque, Iowa)* was based on a sketch Bricher might have made from a boat that bore him north to Prairie du Chien, Wisconsin.[5]

In 1868, two years after his trip to the upper Mississippi, Bricher moved from Boston to New York. It may have been his greater exposure there to the increasingly atmospheric and tonal paintings of Frederick Kensett and Sanford Gifford – two enormously successful artists – that finally persuaded Bricher to reconsider the luminous work of Heade and Fitz Hugh Lane, which he had known in Boston since at least the early 1860s. Bricher was ambitious and had an eye for commercial success; he was not inclined to produce canvases that the public or critics would find esoteric. But after a decade of emulating the subjects and style of Thomas Cole and his followers, and achieving only modest success, Bricher may have recognized that Heade's paintings were less anomalous than they originally had seemed. Indeed, by the late 1860s, the atmospheric experiments of Kensett, Gifford, Heade, and (the late) Lane were at the vanguard of American landscape and marine painting, and more to point for Bricher, they were very much in demand.[6]

In Bricher's *Mississippi River (Dubuque, Iowa)* of 1870, the artist finally allowed himself to veer directly into the aesthetic territory of Kensett and Heade. The painting's austere tonal and chromatic range was a significant departure for Bricher, as was his sparse and assertively horizontal composition dotted only with the carefully placed vertical forms of the sailboat and the grain building. Bricher's paintings of the Mississippi River mark a shift in priority toward more atmospheric subjects stripped of all irrelevant detail, and they represent the first full steps toward the later marine paintings for which he would become best known. Those broad seascapes would become Bricher's trademark and his most profitable subject, but their origins are in the expansiveness he discovered on the banks of the Mississippi River.

27   RAINBOW FALLS, WATKINS GLEN, NEW YORK

James Hope (1818–1892)

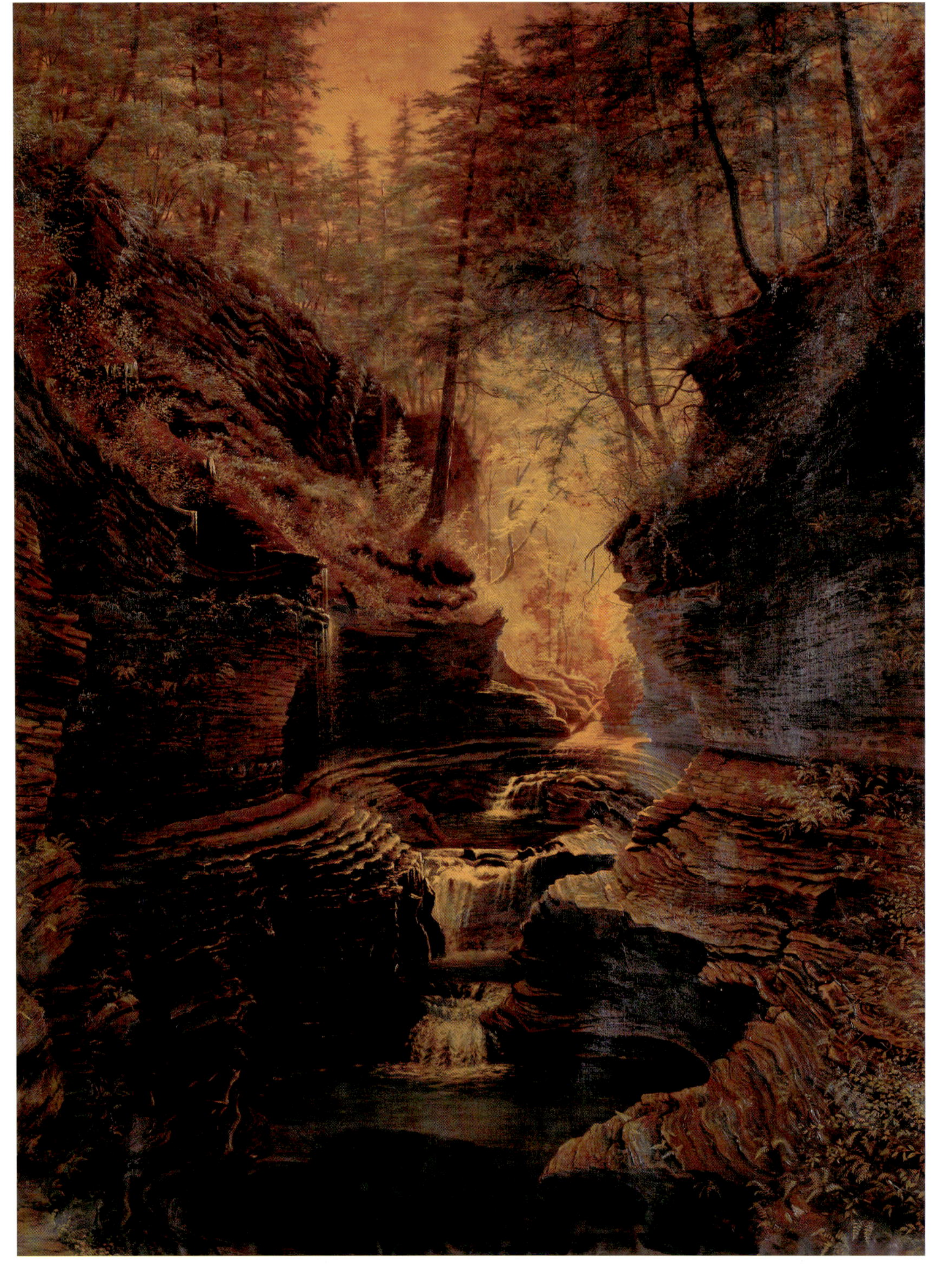

1871 (painted when the artist
was 52–53 years old)
Oil on canvas
78 x 60 in. (198.1 x 152.4 cm)
Signed and dated and lower right:
JHope/1871

Early provenance: From the artist,
Watkins Glen, N.Y., 1871; (moved) to
Glen Art Gallery, Watkins Glen, N.Y.,
1872–1926; (sold) to Otis L. Fowler,
Oakland, N.Y., 1926.
Early exhibition history: (Possibly)
*Forty-seventh Annual Exhibition of
the National Academy of Design*, New
York, spring 1872, no. 312. Glen Art
Gallery, Watkins Glen, N.Y., 1872–1892.
World's Columbian Exposition, Chicago,
1893. *Pan-American Exposition*, Buffalo,
N.Y., 1901.

References: *American Paintings,
Drawings and Sculpture: The Collection of
Arthur and Holly Magill; and a Collection
of Works by Andrew Wyeth*, Sotheby's,
New York, 30 November 2000, no. 128.

James Hope was an orphaned Scottish immigrant who started life as a wheelwright in Fair Haven, Vermont. In the late 1830s, he sustained a terrible ankle injury, and during his slow recovery, he indulged a long-held interest in drawing. A self-portrait caught the attention of friends, and by the time his ankle healed, Hope was supporting himself as a portraitist. He was confident enough in his prospects to have married Julia Smith in 1841, and three years later they moved to Montreal, where he opened a studio and remained for two years. Hope and his wife returned to Vermont in 1846, settling in Rutland, where their children were born. There, Hope met the painter William Hart, one of the many artists credited with persuading the former wheelwright to abandon portraiture for landscape painting.

Little is known about Hope's early life and work, but seemingly he found his way into prominent artistic circles, and contributed to significant exhibitions. Frederic Church is said to have urged the artist to open a studio in New York City, and Asher B. Durand apparently encouraged him to continue (or to begin) painting landscapes. Hope took the advice of both distinguished colleagues, and by 1852, he was spending his winters in New York and his summers painting the picturesque scenery around Castleton, Vermont, where he had built a house in 1851.[1]

At the start of the Civil War, Hope recruited and formed Company B, the 2nd Regiment of the Vermont Infantry, and was appointed its captain. In eighteen months of active duty, he went into battle no fewer than eleven times and saw considerable action before poor health scratched his participation from the Battle of Antietam. He was so ill that he eventually received a medical discharge, but he remained with his company of volunteers throughout the fighting in Maryland. His drawings of the Battle of Antietam would later become a cycle of paintings, and perhaps the most important firsthand representation of Civil War fighting.[2]

After his discharge, Hope returned to his studio in New York and continued to paint the rural landscape around Castleton. For Hope, the postwar years were marked by constant struggle punctuated by only sporadic successes. In December 1870, possibly inspired by Albert Bierstadt, Hope launched a trip to the American West, but never got further than New York's Finger Lakes. His itinerary had taken him near the town of Watkin's Glen, and Hope was captivated by the area's spectacular beauty, and by its most dramatic feature, Rainbow Falls. He sent for his family soon after arriving, and built a house high on the glen, overlooking the waterfall that would be his inspiration for the next twenty years.[3]

The deep limestone gorges near Watkin's Glen were eroded by centuries of water tumbling from Sugar Hill into Glen Creek. Depending upon rain and snowfall, the volume of water varied from season to season and year to year, creating intriguing erosion patterns that resembled stepped shelves. The most impressive of the narrow ravines at Watkin's Glen held Rainbow Falls, which earned its name from the colorful striations that the mineral rich water had left on the limestone walls and ledges. Hope painted Rainbow Falls many times and under a variety of climatic conditions, always capturing the site's dramatically irregular profile and the distinctive rainbow coloring that gave the landmark its name.

Hope's 1871 masterpiece, *Rainbow Falls, Watkin's Glen, New York*, was among the first major canvases he devoted to the falls, and certainly, the painting held some personal significance for the artist. Although views of the colorfully striated chasm would become his trademark, as well as his most bankable subject, Hope retained this early and ambitious interpretation for the remainder of his life. He placed the painting on display in the Glen Art Gallery, a small museum he founded in Watkin's Glen in 1872. The gallery held a large ensemble of Hope's work, but no doubt the centerpiece of the collection was the majestic *Rainbow Falls* of 1871.[4]

The painting remained in the Glen Art Gallery for the last twenty years of Hope's life, and was exhibited at the 1893 and 1901 World's Fairs in Chicago and Buffalo in the first decade after his death. Even as the gallery in Watksin's Glen fell into disrepair after Hope died, *Rainbow Falls, Watkin's Glen, New York* remained in his family's hands until 1926, when it was finally sold. The timing of the transaction was fortunate. *Rainbow Falls, Watkin's Glen, New York* was spared the fate of eighty-two other paintings by Hope that were damaged beyond repair in a devastating flood of 1935.[5]

John Williamson (1826–1885)

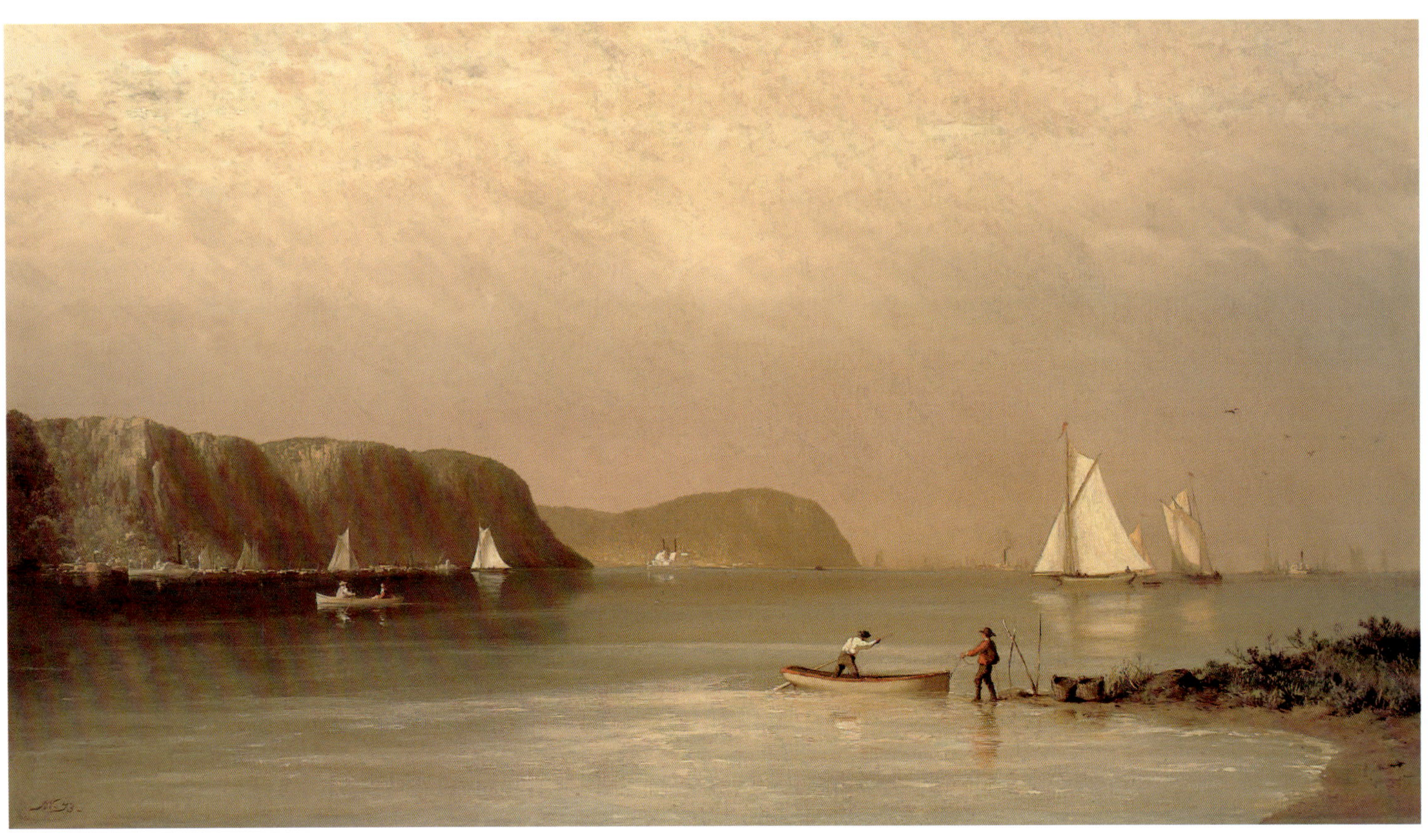

John Williamson was among the gifted painters who prospered in New York during the 1850s. A versatile artist, he produced attractive still life subjects and genre pictures in addition to handsome land-scapes of Adirondack and Catskill scenery. Early in his career, Williamson frequently borrowed from the styles and subjects of more successful New York landscapists whose work he admired. In the 1850s and early 1860s, he produced convincing adaptations of Asher B. Durand's forest interiors, the sunsets of Frederic Church, and airy mountaintop vistas in the manner of Sanford Gifford. But Williamson's most impressive canvases would not come until later in his career, when he painted views of the lower Hudson River where it widens above Dobb's Ferry.[1]

The Hudson River Valley had been a contested territory from the arrival of the first Europeans in 1524. By the late sixteenth century, it was an important commercial artery for French trappers laden with beaver skins, and it was the site of a bustling trade culture by the time Henry Hudson arrived in the early seventeenth century. Native American populations were largely eradicated or forced out of the valley by the mid-eighteenth century, and with French and English militia vying for control of North America, the river became thoroughly colonized, attracting settlers in significant number. Formerly tiny villages such as Yonkers, West Point, Poughkeepsie, and Hudson emerged as viable communities, for which the river pro-vided water, transportation, and news of the outside world, including the first seeds of political dissent that would mature into the American Revolution.[2]

A half-century after nationhood, Thomas Cole journeyed up the Hudson River in search of inspiring landscapes. For all of his cel-ebration of the American wilderness, when he traveled the Hudson, he probably bought a ticket in Manhattan, boarded a steamboat, and encountered lively small communities on his way to the frontier. His decision to disembark near Catskill Creek, a tributary of the great river, and to follow it into the mountains had enormous ramifi-cations for the history of American painting, but he was by no means the first to blaze those trails. Thousands of others had preceded Cole along the very route he traveled, and thousands more would follow, including dozens of painters, among them John Williamson. By Cole's premature death in 1848, the Hudson River had become an

artistic pilgrimage route that took painters to the Catskills, the Adirondacks, Lake George, and Lake Champlain. The river became so identified with the legion of landscapists who trailed in the wake of Cole that by the 1870s, New York art critics would group his crowded flock of followers under the insulting rubric of the Hudson River School.[3]

Williamson may have recognized himself in the critics' dis-dain for the Hudson River School, even if well before the term was actually coined. In 1867, apparently weary of deriving his inspiration from the work of other artists, Williamson auctioned almost every canvas that remained in his studio.[4] And in what would almost seem an act of sheer obstinacy, he began to work in the Hudson River Valley to the near exclusion of every other landscape setting. He would occasionally paint in the nearby Catskills, but for the most part, he worked along the river's commercially active and largely indus-trial stretch between Yonkers and West Point. In 1868, he submitted a view of the Hudson to the National Academy of Design, and for the remainder of his career, he sketched at such relatively accessible points as Glenwood and Tappan Zee, locations he could reach from Manhattan in a matter of hours. In 1882 or 1883, he moved to Yonkers, where he was rarely more than a few minutes walk from the river.[5]

In *Hudson River from Glenwood (Palisades)* of 1873, Williamson captured the river in late afternoon haze as fishermen, steamboats, and schooners made their way to the commercial piers that served dozens of factories and small communities. The Hudson was still a busy and vigorous river in 1873, but it was already much different than it had been even in Cole's day. With the completion of the Hudson River Railroad in 1849, passenger travel on the river was swiftly curtailed, and the great waterway would become less a vital transportation corridor than an artery for sewage and industrial waste.[6] In the foreground of Williamson's painting, two fishermen work a small skiff for gathering oysters, and their large wicker baskets no doubt hold the mollusks they have collected. But just as the era of the Hudson River School painters was coming to an end in the 1870s, the days of fishermen earning a living on the great river were numbered as well.

Francis Augustus Silva (1835–1886)

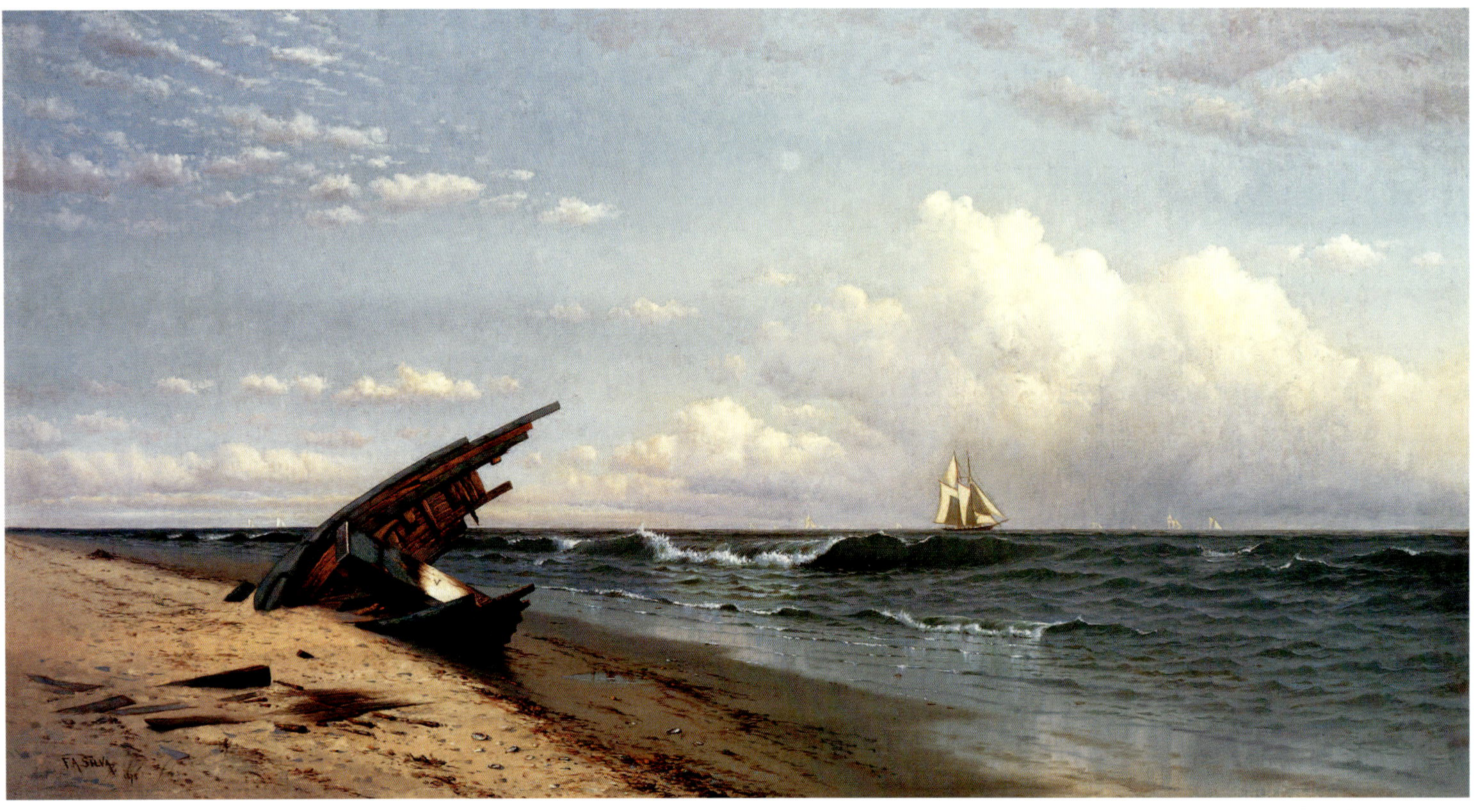

1875 (painted when the artist
was 39–40 years old)
Oil on canvas
20 ⅛ x 38 ⅛ in. (51.1 x 96.8 cm)
Signed and dated at lower left:
F. A. Silva/75

Early exhibition history: Brooklyn Art
Association, November 1875, no. 368 as
A Wreck on Coney Island Beach.
References: Manoogian, 1989, no. 16,
pp. 48–49. Manoogian, 1999, no. 43,
pp. 104–5. Manoogian, 1997, no. 14,
pp. 54–57 and 189–190. Mitchell, 2002,
pp. 35, 89, and 131.

Like much of his generation, Francis A. Silva was deeply affected by his experience of the Civil War. While many were scarred by the carnage and the destruction of the battlefield, young Captain Silva was marked by an unjust dishonorable discharge that stripped him of his command and his unit of New York volunteers. He was eventually restored to his proper rank, and after a long delay, reassigned to a military hospital in Lynn, Massachusetts. But Silva came away from the war having felt its anguish without knowing its redemptive honor, and it would color his perception of the world well after the fighting had stopped.[1]

Before the war's end, Silva had determined to become an artist, and by 1867, he had opened a studio in Manhattan. It is not entirely clear when or how Silva came to understand and to convincingly master the themes and techniques of America's most advanced marine painters. There would have been opportunities to see the work of Fitz Hugh Lane, Frederick Kensett, and Martin Johnson Heade at exhibitions in New York, but Silva's early paintings of the New Jersey shore and his views of Gloucester Harbor are more than the competent replicas of a clever autodidact. Silva's rocky shorelines, lighthouses, moored sailing ships, and vaporous sunsets spoke articulately in the vernacular of contemporary marine painting. But his seascapes also functioned as sophisticated metaphors, addressing issues of exposure, peril, endurance, and fleeting mortality, all of which the artist and the nation had contemplated during the war.[2]

On 11 July 1874, as Silva walked along the beach at Coney Island, he came upon the wreckage of a schooner named *Progress.* Apparently, the large sailing ship had foundered during rough seas on the night of 4 July, and had broken into at least two sections, and probably more. Only the ribbed walls of the bow and a bit of the hull had found the Brooklyn shore on Independence Day, and by the time Silva began to make drawings of the debris a week later, the tide was already burying the vessel fragment in sand.[3]

There was no report in the major New York or Brooklyn newspapers that *Progress* had been lost, but there was fairly broad coverage of the storms that had marred the holiday weekend. The sinking (accidental or otherwise) of outdated sailing vessels had become more and more common in the years after the Civil War, and with steam-propelled merchant ships dominating the sea lanes, the loss of even a large schooner like *Progress* was just barely newsworthy.[4] But it was hardly the importance of the ship that interested Silva and drew him back to Coney Island with his box of pencils and watercolors on 28 July and again on 15 August.[5] It was the intriguing convergence of an evocatively named sailing vessel, the memorable date of its destruction, and the shoreline scenery that was Silva's stock and trade that he found so compelling. If he was not already giving serious consideration to the progress (or the fate) of American marine painting in 1874, the decaying diorama he encountered on Coney Island certainly would have set his thoughts in motion.

By 1874, *Progress*, rotting on the shore, would have appeared to Silva a neat analogy for artistic progress in America. Each day, a steady stream of young American painters returned from the academies of Europe. To Silva's thinking, they were a rabble of unpatriotic "dandies," who had left America more to avoid military service during the Civil War than to train as artists. Their European affectations and flimsy aestheticism were already altering the nature of painting in New York and across the United States, and usurping the native traditions forged by the artists Silva considered more truly American. He would eventually and unfortunately describe the stylistic battle in a chauvinistic article for the *American Art-Union* that he called "American vs. Foreign-American Art."[6]

If Silva was concerned by the larger issue of progress in American art, his own meager professional progress may have troubled him even more. Lane had passed away in 1865, Kensett had died unexpectedly in December 1872, and by 1875, Heade was already on his steady course toward complete obscurity. But even with the premature deaths of Lane and Kensett, all three artists outlived the fashion for luminous marine painting they had come to epitomize, and that Silva had embraced only once it was past its vogue. Gazing upon wrecked *Progress*, Silva realized that he must make changes to salvage his own career. He had to reconsider the way he rendered the sea before his own progress became, like the decaying schooner, so much beached wreckage on the shore of Coney Island.[7]

During the early autumn of 1874, Silva painted the work now known as *Approaching Storm*, a first version of the wrecked schooner *Progress*. He based the canvas on the initial drawing he had made on 11 July 1874, but that modest sketch could scarcely have anticipated

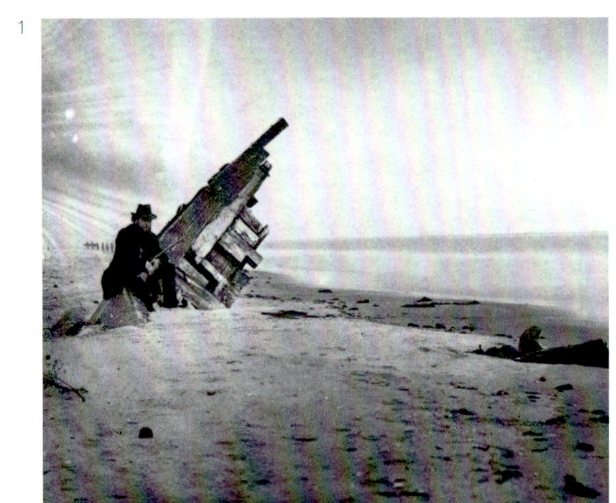

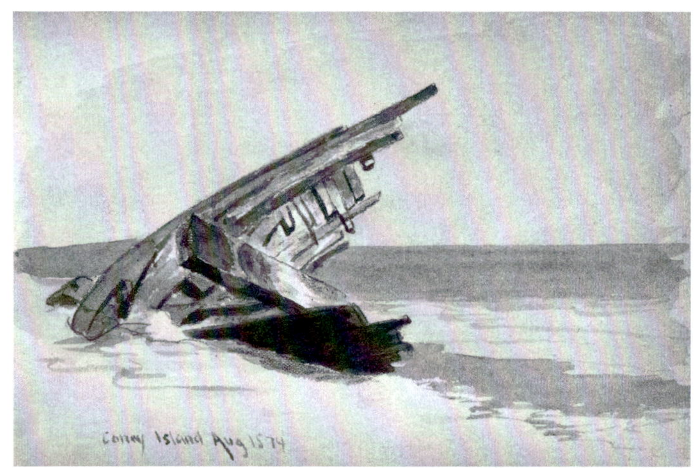

Coney Island Aug 1874

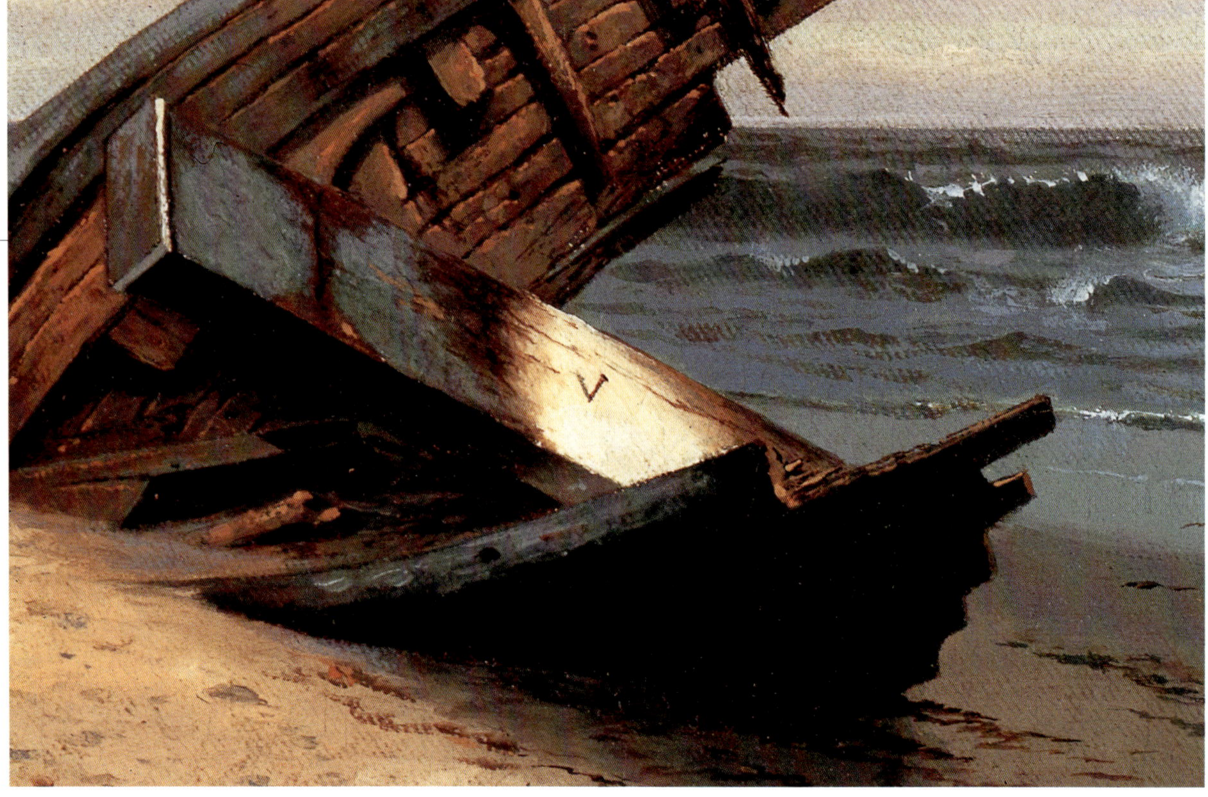

the transition that was about to occur in Silva's work. In *Approaching Storm*, Silva introduced purer color in a broader chromatic range, a clearer quality of light and sharper resolution to a somewhat bolder compositional format. After ten years of laboring in the protected harbors of Fitz Hugh Lane, producing paintings that were all tranquil light effects and atmosphere, a collapsed schooner called *Progress*, a triangle of sand and a view to the open sea marked a significant departure in Silva's approach to marine painting.[8]

In November 1874, Silva submitted *Approaching Storm* to the annual exhibition of the Brooklyn Art Association – a Brooklyn subject for a Brooklyn venue, as was his usual practice. Exhibited as *The Wreck*, the painting now known as *Approaching Storm* went virtually unnoticed in the local press, and while Silva's reaction is unrecorded, he must have been disappointed by the critical void. He was not simply showing a painting in Brooklyn, he was debuting a new phase of his career, and to reinforce the point, he was showing Brooklyn its own Coney Island. By titling the painting *The Wreck*, Silva skirted obvious asides about progress, but he must have counted on Brooklyn's memory of the storm and the wreckage on the beach. He may even have hoped that interested and attentive visitors to the Brooklyn show would study his painting, and then take the short ride down Coney Island Avenue to see for themselves the weathered debris of *Progress*. Perhaps that is what the Brooklyn photographer George Brainerd did on 3 November 1874, when he made his way to Coney Island, camera in hand (*fig. 1*).[9]

Despite the disappointing response in Brooklyn, Silva was far from finished with the remains of *Progress*. In 1875, he painted *The Schooner 'Progress' Wrecked at Coney Island, July 4th, 1874*, a near variant of *Approaching Storm*. Close though it was in handling and color to the picture he had exhibited in Brooklyn the previous autumn, Silva actually based his reprise on the graphite and watercolor drawing that he had made the previous summer and inscribed "Coney Island Aug 15 74" (*fig. 2*). In vantage point, perspective, composition, and all but one detail, the drawing and the finished painting were virtually identical conceptions.[10]

In November 1875, Silva submitted *The Schooner 'Progress' Wrecked at Coney Island, July 4th, 1874* to the annual exhibition of the Brooklyn Art Association, showing the work as *A Wreck on Coney Island Beach*.[11] He reprised and displayed a painting virtually identical to the one he had shown in 1874, but with a title that made its local interest clear. He must have desperately wanted his audience to see what he had seen on the beach at Coney Island, for them to remember the destroyed schooner, and to recognize that no matter how it was defined, progress was wrecked. Whether advancing an old inherited movement or fighting off a new one, progress was nothing more than sandy debris on a beach in Brooklyn. In *The Schooner 'Progress' Wrecked at Coney Island, July 4th, 1874*, Silva allowed himself but one departure from the 15 August 1874 drawing. He painted a tiny and incongruous nail pounded into a bleached white section of a decaying timber, as if to drive his point home (*fig. 3*).

30   CATTLEYA ORCHID, TWO HUMMINGBIRDS AND A BEETLE

Martin Johnson Heade (1819–1904)

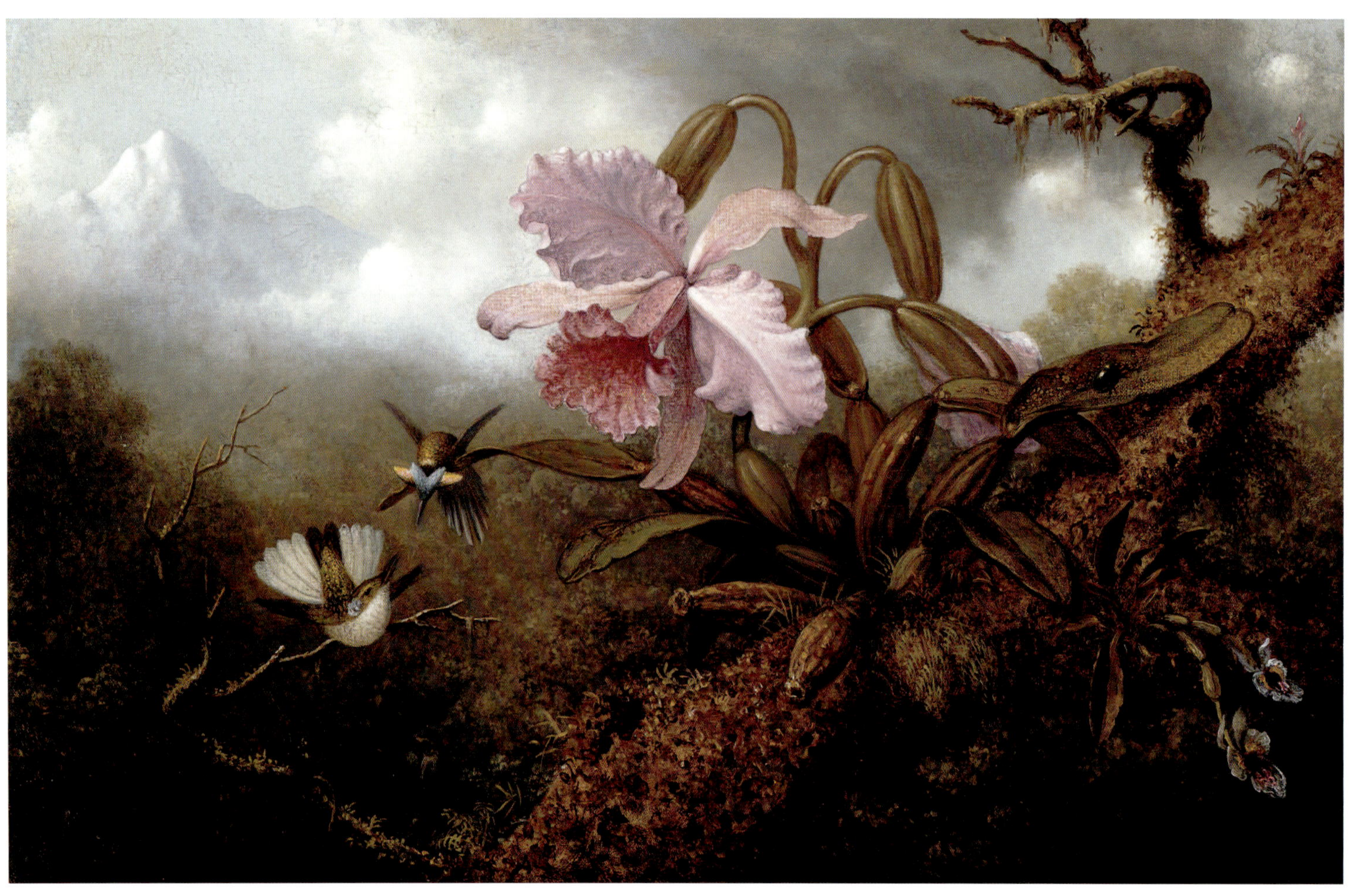

c. 1875–1890
Oil on canvas
14 ¼ x 22 ¼ in. (36.2 x 56.5 cm)   References: Manoogian, 1999, no. 26,
Signed lower right: *M. J. Heade*   pp. 70–71. Stebbins, 2000, no. 503, p. 325.

Martin Johnson Heade and Frederic Church had known each other for years, but beginning in the mid 1860s, they forged a friendship that survived for the rest of their lives. Their deeper amity began when Heade moved into Church's Tenth Street studio in the fall of 1866, and may have been nurtured by their shared experience, if very different opinions, of South American travel (see cats. 8, 18, and 23). Church had launched celebrated journeys to New Granada (now Colombia) and Ecuador in 1853 and 1857, while Heade had undertaken all but calamitous junkets to Brazil in 1863 and to Nicaragua in 1866.[1]

In the mid 1860s, Church was reaching the peak of his international fame, but the peripatetic and somewhat eccentric Heade was still struggling to find an audience for his highly original paintings. Heade's career probably benefited in the late 1860s from its near proximity to the Church mystique, and more pragmatically, to Church's friends and collectors. But Church still felt that his aimless friend required guidance and the steadying influence of his own sound advice. It was probably Church who recommended that Heade make yet another tour of South America, and to follow the itinerary that he himself had imposed upon the region in the 1850s.[2]

In December 1869, Heade made a genuine effort to retrace Church's footsteps in South America, just as Church had traced those of the German naturalist Alexander von Humboldt. But after reaching the coast of New Granada near the town of Barranquilla, Heade found that he had no desire to journey through the jungles of the Magdalena River as Church had done. Instead, he inched along the New Granada coast to Panama, lingered on the isthmus, and much to Church's consternation, produced little work and complained loudly about the discomforts and dangers of the tropics.[3]

Although Heade traveled widely and frequently, he fought an almost instinctive dissatisfaction with any new place he visited. In time, he would warm to most locales, as he did to Rome in the late 1840s and to Rio de Janeiro in 1863. But regardless of where he traveled, Heade generally required a period of acclimation to overcome his near disgust for the unfamiliar, and to gain a sense of the language, customs, and culture of wherever he had just arrived. Heade came away from his journey to New Granada and Panama with a myriad of tales he would later delight in telling. But it was only toward the end of the trip, as he grew accustomed not so much to where he was,

but to the idea of being a traveler, that the excursion became aesthetically useful for Heade. By then, he had abandoned the South American continent and sailed to yet another destination that had been fertile ground for Church — the island of Jamaica — and it would prove a revelation.[4]

After seeing Jamaica, Heade invented yet another of his brilliant variations on conventional nineteenth-century subject matter. In the 1850s, he had dredged salt marshes from the landscape idiom, and in the 1860s he had unleashed his hummingbirds on staid ornithological prints. In the 1870s, inspired by Jamaica, Heade would become the great interpreter of orchids, placing them in natural but aesthetically hybrid settings that were part landscape and part still life. In paintings such as *Cattleya Orchid, Two Hummingbirds and a Beetle*, Heade devised a system of representation that set the languid beauty of orchids against the manic energy of hummingbirds, and their rare, ethereal delicacy opposite the permanence and impenetrability of the rugged landscape. It was a unique and utterly unexpected pictorial invention that defied categorization, and for better or for worse, challenged the nineteenth-century mind for taxonomic order.[5]

Church may been concerned that Heade and his orchids would lapse into another time-consuming but ultimately unprofitable venture. Not long after Heade returned to New York, Church asked, "Are you painting a Jamaica picture?" By that he meant a tropical landscape with plenty of palms and a water view that might tempt collectors who had also visited the island. And in fact Heade did paint at least one significant Jamaican landscape in 1870. But mostly he was occupied with the close inspection of orchids accompanied by hovering, perching, or nesting hummingbirds set against murky skies, dense tropical foliage, and in *Cattleya Orchid, Two Hummingbirds and a Beetle*, a distant snow-peaked mountain. Heade would paint the sensual beauty of orchids for the rest of his career, returning again and again to the unique flower that so ably conveyed the artist's own feverish temperament. Even Church could not resist their hothouse nature, reminiscent of Heade himself, and he had acquired one for his own collection by 1874.[6]

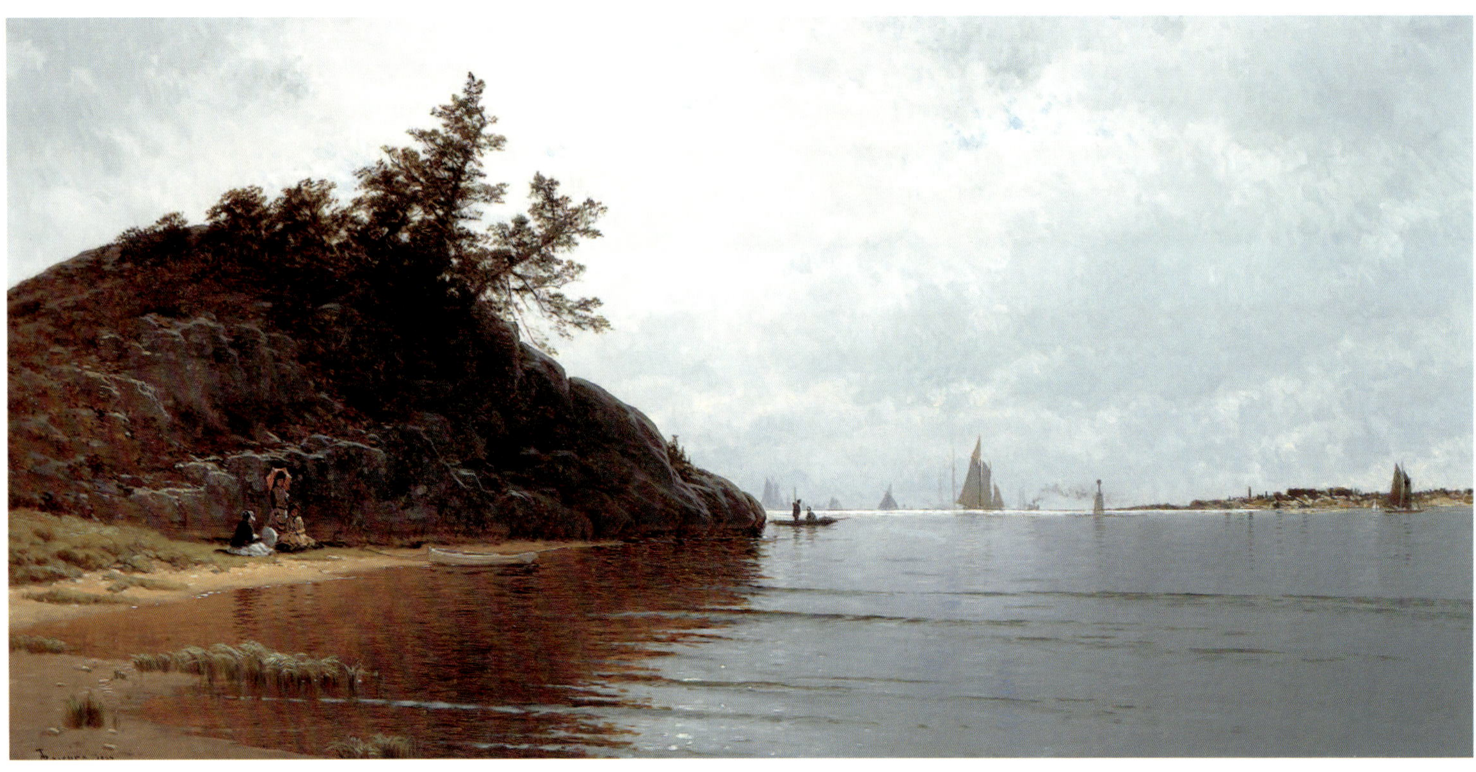

1877 (painted when the artist
was 39–40 years old)
Oil on canvas
25 1/8 x 50 1/8 in. (63.8 x 127.3 cm)
Signed and dated at lower left:
ATBricher 1877

Early provenance: From the artist,
New York, 1877; (sold) to William &
Everett, Boston, 1883.[1]
References: Manoogian, 1989, p. 42.
Manoogian, 1997, no. 15, pp. 58–59 and
190. Manoogian, 1999, no. 5, pp. 28–29.

When Alfred T. Bricher painted *View on the Providence River* in 1877, he was an established New York artist who had made the shorelines of New England his specialty. Bricher's accomplishments as a marine painter from the 1870s through the end of his career came in the face of generally declining interest by critics and major collectors in the traditional seascape genre. America's most highly regarded marine painters of the 1860s, Fitz Hugh Lane and Frederick Kensett, had both died prematurely, and others such as William Bradford (see cat. 34), William Stanley Haseltine (see cat. 20), and Francis A. Silva (see cat. 29) were unable or unwilling to invigorate their own dormant subject matter. It would take a painter of native genius like Winslow Homer, and artists trained in Europe such as James McNeill Whistler and William Merritt Chase to revitalize seascape painting to the satisfaction of American writers and collectors.[2]

Bricher was not considered a major talent in his own time, and indeed was frequently chided by critics for an absence of originality and a tendency to be overly literal. The prominent writer S. G. W. Benjamin echoed the view of more than one detractor when he wrote in 1880 that "A. T. Bricher… renders certain familiar scenes of the Atlantic shore with much realistic force but little feeling for the ideal."[3] Such highbrow criticism would plague the artist throughout his career, but it hardly diminished his popularity with the public. Bricher's first small triumphs in the 1860s had come through his involvement in the mainstream art of chromolithography, and the experience seemingly sharpened his palate for the flavor of popular taste. Despite the dipping fortunes of his chosen style and subject matter, Bricher's seascapes continued to find middle-class buyers and surprisingly broad approval. Unlike the myopic Bradford or the Europeanized Haseltine or the irritable Silva, he remained alert to what the American public wanted.

Benjamin's comments about Bricher were not necessarily mistaken, but they referred to the very qualities that made him successful. While dozens of lesser talents rendered the ocean and its rocky shores in increasingly grandiose terms, for better or for worse, Bricher simply followed the tourists to a quiet stretch of beach. Leisure travel had come of age after the Civil War, and Bricher's luminous views of secluded areas at Narragansett Bay, Marblehead, and Southampton, all fashionable destinations, would prove consistently profitable subjects. The "certain familiar scenes" that may have seemed common by Benjamin's standards appealed to the leisure travelers who supported Bricher.

By the centennial year, Bricher recognized that popular taste was shifting in accord with younger art critics, who were speaking from increasingly prominent platforms. In his review of the 1876 National Academy of Design exhibition, Clarence Cook noted with some satisfaction that the show:

will make itself remembered… as one in which for the first time the influence of the new generation of painters made itself distinctly felt… (and despite reflecting much foreign influence)… there is so much independence and so much feeling shown as to justify us in the hope that the tide has turned.[4]

Cook's new generation was largely made up of figure painters, or at least artists who introduced the figure to their landscapes, such as Thomas Eakins and Homer. Bricher would have noticed the considerable attention that Homer was receiving in the 1870s for his sturdy fisher folk who lived and worked in Gloucester and Manchester, Massachusetts. It may have been in response to Homer's success and the comments of critics such as Cook that Bricher began to place figurative ensembles in his own seaside settings. Although Bricher was never tempted to portray those who lived by the sea, only its fashionable holiday revelers, like the modest women hiding beneath parasols in *View on the Providence River*, his strategy proved effective. He wrote to H. R. Latimer in December 1879, "My works are in much demand now since I have been varying them with human figures."[5]

Bricher's *View on the Providence River* of 1877 was based upon sketches he had made six years earlier from the east side of Narragansett Bay. The rocky formation where three women have oared their small rowboat was perhaps Pomham Rocks in East Providence, an area noted in period guidebooks. But the view across the Providence River and south toward the sea, where a day beacon stands on a narrow neck that juts into the bay, was actually based on drawings that Bricher made much further downstream. Bricher's willingness to marry drawings from two different locations to achieve an ideal formal and scenic arrangement would suggest that Benjamin's discussion of "realistic force" may not have been entirely apt.[6]

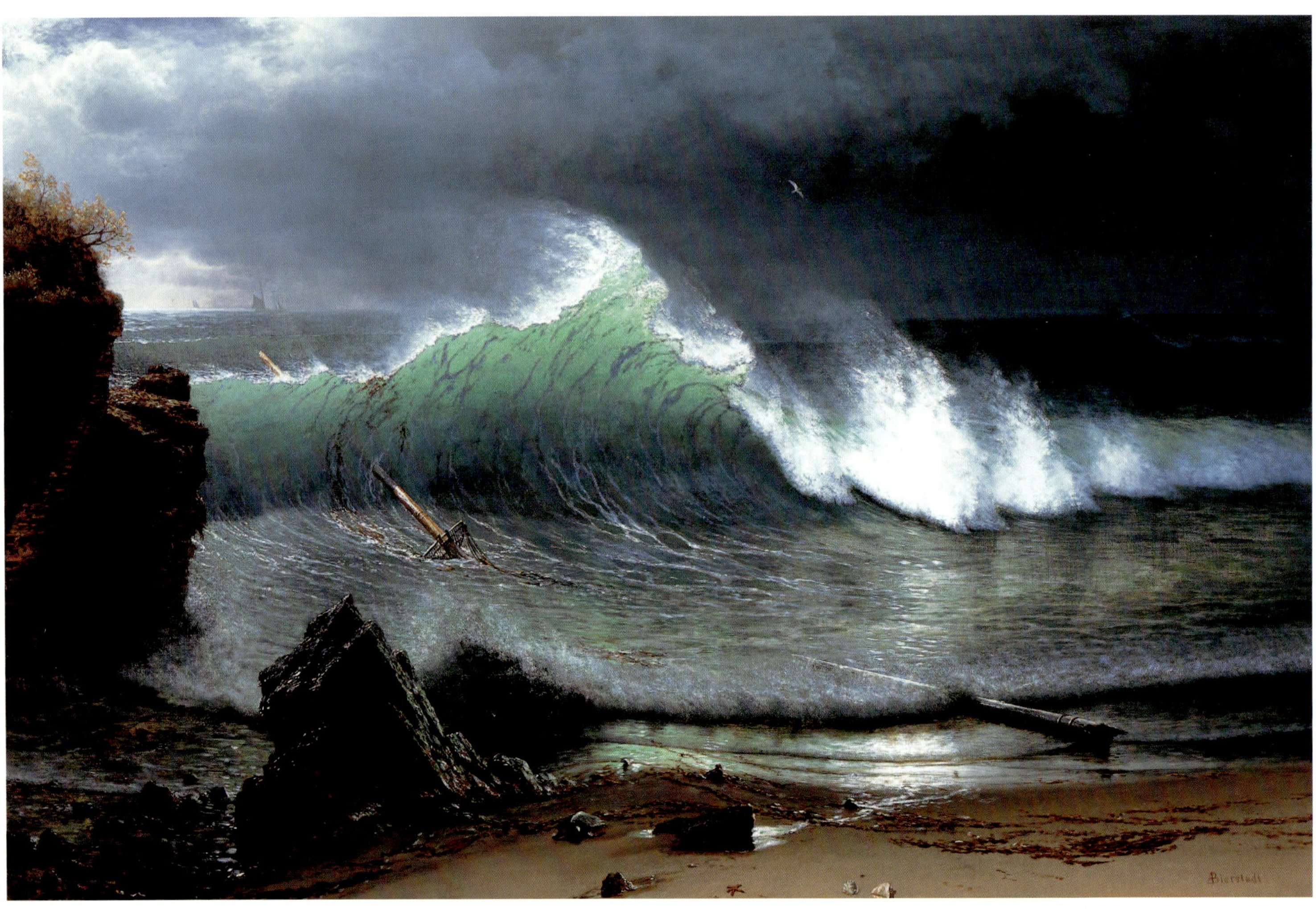

1878 (painted when the artist
was 48 years old)
Oil on canvas
42 ½ x 64 ½ in. (108 x 163.8 cm)
Signed at lower right: *ABierstadt*

Early exhibition history: Union League Club, New York, January 1878. Brainerd Gallery, Boston, February 1878. Union League Club, New York, February 1880. *Fifty-fifth Annual Exhibition of the National Academy of Design*, New York, spring 1880, no. 344 as *The Shore of the Turqoise* [sic] *Sea*.

Early publications: *New York Herald*, 8 October 1877, p. 6. *New York Herald*, 11 January 1878, p. 10. *New York Herald*, 13 January 1878, p. 6. *Boston Herald*, 3 February 1878, p. 4. *Boston Morning Journal*, 9 February 1878, p. 4. *Boston Herald*, 10 February 1878, p. 6. *Boston Daily Evening Transcript*, 9 February 1878, p. 6. *New York Herald*, 13 February 1880, p. 4. *New York Times*, 13 February 1880, p. 5. *New York Tribune*, 13 February 1880, p. 1. *New York Evening Mail*, 14 February 1880, p. 1. *Boston Daily Evening Transcript*, 27 March 1880, p. 1. *New York Sun*, 28 March 1880, p. 5. *New York Herald*, 30 March 1880, p. 12. *New York Independent*, 8 April 1880, p. 6. *New York Tribune*, 18 April 1880, p. 7. S. G. W. Benjamin, *American Art Review*, 1880, p. 350.

References: Manoogian, 1989, no. 18, pp. 52–55.

By the mid 1860s, after a decade of hard work and two well-publicized excursions into the American West, Albert Bierstadt was one of the most famous and commercially successful artists in the United States. His grand manner canvases of the Rocky Mountains and Yosemite attracted collectors of enormous wealth and prestige, and garnered commissions that Bierstadt's colleagues could only look upon with envy. He kept company with European nobles and American *nouveau riche*, with bankers and industrialists, and with senators and presidents. The annual unveiling of his majestically scaled landscapes were gala events attended by thousands. No one reached higher peaks faster than Albert Bierstadt, and no fell further when the fashion abated for American landscape painting.

Bierstadt and his rival, Frederic Church, had been speared by critics if not from the very start, then at least from the moment of their respective apotheoses. By the 1860s, young writers such as Clarence Cook and James Jackson Jarves saw the school of New York landscape painters, clinging to the legend of Thomas Cole, as products of a bygone era, whose work was unbearably old fashioned. But it was easy enough for Bierstadt to ignore such sniping, with audiences from London to New York lined up to see his work, and with such wealthy collectors as Le Grand Lockwood offering $25,000 for a painting of Yosemite.[1]

Ironically, Bierstadt's downfall may have had its origins in the Lockwood commission. Lockwood had expanded his fortune during the Civil War, and was building an enormous mansion in Norwalk, Connecticut. For that imposing monument, he asked Bierstadt to produce *The Domes of Yosemite* on a canvas that was fifteen feet wide. The commission was followed with great interest, particularly when Bierstadt premiered the work at the Tenth Street Studio Building in 1867. But not long after the painting was installed in Norwalk, Lockwood's fortunes turned swiftly and dramatically. Jay Gould and Jim Fisk cornered America's gold supply in 1869, and Lockwood was ruined when prices climbed to unheard of levels and then plummeted on 24 September — Black Friday.[2]

Bierstadt felt badly for his former patron, but he had no idea that Lockwood's reversal would become an index of his own sliding position. At the 1872 auction of Lockwood's mansion and art collection, the architect A. S. Hatch came away with *The Domes of Yosemite* for $5,100, one fifth of its original price. It was not simply that the economy and the market for American landscape painting had changed, although that was part of it. The fashion had also run its course for bigger-than-life pictures by bigger-than-life artist-adventurers. Bierstadt still had his admirers and received lucrative commissions, but by the mid 1870s, the climate for landscape painting had already turned decidedly cool.[3]

In 1877, Bierstadt and his wife, Rosalie, made the first of many excursions to the Bahamas, spending the spring in Nassau to restore Rosalie's continually fragile health. Inspired by the beauty of the Atlantic, Bierstadt occupied himself with drawings of the shoreline near Nassau on the Bahamian island of New Providence. By the following October, the New York press was describing his progress on a large seascape, a "huge wave of that peculiar emerald one only sees in the tropics," and by January 1878, the canvas was far enough along that the artist placed it on view at the Union League Club.[4] The *New York Herald* described *The Shore of the Turquoise Sea* at length, and called it a "successful treatment of a difficult motif." Bierstadt finished the painting by February, and exhibited it in Boston, where it also attracted a good deal of favorable commentary in the press.[5]

Bierstadt's presentation of *The Shore of the Turquoise Sea* in New York and Boston was meant to generate publicity before its appearance in Paris at the 1878 Exposition Universelle. It probably never occurred to Bierstadt that the American selection committee made up of Augustus Saint-Gaudens, D. Maitland Armstrong, and C. E. Detmold, all younger men, would dare to refuse his magnificent green wave. But indeed they did.[6] On 21 February 1878, while *The Shore of the Turquoise Sea* was still on view in Boston, the often bleak Jervis McEntee wrote in his journal: "these are very anxious and discouraging days. No one seems to take the least interest in the work of American artists."[7] That was a common perception within Bierstadt's aging circle, and there was no denying the growing fascination in America for French painting. But the shift was more generational than national, as younger American artists, many of them steeped in European aesthetics, successfully lured dealers and collectors away from the declining landscape school that traced its origins to the 1820s.[8]

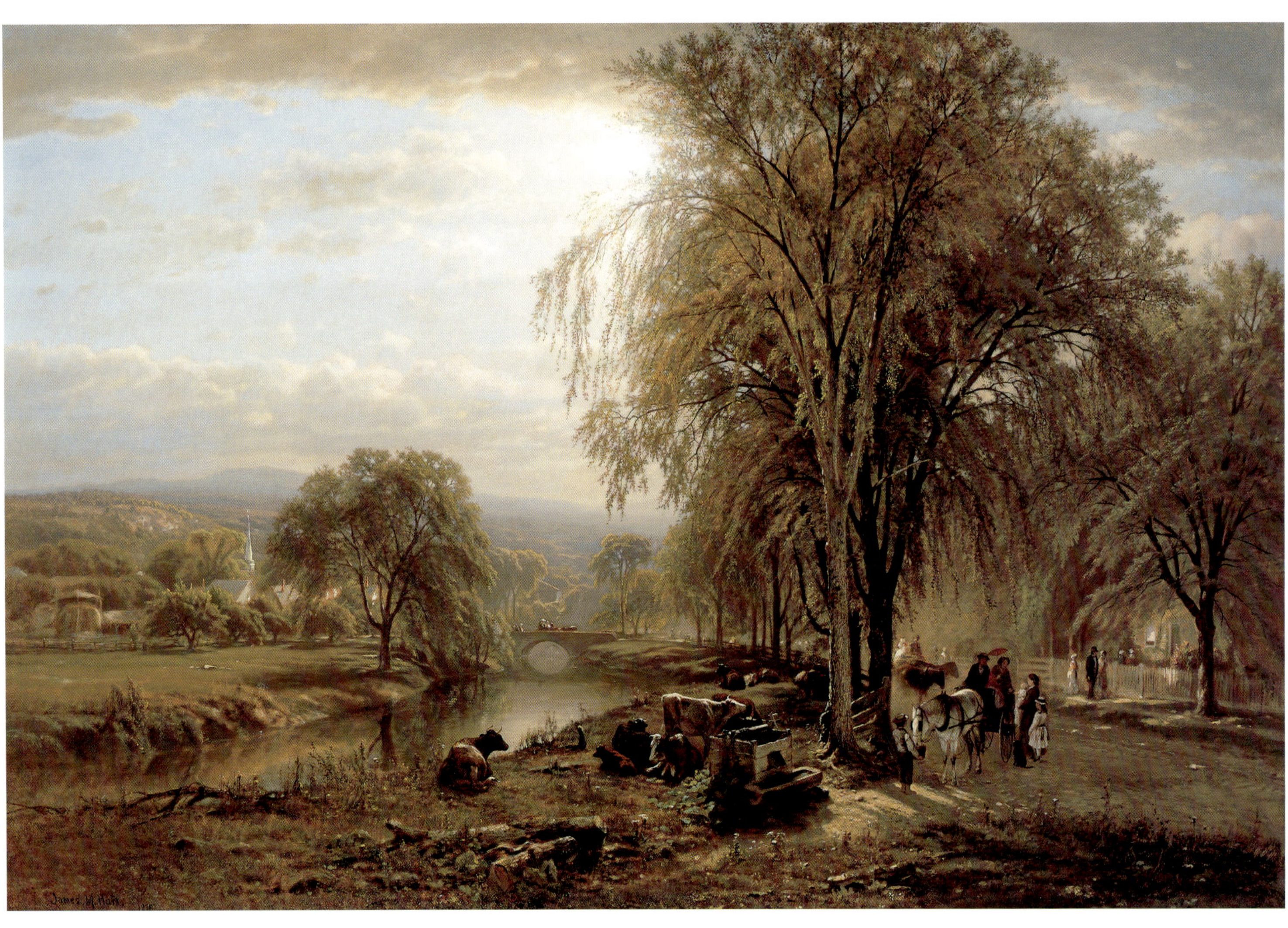

1878 (painted when the artist
was 49–50 years old)
Oil on canvas
40 x 60 in. (101.6 x 152.4 cm)
Signed lower left: *James M. Hart 1878*

In 1878, Americans arrived by the tens of thousands to see the Exposition Universelle in Paris. As they entered the great fair, they passed by (or through) the colossal head of *Liberty*, Antonin Bartholdi's enormous sculpture that would eventually take its place in New York Harbor. Once inside the sprawling exposition, Americans were dazzled by the remarkable new products and machinery that were on display. If Paris's 1867 World's Fair had been a showcase for huge steam engines, vast hydraulic systems, and massive industrial power, the 1878 exposition was about the personal benefits of mechanization and how modern machinery could enhance the life of every man, woman, and child. Among the extraordinary devices on display were Thomas Edison's phonographs and electric light bulbs, the first Singer sewing machines, Alexander Graham Bell's telephone, rubber tires, and the typewriter, among many other labor-saving conveniences. When Edison flipped a switch and Paris's Avenue de l'Opéra was instantly flooded in electric light, a new era was begun. From that moment on, there was no restraining America's consuming fascination for all things modern and urban and new.[1]

By contrast, the handful of American landscape paintings that were exhibited at the 1878 Exposition Universelle must have appeared the product of a bygone era. The American selection committee had outright rejected *The Shore of the Turquoise Sea* (see cat. 32) by Albert Bierstadt, and Frederic Church's *The Parthenon* and *Morning in the Tropics* and Sanford Gifford's *Mount Rainier* probably seemed anachronistic and even tame alongside the more cosmopolitan art of Mary Cassatt, Walter Shirlaw, and J. Alden Weir, and the scenes of African-American life submitted by Winslow Homer. James M. Hart contributed two landscape paintings to the Exposition Universelle, but they attracted little comment in the abundant French and American press coverage. No doubt, Hart's canvases too were viewed as pastoral and nostalgic relics of America's rural past.[2]

By 1878, Hart had been a successful artist for twenty-five years. A native of Scotland, but reared in Albany, New York, Hart had followed his older brother, William, from carriage and sign painting into the fine art studio. More skilled and better trained than his brother, James M. Hart studied in Düsseldorf in the early 1850s alongside such talented Americans as Emanuel Leutze, Worthington Whittredge, and Albert Bierstadt. By the late 1850s, he was a full

Academician at the National Academy of Design, and his work was as much in demand as that of any painter in Manhattan.[3] Describing New York's art market in 1860, an article in the *Cosmopolitan Art Journal* noted that:

> *Church obtains his own price, for he paints only one picture where one hundred are asked. The same thing may be said of no artist in this country, except it be of James M. Hart, whose superb canvasses are daily becoming more difficult to obtain.*[4]

In the last heady hours before the Civil War, Hart's pictures were remarkably desirable, but by the 1870s, like many artists of his generation, he had begun to feel the sting of younger critics, and an accompanying slump in stature and sales. But while some of his colleagues tried to adapt to the newer, more painterly styles, or protested loudly against their intrusion, Hart simply worked in the same manner he always had, remaining aloof of culture wars and the heated debates along generational lines. Within months of painting *Sunday after the Meeting*, the plain spoken Hart tried to characterize his humble aesthetic principles to the writer G. W. Sheldon: "I strive to reproduce in my landscapes the feeling produced by the original scenes themselves. That is what I try for — only that, just that." To such unaffected language, Sheldon could not resist adding his own snide commentary: "Here, then, are no 'symphonies,' or 'nocturnes,' or 'variations,' or 'arrangements' of color, and no improvements upon Nature."[5]

America in the 1870s was on a collision course with modernity and modernism, but already there were some who lamented the loss of simpler ways. Although his prestige had waned since the early 1860s, Hart's pastoral elegies to rural tranquility continued to find buyers and enough appreciative admirers for him to remain viable for the remainder of his career. In *Sunday after the Meeting*, as in so many of his canvases, dappled sunlight filters through leafy trees, where cattle rest peacefully and country people go about their affairs. Such wholesome themes failed to register in Paris in 1878, but in Boston later that same year, Hart's painting *The Oaks near Littleton, N.H.* was awarded a gold medal at the Massachusetts Charitable Mechanic Association in honor of his able representation of "landscape and cattle."[6]

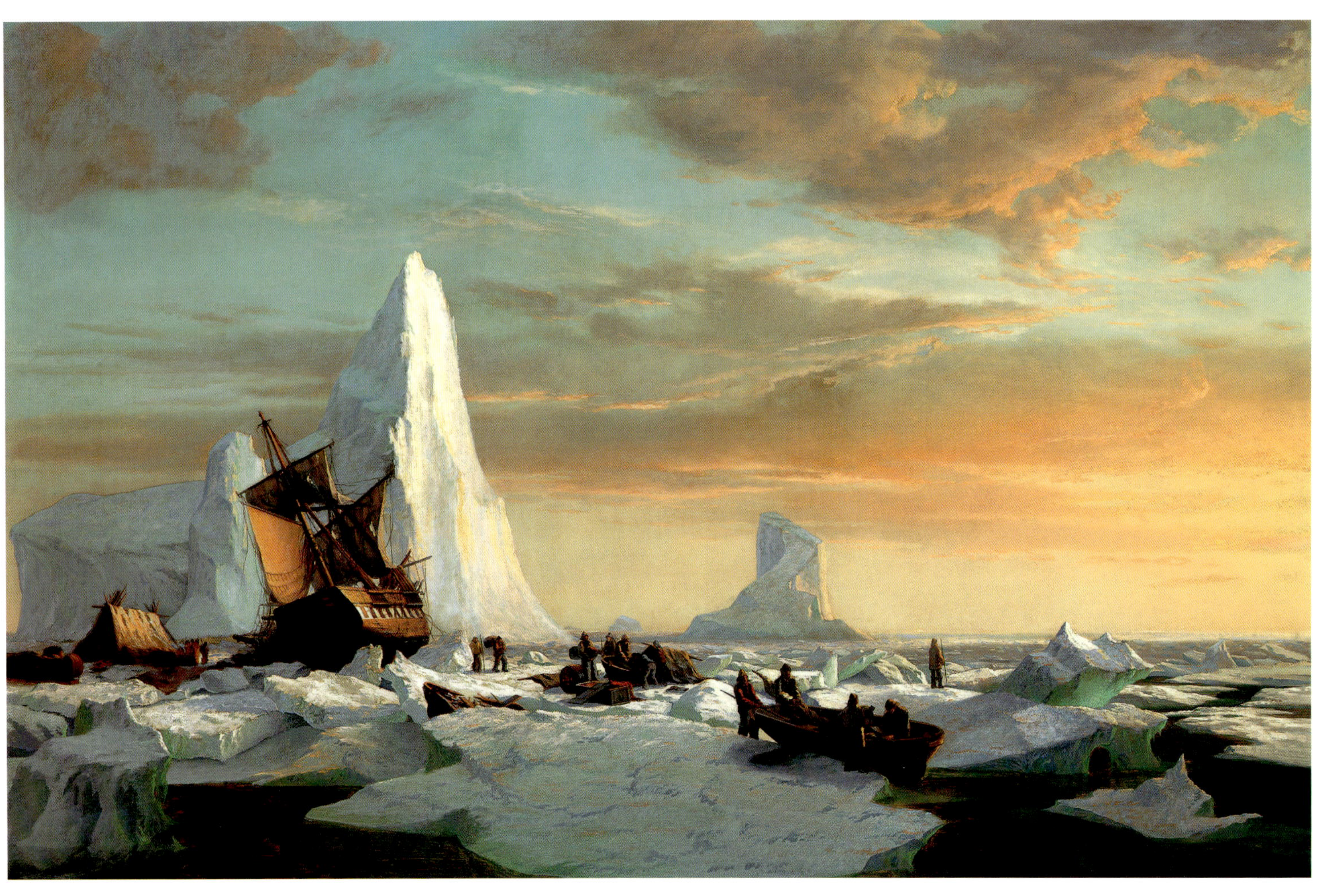

c. 1870–1880
Oil on canvas
28 x 44 in. (71.1 x 111.8 cm)
Unsigned

References: Manoogian, 1989, no. 17,
pp. 50–51.

William Bradford was the seventh generation of his family to live in Massachusetts. Born in Fairhaven, just across the Acushnet River from the whaling port of New Bedford, Bradford turned to painting after failing in the clothing and textile business. He began his career in 1852 making portraits of whaling boats moored in the port of New Bedford and clipper ships anchored in Boston Harbor. In 1854, he traveled to New York, seeking instruction in marine painting, and returned to Fairhaven with the Dutch seascape artist Albert Van Beest. They shared Bradford's studio in Fairhaven and collaborated on a number of steadily more complex nautical subjects.[1]

Their collaboration was relatively successful, but Van Beest's most important contribution to Bradford's development was encouraging him to explore the more advanced aspects of the seascape idiom.[2] During the second half of the 1850s, Bradford forged a more distinctive style of marine painting, but he also made himself better known within local and regional fine art circles. When the New Bedford native Albert Bierstadt returned to his hometown in 1857 after studying in Europe, Bradford contributed to an exhibition he organized of American and European paintings.[3] In 1858, Bradford returned to Boston, where he remained for two years; this time, he produced harbor views and coastal scenes rather than ship portraits, and participated in exhibitions at the Studio Building and in the gallery of Williams and Everett.[4]

In June 1861, Bradford made his first trip to the coast of Labrador in search of icebergs and other arctic subject matter. His reasons for testing the icy northern waters are not entirely clear, but he may have been inspired by Frederic Church's journey to Newfoundland with Louis Legrand Noble in 1859. Noble's popular account of their expedition was published as *After Icebergs with a Painter* in 1861, which coincided with the debut of Church's vast masterwork, *The Icebergs.* But it could be too that Bradford discovered the efficacy of travel in search of exotic subjects through Bierstadt, who had made a very different but no less monumental trek to the remote American West in the summer of 1859 (see cat. 14).[5]

Nearly all of Bradford's professional success derived from his interpretation of frozen shorelines, whaling ships locked in ice, heroic sailors, and the monumental icebergs he encountered during six journeys to Labrador and into the Arctic Circle between 1861 and 1869. Bradford personally organized these expeditions, which involved chartered vessels, paid captains and sailors, photographers, a handful of paying guests, and usually, at least one or two friends of the artist. The longest, the most dangerous, and certainly the most costly of the six was Bradford's final expedition to Melville Bay in Greenland with the noted polar explorer Dr. Isaac Israel Hayes in 1869. The trip was to have been funded by Le Grand Lockwood, an important patron of Bierstadt's. But just as Bradford was returning from Greenland, Lockwood was ruined in the collapse of the gold market in September 1869 (see cat. 16). Bradford was overwhelmed at finding himself personally responsible for such staggering debt, but he had sketched and photographed sights on the 1869 trip that he had never encountered in the relatively tame waters of Labrador. Moreover, it may have been the pressure to recoup financially that spurred his most dynamic period of artistic production and commercial success.[6]

Bradford's *Whalers Trapped in Arctic Ice* was produced during the 1870s, when the artist was actively cultivating an audience for his arctic subjects in England. The English had been pioneers of polar exploration, launching numerous expeditions into the Arctic Circle, including that of Sir John Franklin, who had sailed north in 1845 and, tragically, never returned. In England, Bradford not only found eager collectors among the aristocracy and more commissions for polar seascapes than he could fulfill, but he also became a popular lecturer on arctic exploration. His book *The Arctic Regions,* an oversized folio volume describing his travels and containing photographs of the harsh Greenland coast, was met by largely unanimous acclaim when it appeared in 1873. Bradford probably painted *Whalers Trapped in Arctic Ice* around the same time. The work captured the perilous existence of those who earned their living on the dangerous polar waters, and was typical of the heroic imagery that his audience most admired. A large whaling ship has been trapped by the ice, wrecked, and heaved upon the floe. Whalers salvage what they can from the ship and prepare to set out in small boats in the slim hope of rescue.[7]

35   A BREEZY AUTUMN   George Inness (1825–1894)

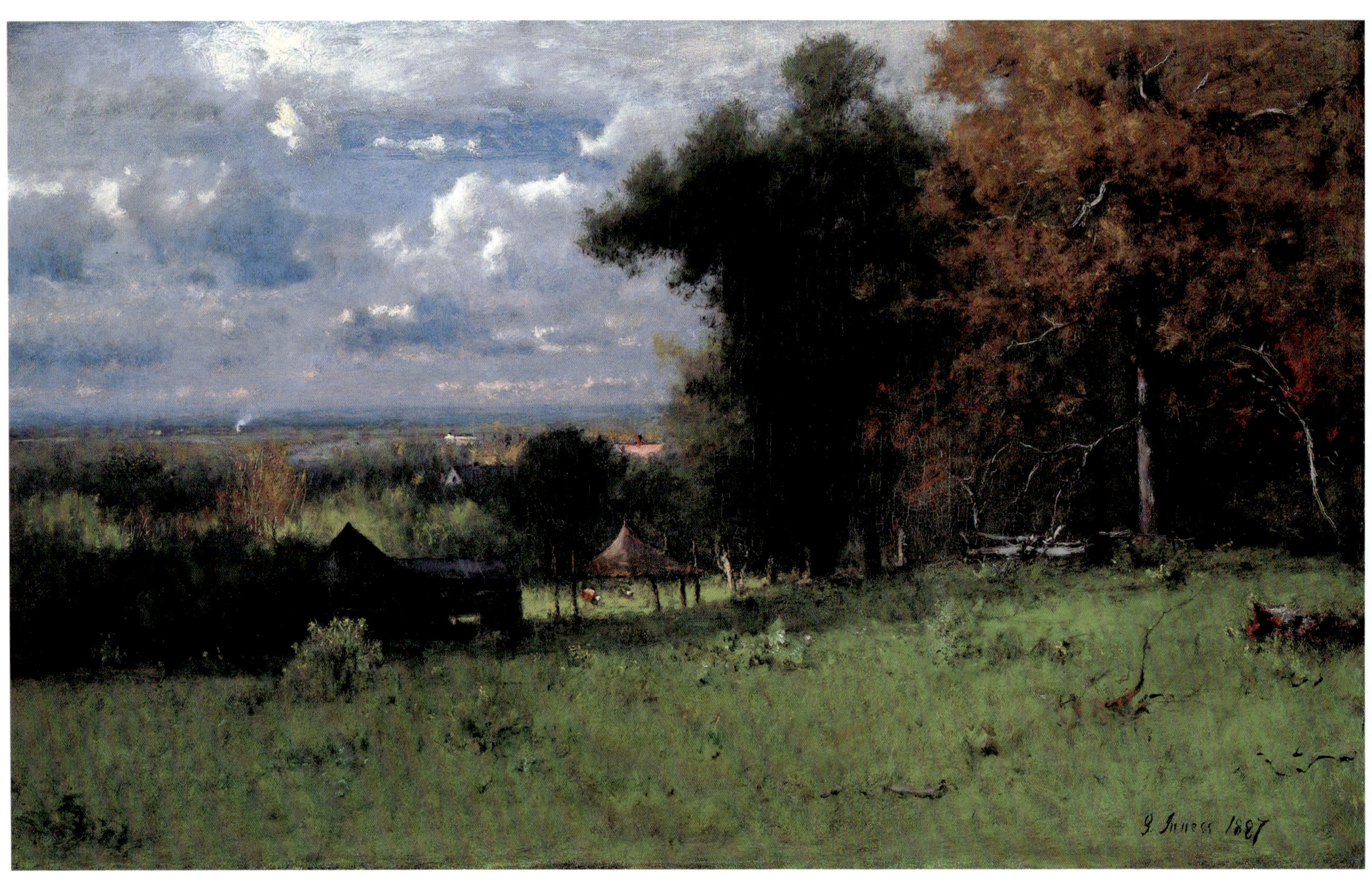

1887 (painted when the artist
was 61–62 years old)
Oil on canvas
30 1/8 x 50 in. (76.5 x 127 cm)
Signed and dated lower right:
G Inness 1887

Early Provenance: From the artist,
New York, 1887; (sold) to Richard H.
Halsted, New York, 1887.
 References: Manoogian, 1989, no. 13,
pp 40–41.

By the 1880s, the first great period of American landscape painting was all but over. The movement that Thomas Cole inaugurated in the 1820s, that Asher B. Durand and Frederick Kensett nurtured in the 1840s and 1850s, and that Frederic Church and Albert Bierstadt expanded into a grand manner aesthetic in the 1860s had run its course, usurped by the bravura modern styles coming out of Munich, Paris, and London. Kensett and Sanford Gifford died prematurely in 1872 and 1880, the ancient Durand finally passed away in 1886, and humbled by rheumatism, Church could barely lift his brush by the 1880s. Jasper Cropsey built a Gothic manor in the heady 1860s, found that his diminishing sales could not support it in the 1870s, and sold it in 1885. Bierstadt's gaudy mansion in Irvington had burned in 1882, and in 1884, Martin Johnson Heade moved virtually unnoticed into a bungalow in St. Augustine, Florida, where he was all but forgotten. An extraordinary era of celebrity landscape painters — darlings of the press, favorites of the public, and companions of the rich and powerful — was drawing to a close, and there would never be anything remotely like it again.[1]

At the same time one group of painters was fading into thorough oblivion, another great artistic movement was poised to begin. The first of the eight French Impressionist exhibitions opened in Paris in 1874, and by the early 1880s, their radical ideas had infiltrated American thinking about the visual arts. Younger American painters banded together in their embrace of avant-garde principles, and a few of the older men such as Worthington Whittredge, Jervis McEntee, and Homer Dodge Martin modified their styles in strained efforts to stay in step with current trends. Only a handful of artists were able to rise above prevailing fashion or to successfully adapt their art to it. Heade had somehow managed to stay aesthetically viable, if professionally obscure, from the beginning to the very end of his career. Thomas Moran's views of the American West remained popular even as the artist approached his ninetieth birthday in 1926. But perhaps the only painter to emerge from the early school of New York landscapists, who successfully transformed his art out of personal vision rather than voguish desperation, was the brilliant George Inness.[2]

Although he was as much as two decades younger in his aesthetic inclinations, Inness was in fact a year older than Church. He had come out of Newark, New Jersey, and was training to be a map engraver when he decided in the early 1840s to become a landscape painter. He made obligatory treks to the Catskills, and his early canvases revealed the common admiration of Cole and Durand, even if he was never quite so smitten as Church. But whereas most of his contemporaries took Cole's theoretical framework and developed variations on it, for Inness, the art of Cole was no more than a logical starting point for a much longer aesthetic journey. In the early 1850s, Inness traveled in Europe, and his exposure to the French Barbizon School, especially Théodore Rousseau, impressed him deeply. In the following decade, Inness was introduced to the ideas of eighteenth-century theologian Emmanuel Swedenborg. Searching for the hand of God in the American wilderness or evidence of human piety in well-tended farms was far from foreign to Cole, Durand or Church, but the spirituality of Inness not only affected what he painted, but how he painted it.[3]

Swedenborg taught that every object in nature was in some way an expression of God's divinity and of a simple spiritual order. In the late 1860s, inspired by Swedenborg, Inness began to think of color in symbolic terms, his brushwork became looser and more fluid, and his compositions developed an overall tonal harmony and unity that reflected the greater arc of God's presence. But Inness also departed from Swedenborgian dogma in his appreciation of man's cultivation of nature, as seen in the pastures, the grazing cattle, the farms, and even the smoke of a distant factory in *A Breezy Autumn*. Inness wrote in 1878: "The highest art is where has been most perfectly breathed the sentiment of humanity. Rivers, streams, the rippling brook, the hill-side, the sky, clouds — all things that we see — can convey that sentiment if we are in the love of God and the desire of truth."[4] By 1887, when he painted *A Breezy Autumn*, Inness was perhaps the most revered and influential artist in the United States. His work had anticipated Impressionism, just coming into fashion, and it was generally agreed that he had waited twenty years for the rest of America to catch up with his innovations.[5]

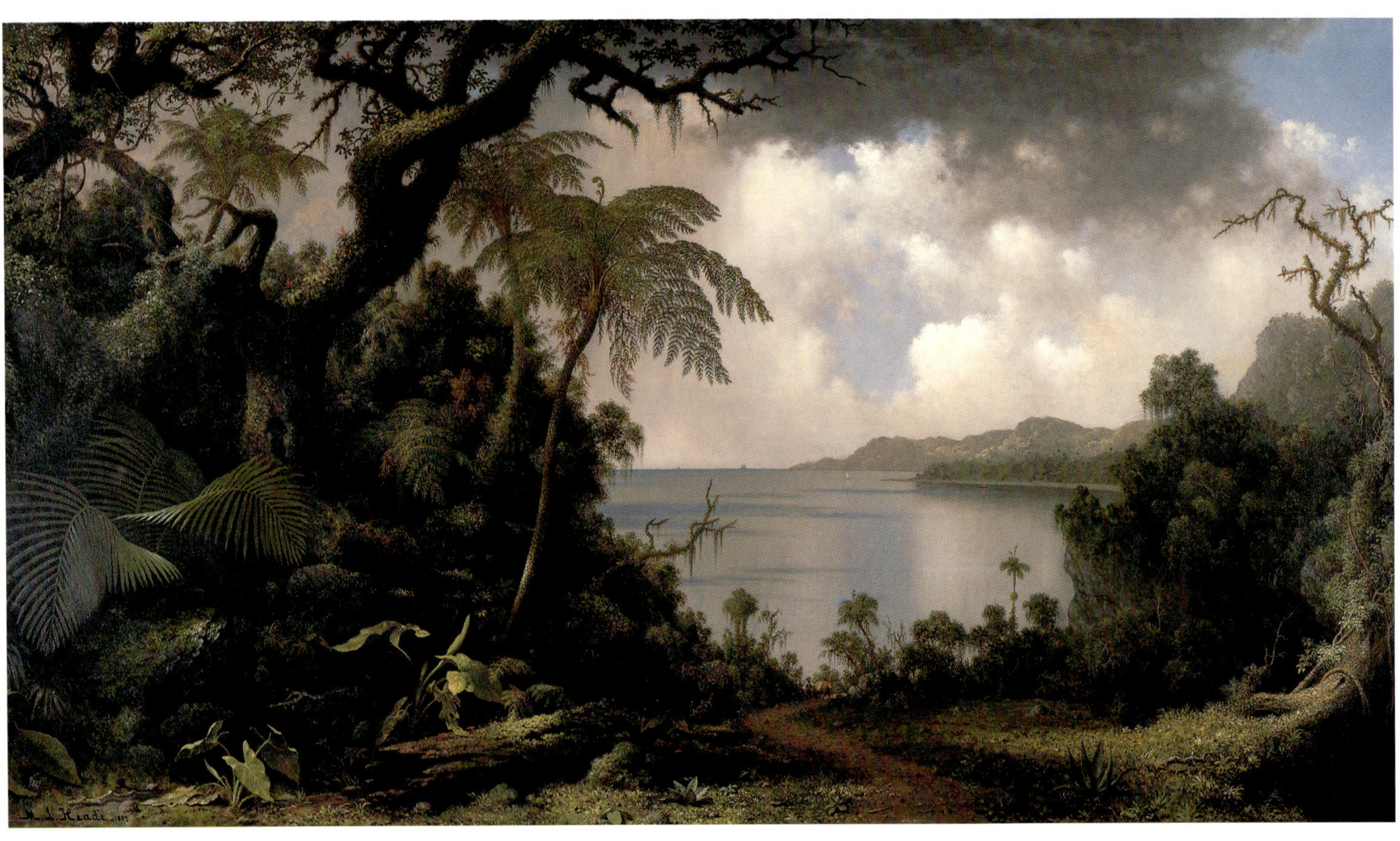

1887 (painted when the artist
was 67 years old)
Oil on canvas
53 x 90 in. (134.6 x 228.6 cm)
Signed and dated at lower left:
M. J. Heade 1887

Early provenance: From the artist,
St. Augustine, Fla., 1887; (sold) to Henry
Morrison Flagler, Ponce de Leon Hotel,
St. Augustine, Fla., 1887.
Early exhibition history: Upper
Rotunda, Ponce de Leon Hotel,
St. Augustine, Fla., 1887 through the
twentieth century.
References: Howat, 1987, pp. 174–76.
Manoogian, 1989, no. 20, pp. 58–59.
Manoogian, 1997, no. 13, pp. 52–53 and 189.
Stebbins, 2000, no. 285, p. 272.

Although the painting by Martin Johnson Heade known as *View from Fern-Tree Walk, Jamaica* is dated "1887" on the canvas, scholars have long considered it to be a work of about 1870. Heade made his only excursion to the Caribbean island early that year, and at least one important painting known to have resulted from the voyage has been unaccounted for since the nineteenth century. The "1887" inscription was thought to have been added by Heade to indicate the year he sold the picture to Henry Morrison Flagler. But perhaps lurking within that reasoning was the assumption that Heade could not have produced such an elaborately detailed but cogently unified masterwork in the late 1880s, as he approached his sixty-eighth birthday. Apparently, however, he not only could, he did.[1]

In 1883, the idiosyncratic, peripatetic, bachelor artist Heade married for the first time at age sixty-four, bought the first house he had ever owned, and settled in St. Augustine, Florida, where he would spend the remainder of his life. Less than a year after Heade and his bride Elizabeth Smith moved into their home on San Marco Avenue, the Standard Oil millionaire Henry Flagler spent his own honeymoon in St. Augustine, and was so taken with the ancient village that he made plans almost immediately to build a luxury hotel there. Heade followed Flagler's construction of the Ponce de Leon Hotel with interest, and by early 1887, the artist and the oilman had become good friends. Flagler had been a man of some cultured impulses before he met Heade, but their association seems to have stimulated his interest in the fine arts. The budding hotelier started thinking of St. Augustine as an artist colony, and he added painting studios to the Ponce de Leon, one of which was occupied by Heade.[2]

Not long after they met, Flagler purchased Heade's large painting now known as *The Great Florida Marsh*, and was so pleased that he commissioned two even more monumental tropical subjects for the Ponce de Leon Hotel. By April 1887, Heade was at work on *The Great Florida Sunset*, and the painting now known as *View from Fern-Tree Walk, Jamaica*. He wryly reported to his friend Eben Loomis that: "I'm painting two landscapes for him (8 ft. long) that will take some thousands out of his pocket, but I think he can stand it." In June, Heade again updated Loomis: "My two big pictures, for the parlor of the big hotel, are nearly completed. One is a Jamaica picture, with tree ferns & things, & I think it's a pretty neat thing — for me."

The paintings may have been intended for the parlor, but Flagler hung them in the more prominent upper rotunda of the Ponce de Leon.[3]

Although the era of monumental landscape painting by bigger-than-life artists such as Albert Bierstadt and Heade's close friend Frederic Church was as all but complete in New York, in the state of Florida, poised for a real estate boom that only a fast-talking oilman like Henry Flagler could envision and pull off, American grand manner landscape painting still had a few final breaths of life. Heade gave Flagler his money's worth ($2,000 each) for the two vast canvases, but more than that, his pictures for the Ponce de Leon Hotel summarized and completed a great era of landscape painting that had begun with Thomas Cole's trek through the Catskills sixty years earlier. If Bierstadt's *The Last of the Buffalo* was an elegy to the vanishing frontier that had inspired America's first great school of art — and perhaps a eulogy to the artists themselves — Heade's paintings of a Jamaican jungle and a Florida sunset were at once familiar summaries of a great era and guideposts to the next frontier, a gilded age of extraordinary fortunes and robber barons.[4]

It was ironic that Heade should have the last word for American landscape painting. He was part of the first circle of New York landscapists, but he had always operated at its fringe. He counted Church, and many influential businessmen, academics, and clergy among his closest friends, yet he was never elected to the National Academy of Design or invited to join the Century Association, the institutional arms of nineteenth-century landscape painting. But by 1887, it no longer mattered. Cole, Louis Remy Mignot, Frederick Kensett, Sanford Gifford, and Asher B. Durand were all dead, Church was hobbled by rheumatism, and Bierstadt had become virtually irrelevant. Only Martin Johnson Heade was left standing, and it was he who gently eased American landscape painting, America's first great art movement, into a Florida retirement.[5]

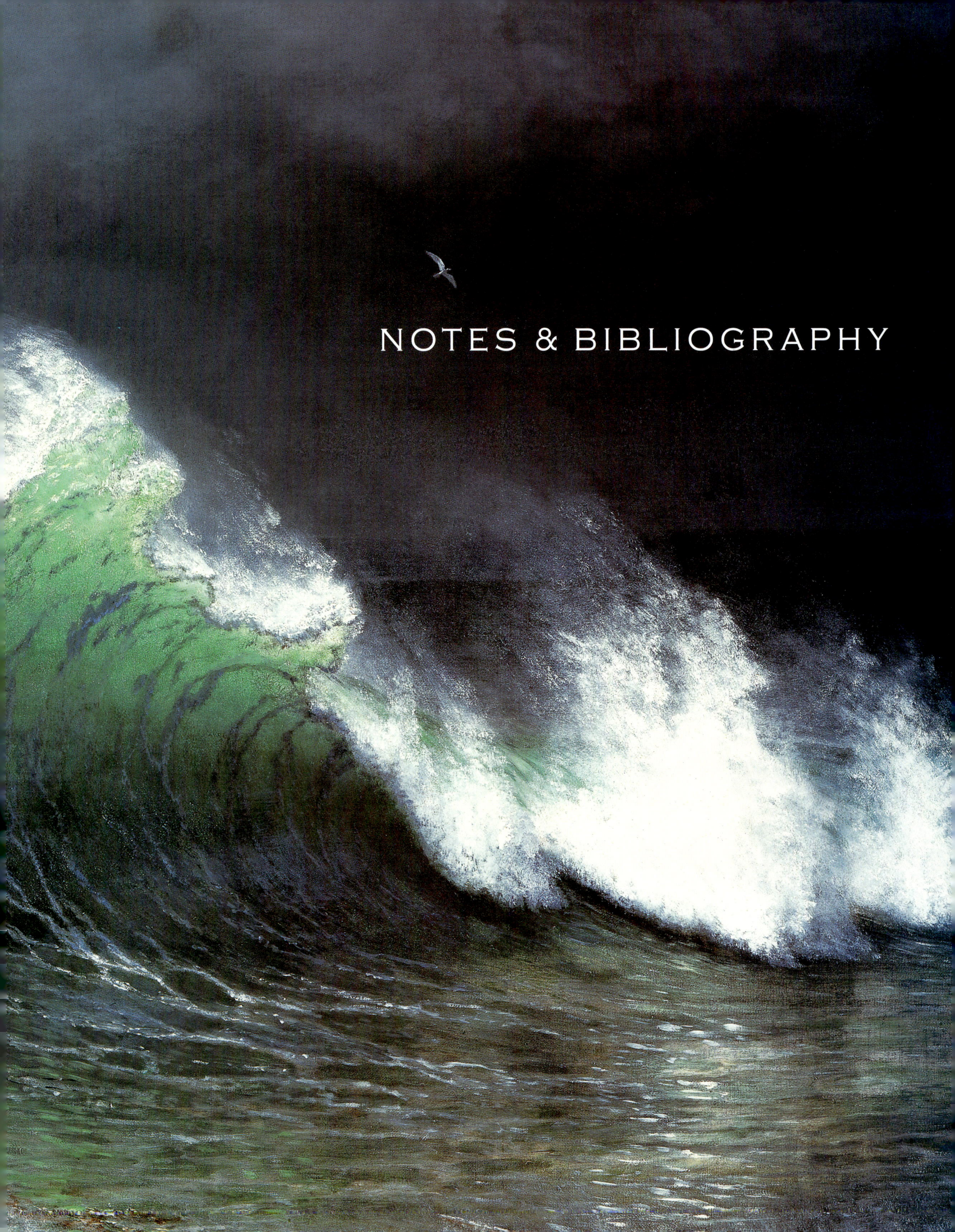
NOTES & BIBLIOGRAPHY

NOTES

A Church on the Magdalena River

1 Any discussion of Thomas Cole is indebted to the impressive scholarly work of Elwood C. Parry III. See Parry, 1988.

2 See the letter from Thomas Cole to Asher B. Durand, 4 January 1838 in Legrand, 1853, p. 185.

3 The relationship between faithful details and general unity in the work of Thomas Cole and Asher B. Durand was noted by at least one perceptive writer: "It is now generally conceded, we believe, that Cole and Durand are the two most prominent landscape painters in this country.... Both of these artists are undoubtedly devoted students, but while one revels upon the whole of a landscape, the attention of the other is invited by an isolated feature of peculiar beauty. Durand paints the better study from nature, so far as individuality is concerned, but Cole produces with greater truth the uncommon effects observable in nature." See *New York Evening Post*, 23 April 1847, p. 2, quoted in Howat, 1987, p. 35.

4 See Sir David Brewster, *A Treatise on Optics,* Philadelphia: Carry, Lea & Blanchard, 1833. Brewster's theories were first published in England in 1831. See also Sir Isaac Newton, *Opticks or A Treatise on the Reflections, Inflections and Colours of Light,* London: W. and J. Innys, 1718.

5 Many of Thomas Cole's sketchbooks are in the collection of the Detroit Institute of Arts. See *Bulletin of the Detroit Institute of Arts,* vol. 66, no. 1, 1990. See also Kathleen Erwin, *Fair Scenes & Glorious Wonders: Thomas Cole in Italy, Switzerland, and England,* Detroit: Detroit Institute of Arts, 1991.

6 There is no question that Asher B. Durand was wounded by criticism that he lacked Thomas Cole's imagination and sense of the ideal. Nearly twenty years after Durand's death, John Durand was still defending his father against charges that he was overly literal and blandly descriptive. See Durand, 1894, pp. 173–75.

7 For a discussion of American critical thought in the 1850s, see Doreen Bolger Burke and Catherine Hoover Voorsanger, "The Hudson River School in Eclipse," in Howat, 1987, pp. 71–90.

8 Frederick Kensett, Sanford Gifford, and Martin Johnson Heade are usually associated with an aspect of mid nineteenth-century landscape painting now known as Luminism. See Wilmerding, 1980.

9 See Thomas Cole, "Essay on American Scenery," in McCoubrey, 1965, pp. 98–109. Quoted in Wilton and Barringer, 2002, p. 39.

10 See Ralph Waldo Emerson, "Nature," *The Best of Ralph Waldo Emerson: Essays, Poems, Addresses,* New York: Walter J. Black, p. 75.

11 Interestingly, unity had also become imperative to the identity of the Hudson River School as a cogent group of artists. By 1858, many of them were working in the same building, and while they were never a school of painters per se, they did benefit from the perceived authority of their collectivity. See Blaugrund, 1997.

12 This is not to say that all Hudson River School paintings were large and formidable. See Oswaldo Rodriguez Roque, "The Exaltation of American Landscape Painting," in Howat, 1987, pp. 45–46.

13 For the ambitions of Frederic Church and Albert Bierstadt, and a discussion of their rivalry, see ibid., pp. 44–45.

14 It is not certain that Gustave Flaubert ever equated God and details. If he did, the axiom does not seem to appear in any of his fiction. The idea of finding larger spiritual truths in the smallest of God's creations is perhaps most consistent with the philosophy of his eager cataloguers Bouvard and Pecuchet. But careful attention was also a trait of the scheming Emma Bovary engrossed in the details of her deceptions, and the pious servant Félicité attending to every detail in *Un Coeur Simple.* See John Bartlett, *Bartlett's Familiar Quotations,* edited by Justin Kaplan, Boston: Little, Brown and Co., 2002.

15 Given the paradise that was the American landscape, it is probably no coincidence that Arcadian themes appear frequently in Hudson River School paintings, and that the Garden of Eden was a favorite subject of Thomas Cole and others. See Cole's *The Garden of Eden* (1828; Amon Carter Museum, Fort Worth, Tex.) and *Expulsion from the Garden of Eden* (1827–28; Museum of Fine Arts, Boston) in Wilton and Barringer, 2002, pp. 91–94.

16 Perhaps not altogether coincidentally, *June Shower* set off a heated argument between George William Curtis, the art critic for the *New York Herald Tribune,* and supporters of Asher B. Durand. Curtis offered sharp criticism of the painting when it was shown at the 1854 exhibition of the National Academy of Design. See the catalogue entry by Franklin Kelly in Manoogian, 1989, pp. 22–23.

17 For Jasper Cropsey's experiences in England, see the catalogue entry by Carrie Rebora for *Autumn – On the Hudson River* (1860; National Gallery of Art, Washington, D.C.) in Howat, 1987, pp. 206–7. See also Richard H. Saunders's catalogue entry for *The Backwoods of America* in Manoogian, 1989, pp. 12–15.

18 For Albert Bierstadt's complicated relationship with Fitz Hugh Ludlow and his wife Rosalie in 1864, see Hendricks, 1974, pp. 113–136. One of Bierstadt's first great landscapes after returning from his second journey to the West with Fitz Hugh Ludlow was *A Storm in the Rocky Mountains – Mount Rosalie* (1866; Brooklyn Museum). See Howat, 1987, pp. 290–93.

19 For discussions of Worthington Whittredge's *Twilight on the Shawangunk Mountains* and Sanford Gifford's *Mount Mansfield,* see the catalogue entries by Franklin Kelly and Christopher Kent Wilson respectively in Manoogian, 1989, pp. 26–29 and 44–47.

20 The compositional device of the figure surveying a landscape is most closely associated with the great French painter Claude Lorraine (1600–1682), an important influence on Thomas Cole and Hudson River School aesthetics.

21 For a thorough discussion of the "magisterial gaze" in the context of Manifest Destiny and American expansionism, see Boime, 1991.

22 George Henry Durrie significantly elevated his ambition with *The Half-Way House.* It seems clear that he was attempting to add texture and nuance, as well as scope and scale to his Connecticut landscape subjects. *The Half-Way House* represented an important step away from the cloying and facile works he generally produced for Currier & Ives, but unfortunately, Durrie died less than two years after completing the canvas. See Sarah Cash's catalogue entry for Durrie's *The Half-Way House* in Manoogian, 1989, pp. 70–71.

23 For a discussion of Luminism, the term applied to the work of Martin Johnson Heade, see Wilmerding, 1980. One hallmark of Luminist painting was its intelligent integration of form and content. See Barbara Novak, "On Defining Luminism" and Lisa Fellows Andrus, "Design and Measurement in Luminist Art" in Wilmerding, 1980, pp. 23–56.

24 For an interesting discussion of Martin Johnson Heade and Darwinism, see Stebbins, 2000, pp. 76–77.

25 For Frederic Church's *Heart of the Andes* (1859; Metropolitan Museum of Art, New York) and *Cotopaxi* (1862; Detroit Institute of Arts), see Howat, 1987, pp. 246–250 and 254–58.

26 For Frederic Church's punning use of quickly sketched chapels combined with his initials to represent his signature, see Manthorne, 1985, p. 151.

Cat. 1

1 In July 1850, the painter Jasper Cropsey visited the widow of Thomas Cole at Cedar Grove, the Coles' home in Catskill. Cropsey wrote to his own wife, "In the house we see the picture that is such a favorite of mine 'Schroon Lake'..." See Parry, 1988, p. 366. For Frederic Church's role in helping Maria Cole sell the painting to William Earl Dodge Jr., see Kelly, 1988, pp. 83 and 153, note 20.

2 John Trumble's frequently quoted remarks about Thomas Cole's work first appeared in William Dunlap, *A History of the Rise and Progress of the Arts and Design in the United States,* 2 vols., New York, 1834, vol. 2, p. 360.

3 For Thomas Cole's description of Schroon Lake from a rowboat, see Noble, 1853, p. 152. For Cole's view from

Mount Holyoke, familiarly known as *The Oxbow* (1836; Metropolitan Museum of Art, New York), see Oswaldo Rodriguez Roque's catalogue entry in Howat, 1987, pp. 125–27. For more on *The Oxbow,* see Allan Wallach, "Making a Picture of the View from Mount Holyoke," *Bulletin of the Detroit Institute of Arts,* vol. 66, no. 1, 1990, pp. 34–45. For Cole's *The Course of Empire* (1836; New-York Historical Society), see Wilton and Barringer, 2002, pp. 95–109 and especially Foshay, 1990, pp. 130–140.

4 Noble, 1853, pp. 151–52.

5 See Thomas Cole's Sketchbook 10 in the Detroit Institute of Arts, 39.568.20–.21. The most fully resolved sketch of Schroon Lake is on page 21. For Cole's description of rowing to a wider place in the lake, see Noble, 1853, p. 152.

6 See Thomas Cole's Sketchbook 10 in the Detroit Institute of Arts, 39.568.78, a drawing Cole described as "Scroon [sic] Mountain from north head of Scroon [sic] Lake."

7 For the drawings of cedar trees, see Thomas Cole's Sketchbook 10 in the Detroit Institute of Arts, 39.568.101, .99, and .96. On the second trip to Schroon Lake, Cole seems to have turned the sketchbook over and worked from the last pages to the first.

8 For a reference to Thomas Cole's composition drawing (c. 1837; Museum of Fine Arts, Boston) for *Schroon Lake,* see the catalogue entry for the painting by Nicolai Cikovsky Jr. in Manoogian, 1989, p. 16, note 6.

9 "Essay on American Scenery" was published in pamphlet form and in the *American Monthly Magazine* in January 1836. It is reprinted in McCoubrey, 1965, pp. 98–110.

10 See the letter from Thomas Cole to Luman Reed, 6 March 1836, in the Thomas Cole Papers, New York State Library, Albany, New York. Quoted in Oswaldo Rodriguez Roque's catalogue entry for *View on the Catskill – Early Autumn* (1837; Metropolitan Museum of Art, New York) in Howat, 1987, p. 128. For a fuller consideration, see Kenneth Maddox, "Thomas Cole and the Railroad: Gentle Maledictions," *Archives of American Art Journal,* vol. 30, 1990, pp. 146–154.

Cat. 2

1 For Joshua Shaw's move from London to Philadelphia, see Judy L. Larsen's catalogue entry for Shaw's *Romantic Landscape* (1835) in *American Paintings from the High Museum of Art,* New York: Hudson Hills Press, 1994, pp. 26–27.

2 See John Hill's prints after Joshua Shaw's watercolors in *Picturesque Views of American Scenery, 1820–1825,* Philadelphia: M. Carey and Son, 1820. The portion of Shaw's statement is quoted in Wilton and Barringer, 2002, p. 43.

Cat. 3

1 Frederic Church is generally considered to be Thomas Cole's first student. See Kelly and Carr, 1987.

2 Frederic Church's father paid Thomas Cole $300 per year for his son's training. Perhaps not altogether coincidentally, Daniel Wadsworth, who had recommended Church to Cole in 1844, purchased Cole's largest, if not his most accomplished, painting, *Mount Aetna from Taormina* (1843; Wadsworth Atheneum, Hartford, Conn.) that same year. In December 1843, Cole completed the large canvas in five days. See Oswaldo Rodriguez Roque's catalogue entry for *Mount Aetna from Taormina* (1844; Lyman Allyn Museum, New London, Conn.) in Howat, 1987, pp. 136–37.

3 For the painting by Thomas Cole known familiarly as *The Oxbow* (1836; Metropolitan Museum of Art, New York), see Howat, 1987, pp. 125–27. For Frederic Church's *The Oxbow (after Thomas Cole)* (1844–46; Mr. and Mrs. Andrew S. Peters, New Jersey), see Wilmerding, 1980, p. 30. For Church's *Hooker and Company Journeying through the Wilderness from Plymouth to Hartford in 1636* (1846; Wadsworth Atheneum, Hartford, Conn), see Kelly and Carr, 1987, pp. 40–42 and Carr, 2000, p. 112, note 6.

4 For the founding of the Wadsworth Atheneum by Daniel Wadsworth and its purchase of Frederic Church's *Hooker and Company Journeying through the Wilderness from Plymouth to Hartford in 1636,* see William G. Delana, "Foremost Upon this Continent: A History of the Wadsworth Atheneum," in Ayres, 1992. For a discussion of Church's relationship to Hartford, see Carr, 2000, pp. 46–47.

5 *Christian on the Borders of the 'Valley of the Shadow of Death,' Pilgrim's Progress* (1847) is in the collection of the Olana State Historic Site, Frederic Church's home and studio near Hudson, N.Y. For a brief description of the American Art-Union, where Church opened his first studio in New York, see Howat, 1987, pp. 53–54. See also Carol Troyen, "Retreat to Arcadia: American Landscape and the American Art-Union," *American Art Journal,* vol. 23, no.1, 1991, pp. 20–37.

6 Thought to be hundreds of years old, the Charter Oak was a Native American landmark well before the ancestors of Daniel Wadsworth and Frederic Church arrived in 1636. Most famously, it was where the Connecticut Charter was hidden from English authorities, an important act of defiance against British tyranny almost a century before the American Revolution. See David E. Philips, *Legendary Connecticut: Traditional Tales of the Nutmeg State,* Willimantic, Conn.: Curbstone Press, 1992. The Charter Oak's history as a symbol of aspirant freedom, not irrelevant to Church, was seized upon by the Abolitionist movement. An anti-slavery newspaper edited by Erasmus Darwin Hudson and published in

Hartford between 1838 and 1848 was called *The Charter Oak.* A few issues from 1838 and 1846 have been preserved on microfilm at the Connecticut State Library in Hartford. The tree finally fell during a windstorm in 1856.

7 See Gerald Carr, "Master and Pupil: Drawings by Thomas Cole and Frederic Church," *Bulletin of the Detroit Institute of Arts,* vol. 66, no. 1, 1990, pp. 56–60. The letter from Frederic Church to Thomas Cole, 17 October 1846 (Thomas Cole Papers, Detroit Institute of Arts, Box 2) is also quoted by Carr in the same article. Church's two paintings of 1846 of the Charter Oak are in the collections of the Olana State Historical Site and the Hartford Steam Boiler Inspection and Insurance Company, Hartford.

8 For Thomas Cole's *The Cross of the World,* a cycle that was still unfinished at the time of his death in February 1848, see Parry, 1988, pp. 315–359.

9 See "The Fine Arts. Exhibitions at the National Academy. Second Saloon," *The Literary World,* 5 June 1847, p. 419, quoted in Manoogian, 1989, p. 18

10 Gerald Carr compares Frederic Church's *July Sunset* to Thomas Cole's *Evening in Arcady* (1843; Wadsworth Atheneum) and *The Mountain Ford* (1846; Metropolitan Museum of Art) in Carr, 2000, p. 47. *July Sunset* would also seem closely related to *Sunset in the Catskills* (1841; Museum of Fine Arts Boston), *Catskill Creek* (1845; New York Historical Society) and *The Old Mill at Sunset* (1845; Location unknown, but see Powell, 1990, p. 117).

11 For the identification of Theodore Cole, see Carr, 2000, p. 47. See also Parry, 1988, p. 317 for William Sidney Mount's *Sketch of Theodore A. Cole* (1843; Toledo Museum of Art). As recently as 1989, *July Sunset* bore the subtitle *Berkshire County, Massachusetts.* See Kelly, 1989, p. 160. That descriptive addition has been dropped in subsequent publications of the painting.

12 For the association of the Charter Oak to Frederic Church's sense of personal and aesthetic independence, see Carr, 2000, p. 47. Similarly, Franklin Kelly discusses Thomas Cole's interest in Associationist theories of Archibald Alison and their relevance to landscape painting. Ironically, Cole probably introduced the idea to Church, who in turn used it to assert his independence from Cole. See Kelly, 1989, pp. 42–43.

13 For Frederic Church's travels in the Berkshire Mountains in 1847, see Carr, 2000, pp. 48–49.

14 For Adrian Janes's acquisition of *July Sunset* and a discussion of Frederic Church's Hartford origins and its effect on his early work, see Carr, 2000, pp. 47–48 and 51–52.

Cat. 4

1 The humility of Asher B. Durand is impressive, given his achievement, but he nearly always deferred to Thomas

Cole in matters of landscape painting. See, for example, Durand's letter to Cole, 5 September 1837, in which he states: "I am still willing to confess myself a trespasser on your grounds, tho' I trust, not a poacher." Quoted in Howat, 1987, p.32. Durand's modesty is more easily grasped when considered in the context of the deep mutual respect that he and Cole shared for each other.

2 For a short biography of Asher B. Durand, see Wilton and Barringer, 2002, pp.252–53.

3 For a discussion of Asher B. Durand's travels in 1848, see the catalogue entry for *Kindred Spirits* (1849; New York Public Library) in Wilton and Barringer, 2002, pp.68–70 and Barbara Ball Buff's catalogue entry for *Kindred Spirits* in Howat, 1987, pp.108–110.

4 See Tuckerman, 1867, p.195. Henry Tuckerman called Durand's *Summer Afternoon* "one of the latest of his pictures." But Tuckerman was prone to frequent miscalculations when assigning dates to paintings by Durand and by other artists as well. Even if he was referring to a painting other than *A Summer Afternoon* in the Manoogian Collection, Tuckerman's description is still apt.

5 Quoted in Barbara Ball Buff's catalogue entry for Asher B. Durand's *Kaaterskill Clove* (1866; Century Association, New York) in Howat, 1987, p.117.

Cat. 5

1 For more on the American Art-Union, see Carol Troyen, "Retreat to Arcadia: American Landscape and the American Art-Union," *American Art Journal,* vol. 23, no. 1, 1991, pp.20–37.

2 For a discussion of the circumstances that contributed to the rise of landscape painting in America, see John K. Howat, "A Climate for Landscape Painters" in Howat, 1987, pp.49–70.

3 See William Cullen Bryant, *A Funeral Oration occasioned by the death of Thomas Cole, delivered before the National Academy of Design, 4 May 1848,* New York, 1848.

4 For Frederick Kensett's participation in the 1845 and 1847 National Academy of Design exhibitions and his sale of paintings to the American Art Union in 1846, see Jonathan P. Harding's catalogue entry for Kensett's *The Bash-Bish* in Abigail Booth Gerdts, *An American Collection: Paintings and Sculpture from the National Academy of Design,* New York, 1989, p.38.

5 See Frederick Kensett to Elizabeth Kensett, 16 December 1844, James R. Kellogg Collection, Archives of American Art, Smithsonian Institution, Washington, D.C., roll no. N68–84. Quoted in Driscoll and Howat, 1985, p.62.

6 The most significant and useful study of Frederick Kensett's life and work remains Driscoll and Howat, 1985.

7 For Frederick Kensett's submission of American landscape paintings to the 1850 National Academy of Design exhibition, see Donelson Hoopes's catalogue entry for Kensett's *Camel's Hump from the Western Shore of Lake Champlain* in *American Paintings from the High Museum of Art,* New York: Hudson Hills Press, 1994, pp.50–51. For Kensett's *The White Mountains – Mt. Washington* (1851; Wellesley College Museum) and its indication of a shift in the artist's ambition and fortunes, see Carol Troyen's catalogue entry in Howat, 1987, pp.149–151.

8 See Tuckerman, 1867, p.513.

9 Frederick Kensett exhibited *Reminiscence of the White Mountains* at the 1852 exhibition of the National Academy of Design, where it was noted and described in [George William Curtis], "The Fine Arts; Exhibition of the National Academy; II," *New York Tribune,* 1 May 1852, p.3. Franklin Kelly identified the Kensett painting in the Manoogian Collection as the work exhibited in 1852. See Manoogian, 1989, p.20.

10 For a discussion of the particular mountain peak Frederick Kensett remembered, see Franklin Kelly's catalogue entry for *Reminiscence of the White Mountains* in Manoogian, 1989, pp.20–21 and especially note 1.

11 For Asher B. Durand's merging of idealism and realism, see his "Letter" in *The Crayon,* 6 June 1855, p.354, quoted in Howat, 1987, p.37. For George Inness's remark, see Reginald Coxe, "George Inness," *Scribner's Monthly,* vol. 44, October 1908, p.511, quoted in Manoogian, 1989, p.38.

12 [George William Curtis], "The Fine Arts; Exhibition of the National Academy; II," *New York Tribune,* 1 May 1852, p.3. Franklin Kelly identified the unnamed writer as George William Curtis. See Manoogian, 1989, pp.20–21.

13 George William Curtis was an important figure in American letters, but also an outspoken advocate of women's suffrage and other social issues. In 1852, he published *Lotus Eating: A Summer Book,* which was illustrated by Frederick Kensett. See George William Curtis, *Lotus Eating: A Summer Book,* New York: Harper and Brothers, 1852. The literary device of lotus eating dates as far back as Homer's *Odyssey,* and was then tantamount to a mind-altering experience. By the nineteenth century, lotus-eating was equated with the euphoria of pleasant experience, such as remembering a satisfying trip to the White Mountains.

Cat. 6

1 Franklin Kelly noted the exhibition of storm scenes by Jasper Cropsey, Frederic Church, and others in his catalogue entry for Asher B. Durand's *June Shower* in Manoogian, 1989, p.22.

2 *The Crayon,* 17 January 1855, p.34, quoted in Howat, 1987, p.36.

3 See Tuckerman, 1867, p.189.

Cat. 7

1 In Manoogian, 1989, p.78 and Manoogian, 1999, p.110, Arthur Fitzwilliam Tait's *The Life of a Hunter: A Tight Fix* has been misdated to 1858. The painting is clearly inscribed by Tait beneath his signature at the lower right: NY 56. The mistaken later date may derive from Tait's decision to withhold the painting from public exhibition in New York (but not Philadelphia; see below) until 1858.

2 Arthur Fitzwilliam Tait may have been encouraged to try his luck in the United States after meeting the American painter, George Catlin, who toured his Indian Gallery in Europe and England from 1840 until 1843. See Adirondack Museum, 1974, p.15.

3 For Arthur Fitzwilliam Tait's relationship with the firm of Currier & Ives, see Adirondack Museum, 1974, p.9.

4 For the identification of the subjects in *Arguing the Point: Settling the Presidency* (1854; R. W. Norton Art Gallery, Shreveport, La.) and *Still Hunting on First Snow: A Second Shot* (1855; Adirondack Museum, Blue Mountain Lake, N.Y.), see Adirondack Museum, 1974, nos. 7 and 9. For Arthur Fitzwilliam Tait's election to the National Academy of Design, see Clark, 1954, p.271.

5 In his catalogue entry for Arthur Fitzwilliam Tait's *The Life of a Hunter: A Tight Fix* in Manoogian, 1989, pp.78–81, Warder H. Cadbury references a number of bear tales that originated in the Adirondacks. His interesting sources include Paul Shepard and Barry Sanders, *The Sacred Paw: The Bear in Nature, Myth and Literature,* New York: Viking Publishers, 1985.

6 Arthur Fitzwilliam Tait sent *The Life of a Hunter: A Tight Fix* to the 1856 exhibition of the Pennsylvania Academy of the Fine Arts, but kept it from his primary audience in New York for nearly two years. See Adirondack Museum, 1974, p.30. Tait may have moved the hunter's right arm, and perhaps added the knife and the distant rifleman after the fact as well. Although well separated in terms of spatial illusion, on the surface of the canvas, the arm, the knife, and the rifleman physically connect, and would have required only minimal scraping and repainting. Advanced imaging technology would be necessary to determine the full extent of Tait's alterations.

Cat. 8

1 Thomas Cole's death was sudden, and considered nothing less than a national tragedy. See Tim Barringer's catalogue entry for Asher B. Durand's *Kindred Spirits* (1849, Metropolitan Museum of Art, New York) in Wilton and Barringer, 2002, pp.68–70.

2 For Worthington Whittredge's description of Frederic Church, see Baur, 1969, p.28.

3 The literature on Frederic Church's work is deservedly large, and there has been perhaps more recent scholarship devoted to Church than to any of his colleagues. See the bibliography in this volume for a listing of useful monographs by Gerald L. Carr, Franklin Kelly, and Katherine E. Manthorne, among others. For a concise survey of Church's achievements, see Howat, 1987, pp. 238–265.

4 The success of Frederic Church's early paintings is on a certain level subjective. Daniel Huntington considered *New England Scenery* (1851; George Walter Vincent Smith Art Museum, Springfield, Mass.) the "masterpiece of Church's youth." See Huntington, 1966, p. 34.

5 For Frederic Church's American travels and particularly his 1851 trip to Virginia and Kentucky, see Carr, 2000, pp. 53–54. For Church's debt to Alexander von Humboldt, see Huntington, 1966, and more recently, Mathorne, 1989, pp. 9–10 and 31–38. Manthorne's bibliography is useful, as is her narrative devoted to the translation of Humboldt's work into English. See Manthorne, 1989, p. 34.

6 For Frederic Church's first trip to South America, see Carr, 2000, pp. 61–66 and Manthorne, 1989, pp. 67–77.

7 For one of Thomas Cole's most impressive views of Mount Etna, see *Mount Aetna from Taormina* (1844; Lyman Allyn Museum, New London, Conn.) in Howat, 1987, pp. 136–37. The most interesting comparison of Frederic Church's and Cole's respective responses to the experience of volcanoes is in Manthorne, 1989, p. 74.

8 Frederic Church's last great painting of South America is *Morning in the Tropics,* (1877; National Gallery of Art, Washington, D.C.). It was produced twenty-four years after his first trip to Colombia and Ecuador. See Wilmerding, 1980A, pp. 100–101.

9 See the letter from Thomas Cole to Asher B. Durand, 4 January 1838 in Legrand, 1853, p. 185. He wrote: "I never succeed in painting scenes, however beautiful, immediately on returning from them. I must wait for time to draw a veil over the common details, the unessential parts, which shall leave the great features, whether the beautiful or the sublime dominant in the mind."

10 For Frederic Church's four submissions to the 1855 National Academy of Design exhibition, see Carr, 2000, p. 65. The paintings were *Tequendama Falls* (1854; Cincinnati Art Museum), *Cotopaxi* (1854; Smithsonian American Art Museum, Washington, D.C.), *The Cordilleras: Sunrise* (1854; private collection) and *Scene on the Magdalene* (1854; National Academy of Design, New York).

11 Frederic Church made trips to Niagara Falls in March, July, and October 1856, producing several drawings and oil sketches in preparation for *Niagara* (1857; Corcoran Gallery of Art, Washington, D.C.). See Wilton and Barringer, 2002, pp. 152 and 164–66. For Thomas Cole's

Distant View of Niagara Falls (1830; Art Institute of Chicago), see Kimberly Rhodes's catalogue entry in Barter, 1998, pp. 149–151.

12 For the 1857 exhibition of *View on the Magdalena River,* see Franklin Kelly's catalogue entry in Manoogian, 1989, p. 56. Gerald Carr suggested that the distant mountain in *Scene on the Magdalene* (1854; National Academy of Design, New York), and by extension, *View on the Magdalena River,* was Mount Puracé. See Carr, 2000, p. 65.

Cat. 9

1 For a brief biography of Jasper Cropsey and his participation in the National Academy of Design exhibitions, see Howat, 1987, p. 200.

2 For the early meeting of Frederic Church and Jasper Cropsey, see Gerald Carr, "Master and Pupil: Drawings by Thomas Cole and Frederic Church," *Bulletin of the Detroit Institute of Arts,* vol. 66, no. 1, 1990, pp. 54 and 60, footnote 19.

3 Typescript copies of Jasper Cropsey's "Natural Art" for the American Art-Union are in the Museum of Fine Arts Boston and the Newington-Cropsey Foundation, Hastings-on-Hudson, N.Y. See Spassky, 1985, p. 185. For Cropsey's move into Thomas Cole's former studio in Rome, see Wilton and Barringer, 2002, p. 256.

4 For Jasper Cropsey's travels in the White Mountains in 1849, see Richard H. Saunders entry for *The Backwoods of America* in Manoogian, 1989, pp. 12–15. For Cropsey's allegorical landscapes see the catalogue entries for *The Spirit of Peace* (1851; Woodmere Art Museum, Philadelphia) and *The Millennial Age* (1854; Newington-Cropsey Foundation, Hastings-on-Hudson, N.Y.) in Wilton and Barringer, 2002, pp. 110–113. For Cole's *The Course of Empire* (1836; New York Historical Society), see Foshay, 1990, pp. 78–82 and 130–140.

5 For the auction of works that remained in Jasper Cropsey's studio in 1856, see Tuckerman, 1867, p. 532 and Spassky, 1985, p. 186

6 For Frederic Church's exhibition of *Niagara* (1857; Corcoran Gallery of Art, Washington, D.C.) in London, see Wilton and Barringer, 2002, p. 55, and Howat, 1987, pp. 243.

7 See John W. Coffey's catalogue entry for Jasper Cropsey's *Eagle Cliff, Franconia Notch, New Hampshire* (1858; North Carolina Museum of Art, Raleigh) in *North Carolina Museum of Art Handbook of the Collection,* edited by Rebecca Martin Nagy, Raleigh, N.C.: North Carolina Museum of Art, 1999, p. 199. Coffey notes that the painting was based on Cropsey's drawings.

8 For Jasper Cropsey's description of the cabin he saw in the White Mountains, see Richard H. Saunders's catalogue entry for *The Backwoods of America* in

Manoogian, 1989, p. 12. The shift may also have been Cropsey's comment upon his own unfinished business.

9 Jasper Cropsey recounted his time in London in an 1867 "Autobiographical Sketch," a transcription of which is in the Cropsey Papers at the Newington-Cropsey Foundation, Hastings-on-Hudson, N.Y. He wrote that "While in London [I] painted many pictures, but those that attracted the greatest attention were 1st 'The Back-Woods of America' exhibited in the Royal Academy." The passage is quoted in Carrie Rebora's catalogue entry for Cropsey's *Autumn – On the Hudson River* (1860; National Gallery of Art, Washington, D.C.) in Howat, 1987, p. 207, footnote 2.

10 See Wilton and Barringer, 2002, p. 137.

11 See Manoogian, 1989, p. 12. Jasper Cropsey was not the only artist to paint smaller, less expensive canvases to earn a living, while wishing to produce major works to further his reputation. See "The Dollars and Cents of Art," *Cosmopolitan Art Journal,* vol. 4, March 1860, p. 30. The unidentified author wrote that a good painter could "average about three hundred dollars for their medium sized works" but that "works worth more than five hundred dollars are in such slow demand that the artists are rarely tempted to paint their composition." Cropsey was presented to Queen Victoria in 1861, largely on the strength of his painting *Autumn – on the Hudson River* (1860; National Gallery of Art, Washington, D.C.). See Carrie Rebora's catalogue entry in Howat, 1987, p. 206.

Cat. 10

1 Sanford Gifford's *Mount Mansfield* was misdated (to 1858) in Manoogian, 1989, p. 44 and in Wilton and Barringer, 2002, p. 144. Gifford clearly inscribed the year 1859 at the lower right of the canvas. Christopher Kent Wilson's catalogue entry for *Mount Mansfield* in Manoogian, 1989, pp. 44–47 suggests that the painting was completed in 1859 even as the heading bears the incorrect year.

2 For a discussion of the Vermont Native American population, see Novak and Blaugrund, 1980, pp. 44–45. For the relatively late commercial development of Mount Mansfield, see Manoogian, 1989, p. 44.

3 See Manoogian, 1989, p. 44.

4 For Jerome Thompson's painting, *The Belated Party on Mount Mansfield* (1858; Metropolitan Museum of Art, New York), see Howat, 1987, pp. 146–47.

5 For a different interpretation of Sanford Gifford's 1856–57 travels in Europe, see Wilton and Barringer, 2002, pp. 144–45. For a discussion of Gifford's intentions at Mount Mansfield and the number of paintings he produced based on the trip, see Novak and Blaugrund, 1980, pp. 44–45. See also the catalogue entry by John Davis for Gifford's *Mount Mansfield* (1859; National Academy of Design,

New York) in Abigail Booth Gerdts, *An American Collection: Paintings and Sculpture from the National Academy of Design,* New York: National Academy of Design, 1990, pp. 40–41.

Cat. 11

1 See Father Louis Hennepin, *A Description of Louisiana,* translated by John Gilmary Shea, New York: John G. Shea, 1880.

2 See William Irwin, *The New Niagara: Tourism, Technology and the Landscape of Niagara Falls, 1776–1917,* University Park, Penn.: Pennsylvania State University Press, 1996, pp. 12–18.

3 See the letter from Thomas Cole to Robert Gilmor, 26 April 1829 in Howard S. Merritt, "Correspondence between Thomas Cole and Robert Gilmor, Jr.," *Baltimore Museum of Art Annual,* vol. 2, 1967, p. 67. Cole's painting, *Distant View of Niagara Falls* (1830; Art Institute of Chicago), was produced in London, as was a larger, seven-foot version of the subject that is now lost. See Kimberly Rhodes catalogue entry for Cole's *Distant View of Niagara Falls* in Barter, 1998, pp. 149–151.

4 For the introduction of the railroad and for tourism statistics, see William Irwin, *The New Niagara: Tourism, Technology and the Landscape of Niagara Falls, 1776–1917,* University Park, Penn.: Pennsylvania State University Press, 1996, pp. 17–18. For Frederick Kensett's *Niagara Falls and Rapids* (c. 1851–52; Museum of Fine Arts Boston), see Wilton and Barringer, 2002, p. 158. For Frederic Church's famous *Niagara* (1857; Corcoran Gallery of Art, Washington, D.C.), see among many other sources Adamson, 1981, Adamson, 1985 and Howat, 1987, pp. 243–46. Church may have based his later *Niagara Falls from the American Side* (1867; National Gallery of Scotland, Edinburgh) on a photograph. See Wilton and Barringer, 2002, p. 152.

Cat. 12

1 George Henry Durrie's father was a founder of Durrie and Peck, a publishing firm in New Haven, Conn. that was active between 1836 and 1885.

2 For George Henry Durrie's relationship with Currier & Ives, see Hutson, 1977, pp. 166–181.

3 For the appearance of George Henry Durrie's *The Half-Way House* at the National Academy of Design, see Sarah Cash's catalogue entry in Manoogian, 1989, pp. 70–71.

4 For a compelling discussion of the ideological landscape, see Andrew Walker and Steven Conn, "The History in the Art: Painting the Civil War," *Terrain of Freedom: American Art and the Civil War,* edited by Andrew Walker, Chicago: Art Institute of Chicago (*Museum Studies,* vol. 27, no. 1), 2001, pp. 74–75.

5 Robert L. Stuart bought George Henry Durrie's painting, *Old Mill in Winter* (1861; New York Historical Society) at the Snedicor and Co. sale for eighteen dollars, less than Currier & Ives would have paid for the reproduction rights alone. See the online catalogue for the Henry Luce III Center for the Study of American Culture at www.nyhistory.org. The sale is also cited in Hutson, 1977, p. 190 and in Manoogian, 1989, p. 70. Durrie made one final submission to the National Academy of Design in 1863, exhibiting *Autumn – Making Cider* (no. 174). Like *The Half-Way House* of the year before, it was listed as for sale.

Cat. 13

1 Louis Rémy Mignot's mother died in 1834. His father remarried, but Mignot was raised by his maternal grandfather, a wealthy confectioner in Charleston. When his father died in 1848, Mignot was not the beneficiary of his estate. See Manthorne and Coffey, 1996, p. 210.

2 For Louis Rémy Mignot and the interesting origins of the Tenth Street Studio Building, see Blaugrund, 1997, p. 134. For Mignot's work with Eastman Johnson, see Teresa A. Carbone, "From Crayon to Brush: The Education of Eastman Johnson, 1840–1858," *Eastman Johnson: Painting America,* Brooklyn, N.Y.: Brooklyn Museum of Art, 1999, pp. 22–23 and 36. For Mignot's collaboration with Thomas P. Rossiter on *Washington and Lafayette at Mount Vernon, 1784* (1859; Metropolitan Museum of Art, New York), see Spassky, 1985, pp. 87–91. The dates of Mignot's entry into the National Academy of Design vary. See Clark, 1954, p. 264, which makes Mignot an ANA in 1858 and an NA in 1859. Spassky 1985, p. 88 gives the dates as 1859 and 1860.

3 For Louis Rémy Mignot's reaction to the start of the Civil War, his trip to Lake George, and his move to London, see Manthorne and Coffey, 1996, pp. 119–138. See also James W. Tottis's catalogue entry for *Autumn, Lake George* in Manoogian, 1997, p. 188.

4 For the sale of Mignot's studio, see *Catalogue of a Choice Collection of Paintings, and Studies from Nature, Painted by Louis R. Mignot …,* New York: Henry H. Leeds & Co., 1862. The catalogue is transcribed and reproduced as an appendix in Manthorne and Coffey, 1996. The sale netted Mignot $5,000. See Spassky, 1985, p. 88.

5 See Steven Conn and Andrew Walker, "The History in the Art: Painting the Civil War," *Terrain of Freedom: American Art and the Civil War,* edited by Andrew Walker, Chicago: Art Institute of Chicago (*Museum Studies,* vol. 27, no. 1), 2001, pp. 71–79.

6 See Tuckerman, 1867, pp. 563–64. For a more nuanced interpretation of Louis Rémy Mignot's work, see Manthorne, 1989, pp. 133–157.

Cat. 14

1 Albert Bierstadt exhibited *Lake Lucerne* (1858; National Gallery of Art, Washington, D.C.) in 1858. See Hendricks, 1974, p. 94. For the long obscure and frequently misidentified Francis Seth Frost, see Jourdan Houston, "Francis Seth Frost (1825–1902): Beyond Bierstadt's Shadow," *American Art Review,* vol. 6, no. 4, April 1994, pp. 146–157.

2 For a detailed description of Albert Bierstadt's travels in the west, see Anderson and Ferber, 1990, pp. 143–45.

3 Albert Bierstadt's letter of 10 July 1859 was published in *The Crayon,* vol. 6, September 1859, p. 287. It is quoted at length in Hendricks, 1974, pp. 70–76.

4 The Tenth Street Studio Building was apparently full when Albert Bierstadt initially sought quarters there in November 1859, but by 19 January 1860, he had been accommodated. See Anderson and Ferber, 1990, p. 146.

5 For *The Base of the Rocky Mountains, Laramie Peak* (1860; Location unknown), see Anderson and Ferber, 1990, pp. 146–47.

6 Albert Bierstadt was relatively sensitive to the changing circumstances that white settlers introduced to Native American life, but he was not without the prejudices of his era. Many of Bierstadt's condescending comments in *The Crayon* about Native Americans repeated nearly verbatim an article that had appeared in the same periodical three years earlier. An unidentified writer remarked, "As an accessory to in landscape, the Indian may be used with great effect." And like Bierstadt, the writer also noted that the native population was "fast passing away from the face of the earth." See "The Indians in American Art," *The Crayon,* vol. 3, January 1856, p. 28, quoted in Howat, 1987, p. 219.

7 Quoted in Hendricks, 1974, p. 70.

8 For interesting discussions of *The Rocky Mountains, Lander's Peak* (1863, Metropolitan Musuem of Art, New York), see Gerald L. Carr's catalogue entry in Howat, 1987, pp. 285–88. See also Spassky, 1985, pp. 321–26. In its original conception, the painting did not include the Shoshone village in the foreground. See Spassky, 1985, p. 322. Not every critic found the Native American village a successful addition to the painting. See *The Round Table,* vol. 1, 27 February 1864, p. 169, quoted in Spassky, 1985, p. 322.

Cat. 15

1 See the *New Bedford Daily Mercury,* 14 September 1859, p. 2, quoted in Hendricks, 1974, p. 86.

2 See Gerald L. Carr's catalogue entry for *The Rocky Mountains, Lander's Peak* (1863, Metropolitan Musuem of Art, New York) in Howat, 1987, p. 286.

3 For Albert Bierstadt's paid draft exemption, see Hendricks, 1974, pp. 131–32. The National Conscription Act went into effect in the summer of 1863, and was

a catalyst for the explosive New York draft riots of
13–16 July. See Burrows and Wallace, 1999, pp.887–899.

4 Albert Bierstadt also exhibited *Mountain Brook* (1863;
Art Institute of Chicago), see Barter, 1998, pp.190–93.
William H. Gerdts has identified *Platte River, Nebraska* as
the painting Albert Bierstadt exhibited at the National
Academy of Design in 1863 as *North Fork of the Platte,
Nebraska*. See Manoogian, 1996, p.30. See also Anderson
and Ferber, 1990, p.177.

5 See [Fitz Hugh Ludlow], *New York Daily Post,* 22 May 1863,
quoted in Hendricks, 1974, p.117.

6 Fitz Hugh Ludlow seemed to hold up well, and wrote dispatches about buffalo hunting, Mormons, and the glories
of Yosemite and Mount Shasta to New York newspapers,
just as he had agreed to. He would, however, contract
pneumonia in Oregon, and only Albert Bierstadt's attentive
nursing saved his life. It was a noble effort on Bierstadt's
part, given that he was already in love with Ludlow's wife
Rosalie. Rosalie eventually divorced Ludlow and married
Bierstadt. Ludlow's essays about his Western travels with
Bierstadt were compiled in *The Heart of the Continent,* New
York: Hard and Houghton, 1870. By far Ludlow's most famous
book was his *The Hasheesh Eater,* New York: Harper, 1857.
For more on Ludlow, see Hendricks, 1974, pp.113–134.

Cat. 16

1 See Anderson and Ferber, 1990, pp.177–79.

2 For the exhibition of Albert Bierstadt's *The Rocky
Mountains, Lander's Peak* (1863, Metropolitan Museum
of Art, New York) in Boston, New Bedford, at the Seitz
and Noelle Gallery on Broadway in Manhattan, and at
the Metropolitan Fair, see Spassky, 1985, pp.321–26. For
Frederic Church's *Heart of the Andes* (1859; Metropolitan
Museum of Art, New York), see Spassky, 1985, pp.269–275.

3 See Jarves, 1864, pp.232–33. See also Fitz Hugh Ludlow,
Atlantic Monthly, vol. 13, June 1864, quoted in Spassky,
1985, pp.326–27.

4 In addition to *Platte River, Nebraska* (cat. 15), Albert
Bierstadt exhibited *Mountain Brook* (1863; Art Institute of
Chicago) at the National Academy of Design in 1863. See
Barter, 1998, pp.190–93.

5 For Albert Bierstadt's exhibition of Native American artifacts at the Metropolitan Fair in New York, and for his
work during 1864 and early 1865 on both Western and
White Mountain subjects, see Anderson and Ferber,
1990, pp.179–181.

6 See *The Crayon,* January 1861, p.22, and *New York Leader,*
17 January 1863, both quoted in Anderson and Ferber,
1990, pp.147 and 149.

7 For a discussion of the emblematic quality of haying and
for references to other literary and artistic sources, see
Stebbins, 2000, pp.125–27.

Cat. 17

1 For a short biography of Homer Dodge Martin, see
Spassky, 1985, pp.420–22.

2 The paintings that Fitz Hugh Lane, Frederick Kensett,
Martin Johnson Heade, and many others produced in the
1850s and beyond have come to be grouped under the
rubric "Luminism." The term was invented by the art historian John I.H. Baur in the late 1940s, and has come to
define a late development within the Hudson River School
idiom. See John I.H. Baur, "Early Studies in Light and Air
by American Painters," *Brooklyn Museum Bulletin,* vol. 9,
no. 2, winter 1948. For one of the more important studies of
American Luminism, see Wilmerding, 1980.

3 See Mather, 1912, pp.37–38, quoted in Spassky, 1985,
p.421.

Cat. 18

1 This catalogue entry borrows heavily from the impres-
sive work on Martin Johnson Heade by Theodore E.
Stebbins Jr., and his colleagues, Janet L. Comey and
Karen E. Quinn. See Stebbins, 2000.

2 Martin Johnson Heade was not only a brilliant painter,
but he was also a gifted naturalist, and wrote many arti-
cles for *Field and Stream.* For a bibliography of Heade's
published essays, see Stebbins, 2000, pp.178–79. For the
quoted passage, see Didymus [Martin Johnson Heade],
"Taming Hummingbirds," *Field and Stream,* vol. 38, no. 15,
14 April 1892, p.348.

3 See Stebbins, 2000, p.62.

4 Ibid., p.64.

5 Ibid., pp.65–66 and 73.

6 Theodore E. Stebbins Jr. identifies a number of ornithological publications of the early and mid nineteenth
century that influenced Martin Johnson Heade, but also
provided competition for his own project. Perhaps most
notable among these books, albums, and folios was
John Gould, *A Monograph of Trochilidae, or Family of
Hummingbirds,* 5 vols., London: John Gould, 1861. See
Stebbins, 2000, p.62. Based on the comments of Henry
Tuckerman (Tuckerman, 1867, p.542), Stebbins suggests
that Heade brought the painted versions of *The Gems
of Brazil* back to the United States. But Tuckerman never
mentions *The Gems of Brazil* by name, and his comments
about Heade's South American studies ring with the
flimsy authority of secondhand information. See
Stebbins, 2000, pp.81 and 189, note 117.

7 See Stebbins, 2000, p.71.

8 Ibid., pp.71–72.

9 See Clara Erskine Clement and Laurence Hutton, *Artists
of the Nineteenth Century and Their Works,* Boston,
Mass.: Houghton Osgood, 1879, p.340, quoted in
Stebbins, 2000, pp.71 and 187, note 58.

Cat. 19

1 For a biographical sketch of Alfred T. Bricher, see Brown
and Lee, 1973, which remains the only significant monograph devoted to the artist. Most brief accounts of
Bricher's life suggest that he worked in a dry goods store,
but Brown and Lee also noted the possibility that he was
employed by a bookseller. See Brown and Lee, 1973, p.13.

2 For Martin Johnson Heade's first trip to Newburyport,
Mass., see Stebbins, 2000, p.28. For Alfred T. Bricher's
1859 trip to Mount Desert Island, see Brown and Lee,
1973, pp.13–14, who mistakenly date the trip to 1858. See
also Wilmerding, 1994, pp.139–140, who suggests that
Bricher met Frederic Church on the same trip, but certainly did not. Given the paucity of evidence, Brown and
Lee quite reasonably suggest that Bricher and Heade did
not encounter one another until 1862 in Boston's Studio
Building. See Brown and Lee, 1973, p.15. Bricher does
not even appear in the index of Stebbins, 2000, p.379.

3 Alfred T. Bricher listed his most important early works,
including paintings that derived from his trips to the
Catskills and to the White Mountains, in what Brown and
Lee call Sketchbook A. See Brown and Lee, 1973, p.14.
For Albert Bierstadt's trip to the White Mountains in
September 1861, see Anderson and Ferber, 1990, p.147.

4 For a synopsis of Martin Johnson Heade's many studios
and travels in the early 1860s, see Stebbins, 2000,
pp.172–73.

5 For Alfred T. Bricher's relationship with Louis Prang and
Co. in Boston, see Brown and Lee, 1973, pp.16 and 34 and
Howat, 1987, p.323. See also Katherine M. McClinton,
The Chromolithographs of Louis Prang, New York: C.N.
Potter, 1973. One of the more significant figures in
Martin Johnson Heade's *The Gems of Brazil* project was
the Reverend James Cooley Fletcher, who provided
Heade with a number of important contacts and a good
deal of information about Rio de Janeiro. The Reverend
Fletcher lived in Newburyport, Massachusetts. See
Stebbins, 2000, p.28.

6 It is difficult to determine with any certainty the specific
works Alfred T. Bricher listed in Sketchbook A. The painting now known as *View of Mount Washington* must certainly be among those listed, and may be *Mt. Washington
from the Saco* or *Autumn, on the Saco* or *On the Saco,
Conway.* See Brown and Lee, 1973, p.14, note 12.

7 For the death of William Bricher, see Brown and Lee,
1973, p.13.

Cat. 20

1 For William Stanley Haseltine's early life and education,
see the very useful chronology in Simpson, 1992, pp.154–59.

2 For William Stanley Haseltine's studio on Tenth Street,
see Blaugrund, 1997, p.133. For the works Haseltine

exhibited in the early 1860s and the critical reaction to
them, see Simpson, 1992, pp.160–173.

3 For the critical backlash, see "Art and the Century Club,"
The Round Table, vol. 1, no. 9, 13 February 1864, p.139,
quoted in Simpson, 1992, p.21. For the death of Helen Lane
Haseltine and her newborn son, see Simpson, 1992, p.22.

4 See "Among the Studios," *Watson's Weekly Art Journal,*
vol. 1, no. 24, 8 October 1864, p.372, quoted in Simpson,
1992, p.171.

5 See "Among the Studios," *Watson's Weekly Art Journal,*
vol. 2, no. 6, 3 December 1864, p.83. See also "Fine Art
Gossip," *Watson's Weekly Art Journal,* vol. 2, no. 10, 31
December 1864, p.147. See also "Among the Studios,"
Watson's Weekly Art Journal, vol. 2, no. 13, 21 January
1864, p.195. All are quoted in Simpson, 1992, p.172. For
the important group of Nahant paintings William Stanley
Haseltine produced in 1864 and 1865, see Simpson, 1992,
pp.100–105. William Bradford painted the same spot in
the mid 1850s. See Kugler, 2003, no. 66, p.151. The formation at Nahant known as Pulpit Rock collapsed at some
point after World War II.

6 Two other Nahant paintings submitted by William
Stanley Haseltine to the 1865 National Academy of
Design exhibition had already been acquired by Levi P.
Morton. By the end of May the dealer, Samuel P. Avery,
owned another. See Simpson, 1992, p.173.

7 See "National Academy of Design. North Room," *New
York Times,* 29 May 1865, quoted in Simpson, 1992, p.173.

8 See Tuckerman, 1867, p.557. For the influence of science
on William Stanley Haseltine, see Simpson, 1992, pp.17–18.

Cat. 21

1 For the early provenance of Thomas Moran's *Under the
Trees (The Autumnal Woods),* see Barbara Dayer
Gallatti's catalogue entry in Ferber and Gerdts, 1985,
p.274. The painting was already owned by Mr. Baird
when it was submitted to the National Academy of
Design exhibition in 1866.

2 See Kinsey, 1992, p.12.

3 Ibid., pp.58–67 and 125–137.

4 For *Modern Painters,* see *The Works of John Ruskin,*
edited by E. T. Cook and Alexander Wedderburn, London,
1903–1912. See also Linda Ferber, "'Determined
Realism': The American Pre-Raphaelites and the
Association for the Advancement of Truth in Art," in
Ferber and Gerdts, 1985, pp.11–16 and 24–31.

5 See Susan Casteras, "The 1857–58 Exhibition of
English Art in America and Critical Responses to
Pre-Raphaelitism," in Ferber and Gerdts, 1985, pp.109–133.

6 For the connection between Thomas Moran and Pre-
Raphaelitism, see the catalogue entry by Nancy Anderson
of Moran's *Under the Trees* in Manoogian, 1989, pp.30–31.

7 For a group so small, the Association for the
Advancement of Truth in Art had tremendous ambition,
and they made numerous lofty proposals, but put few
into action. Their primary accomplishment as an organi-
zation was the publication of a journal called *The New
Path.* See Ferber and Gerdts, 1985.

8 Ferber and Gerdts, 1985, p.28.

9 Ibid., p.15.

10 It has been suggested that the bearded figure may be a
self-portrait. See Barbara Dayer Gallati's catalogue
entry for *Under the Trees* in Ferber and Gerdts, 1985,
p.274. John Ruskin's leaf is from a passage in *Modern
Painters.* See *The Works of John Ruskin,* edited by
E. T. Cook and Alexander Wedderburn, London, vol. 5,
1903–1912, p.52, quoted in William H. Gerdts, "Through a
Glass Brightly: The American Pre-Raphaelites and Their
Still Lifes and Nature Studies," in Ferber and Gerdts,
1985, p.42.

Cat. 22

1 Worthington Whittredge was the model for George
Washington and the steersman in Emanuel
Leutze's *Washington Crossing the Delaware* (1851;
Metropolitan Museum of Art, New York). See Spassky,
1985, p.17.

2 The passage is from Worthington Whittredge's autobiography, which he started in about 1905, after his eighty-
fifth birthday. Having outlived most of his colleagues,
Whittredge produced an account of the interesting
milieu he once inhabited. But by the time he wrote his
life story, nineteenth-century landscape painting was
well out of fashion, and his manuscript remained unpub-
lished until 1942. See Bauer, 1969.

3 Worthington Whittredge kept his studio in the Tenth
Street Studio Building for more than forty years. See
Blaugrund, 1997, p.134. Emanuel Leutze painted his portrait, *Worthington Whittredge in His Tenth Street Studio*
(1865; Reynolda House Museum of American Art,
Winston-Salem, N.C.) the same year that Whittredge
completed *Twilight on the Shawangunk Mountains.* See
Blaugrund, 1997, p.61. A print of S. Beer's 1866 stereoscopic view of Whittredge's studio filled with artists still
survives. See Blaugrund, 1997, p.58.

4 For a useful description of the area represented in
Worthington Whittredge's *Twilight on the Shawangunk
Mountains,* see Franklin Kelly's catalogue entry in
Manoogian, 1989, pp.7–10. Jervis McEntee not only
worked in the Tenth Street Studio Building, he and his
wife lived there. See Blaugrund, 1997, p.54. For the 1861
trip made by Whittredge, McEntee, Sanford Gifford, and
John White to the Shawangunk Mountains, see Harvey,
1998, p.215 and Wilton and Barringer, 2002, p.163.

For Gifford's work in the Shawangunk Mountains in 1864,
see Howat, 1987, p.77.

5 For Frederic Church's *Twilight in the Wilderness* (1860;
Cleveland Museum of Art), see Wilton and Barringer,
2002, pp.129–131. For the development of cadmium reds
and yellows, see Richardson, 1965, p.219. For
Worthington Whittredge's use of the new materials, see
Esther T. Thyssen's catalogue entry for *Twilight on
Shawangunk Mountain* in Howat, 1987, pp.182–83.

6 See Jarves, 1864, pp.231 and 193, quoted in Wilmerding,
1980, pp. 15 and 86.

7 See Tuckerman, 1867, p.518.

8 Worthington Whittredge's *Twilight on the Shawangunk
Mountains* was exhibited in January 1866 at the gallery of
S. P. Avery along with Frederic Church's *Twilight in the
Wilderness* (1860; Cleveland Museum of Art). See
Manoogian, 1989, p.29, note 16. For Winthrop B. Smith,
see Mauck Brammer, "Winthrop B. Smith: Creator of the
Eclectic Educational Series," *Ohio History: The Scholarly
Journal of the Ohio Historical Society,* vol. 80, no. 1, winter
1971, pp.45–59. Smith already owned one painting by
Whittredge, *The Pilgrims of St. Roche* (c.1850s; Location
unknown), when he acquired *Twilight on the Shawangunk
Mountains.* See Tuckerman, 1867, pp.516–17.

Cat. 23

1 Theodore E. Stebbins Jr. does not identify the work that
Martin Johnson Heade showed in 1867 at the Goupil
Gallery, but *Sunset on the Marshes* would have to be a
likely candidate. See Stebbins, 2000, p.173.

2 For Frederic Church's offer to let Martin Johnson Heade
store paintings in his studio while he traveled to
Nicaragua, see Stebbins, 2000, p.188, note 102.

3 See the letter from Martin Johnson Heade to John Russell
Bartlett, 10 August 1866, quoted in Stebbins, 2000, p.78.
The Somerville Gallery was at Fourteenth Street and
Fifth Avenue. For Frederic Church's offer to lease his stu-
dio to Heade, see Stebbins, 2000, pp.80 and 188, note 114.
It was Heade's second occupancy of the Tenth Street
Studio Building. He had worked there from late 1858 until
1861. See Stebbins, 2000, p.21 and Blaugrund, 1997,
p.133. The building's address changed from 15 to 51 Tenth
Street in 1866. See Blaugrund, 1997, p.17.

4 See "Pictures at the National Academy," *The Round
Table,* 18 May 1867, p.310, quoted in Stebbins, 2000,
no, 169, p.243.

5 See Stebbins, 2000, pp.117–127.

6 For Martin Johnson Heade's large landscape canvases of
the early 1860s, see Stebbins, 2000, nos. 65, 71–72, 82, 84,
86, 89, 91, 94–95, 98, 107–108, 116, and 119. All of these
paintings measured forty inches or wider. The main reason Heade worked on a smaller scale in Rio and London

was that he was largely engaged in his hummingbird subjects, which he generally painted to scale.

7   For Michael Knoedler's commission of Frederic Church to paint a view of *Niagara Falls from the American Side* (1867; National Gallery of Scotland, Edinburgh), see Wilton and Barringer, 2002, pp. 152–54. The painting that Church produced for Knoedler did not appear at the 1867 Exposition Universelle after all.

Cat. 24

1   For Robert S. Duncanson's parents, his early life in Monroe, Michigan, and his move to Cincinnati, see Ketner, 1993, p. 11–14. There is some debate among scholars of Duncanson's work about his early biography, especially his parentage and his parents' experience of slavery. Ketner describes Duncanson's father and mother as having come out of Virginia, meaning that both were born slaves. It also has been suggested that Duncanson was "the son of a free black or mulatto mother and a Scottish-Canadian father." See Lynda Roscoe Hartigan, "Robert Scott Duncanson," *Sharing Traditions: Free Black Artists in Nineteenth-Century America,* Washington, D.C.: Smithsonian Institution Press, 1985, p. 51. Ketner clearly disputes this ancestry.

2   For *Cliff Mine, Lake Superior, 1848* (1848; F. Ward Paine, Jr., Portola Valley, Calif.), see Ketner, 1993, p. 192. See also Ketner, 1993, pp. 25–27 and 117.

3   Thomas Cole painted the first version of his series of four paintings, *The Voyage of Life* (1839–1840; Munson-William-Proctor Institute, Utica, N.Y) for the banker Samuel Ward. See *Masterworks of American Art from the Munson-Williams-Proctor Institute,* edited by Paul D. Schweizer, New York: Harry N. Abrams, Inc., Publishers, 1989, pp. 38–45. The suite that Robert S. Duncanson saw belonged to the abolitionist minister, Reverend Elias Lyman Magoon (1841–42; National Gallery of Art, Washington, D.C.). See Wilmerding, 1980A, pp. 88–89. For Cole's "Essay on American Scenery," see McCroubey, 1965, pp. 98–109. For Cole's *The Garden of Eden* (1828; Amon Carter Musuem, Fort Worth, Tex.), see Wilton and Barringer, 2002, p. 93. For Duncanson's *The Garden of Eden* (1852; High Musueum of Art, Atlanta, Ga), see Ketner, 1993, p. 118.

4   Accounting for race in the art of Robert S. Duncanson is a difficult problem. Duncanson was a free man and a serious painter. He shared the same aesthetic goals and professional ambitions for himself and his art as his white colleagues. On the other hand, he was a black man living in a time and near a place where other black men were slaves. He was supported by collectors of art, who were also abolitionists, and Duncanson was not above pandering to his audience. Race certainly factors into the equation,

but to what degree? For a discussion of race, racial identity, history, and the art of Duncanson, see Margaret Rose Vendryes, "Race Identity/Identifying Race: Robert S. Duncanson and Nineteenth-Century American Painting," *Terrain of Freedom: American Art and the Civil War,* edited by Andrew Walker, Chicago: Art Institute of Chicago (*Museum Studies,* vol. 27, no. 1), 2001, pp. 82–99.

5   See Ketner, 1993, pp. 114, 134, and 137. For *Minnehaha Falls* (1862; Howard University Art Gallery, Washington, D.C.) and *Minnenopa Falls* (1862; The Proctor and Gamble Company, Cincinnati), see Ketner, 1993, p. 199.

6   Robert Duncanson had exhibited *The Land of the Lotus Eaters* (1861; Collection of His Royal Majesty, the King of Sweden) and *Western Tornado* (1861; Location unknown) at Joseph's Jewelry Store in Toronto in November 1861. See Ketner, 1993, p. 198. He planned to take these same two pictures on an exhibition tour of Europe, and a Canadian passport was more easily attained by African Americans than one from the United States.

7   Robert Duncanson's small oil sketch of *Vale of Kashmir* was mentioned in the *Cincinnati Daily Enquirer* on 24 March 1863. See Ketner, 1993, p. 199. See also Ketner, 1993, p. 141.

8   See Ketner, 1993, pp. 152–54. For *Western Tornado* (1861; Location unknown), *Prairie Fire* (1862; Location unknown), *Niagara* (1863; Location unknown), and *Oenone* (1863; Location unknown), see Ketner, 1993, pp. 198–99.

9   See Ketner, 1993, p. 155.

10 Robert Duncanson was long interested in photographic processes, having experimented with "Chemical Paintings" as early 1844. He painted a view of Cincinnati in about 1851 after a daguerreotype printed in *Graham's Magazine* in 1848. In the mid 1850s, he worked in the studio of Ball's Daguerreotype Gallery in Cincinnati, and was himself listed in a local directory of 1853 as a "daguerreotype artist." When Duncanson arrived in Montreal, one of the first people he sought out was William Notman, an important figure in Canadian cultural affairs and a pioneering photographer. Notman photographed two of Duncanson's paintings for his album of reproductions modestly entitled *Photographic Selections.* There is no evidence that Notman also photographed the 1864 *Vale of Kashmir,* but given Duncanson's abiding interest in the medium, and his manifold uses of it, the marketing potential of photo-reproductions may not have escaped his attention. See Ketner, 1993, pp. 137–39.

Cat. 25

1   Jervis McEntee kept a diary from 1872 until his death in 1891, making him the unofficial historian of the Tenth Street Studio Building. See Garnett McCoy, "Jervis

McEntee's Diary," *Archives of American Art Journal,* vol. 8, nos. 3–4, July and October 1968 and Garnett McCoy, "Jervis McEntee's Diary," *Archives of American Art Journal,* vol. 31, no. 1, 1991. See also Blaugrund, 1997, p. 54. For McEntee's involvement with the National Academy of Design, see Clark, 1954, p. 263. For McEntee's melancholy, see David Steinberg's catalogue entry for *Autumn, Landscape* (the present work) in Howat, 1987, pp. 279.

2   For Jervis McEntee's *Melancholy Days* (1860, Location unknown), see Howat, 1987, p. 278.

3   For Jervis McEntee's preference, see the letter from McEntee to Geroge Ripley, 28 October 1874, Archives of American Art, roll no. DDUI, frame nos. 382–83, quoted in Howat, 1987, p. 378. For McEntee's education, see T. B. Thorpe, "Painters of the Century. No. VII. Our Successful Artists – Jervis McEntee," *Baldwin's Monthly,* vol. 13, July 1876, p. 1, quoted in David Steinberg's catalogue entry for *The Ruins of Caesar's Palace* (c. 1869; Pennsylvania Academy of the Fine Arts, Philadelphia, Pa.) in Howat, 1987, p. 281.

4   See "The National Academy of Design," *New York Times,* 14 April 1867, p. 4, quoted in Howat, 1987, p. 278.

5   See Carol Troyen, "Innocents Abroad: American Painters at the 1867 Exposition Universelle, Paris," *American Art Journal,* vol. 16, no. 4, autumn 1984, pp. 2–29. For the 1868 excursion to Rome, see among other sources, John Davis, *The Landscape of Belief: Encountering the Holy Land in Nineteenth-Century American Art and Culture,* Princeton, N.J.: Princeton University Press, 1996, pp. 168–207. See also Andrea Henderson, "Haseltine in Rome," in Simpson, 1992, pp. 33–50.

6   For the location of Jervis McEntee's studio in Rome, see Simpson, 1992, p. 180. McEntee exhibited *Autumn Afternoon* at the 1868 National Academy of Design exhibition (no. 413), but distinguishing his autumn subjects can be difficult.

7   See G. W. Sheldon, *American Painters: with Eighty-three Examples of Their Work Engraved on Wood,* New York: D. Appleton and Co., 1879, p. 543, quoted in Howat, 1987, p. 279.

Cat. 26

1   For Alfred T. Bricher's journey up the Mississippi River, see Rene Neumann Coen, "Alfred Thompson Bricher's early Minnesota Scenes," *Minnesota History,* vol. 46, summer 1979, pp. 233–36.

2   See Rene Neumann Coen, "Alfred Thompson Bricher's early Minnesota Scenes," *Minnesota History,* vol. 46, summer 1979, p. 236, note 9. See also Katherine M. McClinton, *The Chromolithographs of Louis Prang,* New York: C.N. Potter, 1973, pp. 190–91. Bricher apparently submitted paintings of the Mississippi River

to Louis Prang, but they were never translated into chromolithographs.

3 For a concise accounting of Martin Johnson Heade's travels, see Stebbins, 2000, pp. 171–77. On the idea of horizontal grandeur, Worthington Whittredge wrote of his first experience of the American west: "I had been accustomed to measure grandeur, at the most, by the little hills of Western Virginia; I had never thought it might be measured horizontally as on our great Western plains. In fact, I believe it is the accepted idea that all grandeur *must* be measured up and down …" See Baur, 1969, p. 31.

4 Alfred T. Bricher's Sketchbook F contains drawings from his excursion up the Mississippi River, including his stay in Dubuque, Iowa. A drawing of the Mississippi River at Dubuque dated 2 June 1866 is the basis for the painting in the Manoogian Collection. See Brown and Lee, 1973, p. 17. In 1973, most of Bricher's sketchbooks were still with the family. See Brown and Lee, 1973, pp. 89–90.

5 For Dubuque, Iowa, see John T. Tigges and James L. Shaffer, *Dubuque, the 19th Century,* Charleston, S.C.: Arcadia Publishing, 2000. For Alfred T. Bricher's *The Sidewheeler 'The City of St. Paul' on the Mississippi River, Dubuque, Iowa* (1872; Terra Museum of American Art, Chicago), see *A Proud Heritage: Two Centuries of American Art,* edited by Terry A. Neff, Chicago: Terra Museum of American Art, 1987, p. 161.

6 An index of the growing demand for what are now called Luminist paintings is the sale of Frederick Kensett's studio after his death in 1872. That auction achieved $136,312, a remarkable sum for that era. See Brown and Lee, 1973, p. 12.

Cat. 27

1 See "Extract," *A Biographical Record of Schuyler County, New York, 1903,* Schuyler County, New York: S. J. Clarke Publishing Co., 2001.

2 For the Battle of Antietam, see *The Antietam Campaign,* edited by Gary W. Gallagher, Chapel Hill, N.C.: University of North Carolina Press, 1999.

3 In 1999, thirty paintings by James Hope and a cache of his correspondence were uncovered by the Vestal, N.Y., auctioneer David Mapes in the estate of Ruth Champion, the artist's great-granddaughter. See "Mapes Has Plenty of Hopes," *Maine Antiques Digest,* February 2000.

4 Apparently, James Hope's first painting of Rainbow Falls was owned by H. D. Rolfe of New York, who submitted it to the 1872 National Academy of Design exhibition as *Rainbow Falls, Watkin's Glen, New York* (no. 312). See "Extract," *A Biographical Record of Schuyler County, New York, 1903,* Schuyler County, New York: S. J. Clarke Publishing Co., 2001. Hope could have produced two

versions in 1871–72 of *Rainbow Falls, Watkins Glen, New York,* but it could also be that Rolfe, about whom nothing else is known, was posing as the owner of a painting that Hope did not intend to sell. No second version of *Rainbow Falls, Watkins Glen, New York* is known to exist.

5 The catalogue entry in *American Paintings, Drawings and Sculpture: The Collection of Arthur and Holly Magill; and a Collection of Works by Andrew Wyeth,* Sotheby's, New York, 30 November 2000, no. 128 incorrectly describes the flood of 1935 that destroyed so many of James Hope's paintings as the Johnstown Flood. That disaster occurred in 1889 in southwestern Pennsylvania.

Cat. 28

1 Published information about John Williamson is fairly slim. He was born in Tollcross, Scotland, near Glasgow, but came to America as a child with his family. He may have traveled to the American West in the late 1850s, and perhaps made at least one sketching tour of Europe, but given his propensity for trading on the subjects of other artists, his surviving Western landscapes and his views of Italy may have been painted from secondhand sources.

2 For the Hudson River in the early eighteenth century, and its role in fomenting American Revolution, see Burrows and Wallace, 1999, pp. 116–17 and 203–4.

3 It is not clear who coined the name Hudson River School, but it was certainly not invented by the artists the term was intended to describe. It probably came out of common usage in the 1870s to distinguish the young, modern, European-trained painters from the older men and younger followers still working in the idiom of Thomas Cole. It seems to have first appeared in print in 1879, but could have been used in vernacular form for years prior. The designation was certainly meant to be an insult, but it quickly became a useful descriptive term to identify Cole and the other landscape painters who were based in New York from the 1840s until the 1870s and beyond. For a thorough investigation of the name and its origins, see Kevin J. Avery, "The Historiography of the Hudson River School," in Howat, 1987, pp. 3–7.

4 For the sale of John Williamson's studio contents, see *Catalogue. The Entire Collection of Pictures and Sketches. Painted by Mr. John Williamson. Consisting of Landscapes, Fruit and Flower Pieces, &c.,* New York: Henry H. Leeds and Miner, 1867. Another reason for the sale was that Williamson moved his studio from 137 Montague Street in Brooklyn to 161 Montague Street probably that same year. In 1869, he moved to 6 Astor Place in Manhattan. See Naylor, 1973.

5 John Williamson submitted *Foggy Morning, Autumn, – View from the Garrisons on the Hudson* (Date and Location unknown) to the 1868 National Academy of

Design exhibition (6). For Williamson's move to Yonkers, see Naylor, 1973.

6 John Williamson contributed a painting to the 1876 National Academy of Design exhibition (276) that he entitled *From Glenwood, Hudson River.* It could be the present work, although given the single-mindedness of his vision and the many similarities between his canvases, that identification is not certain. For a discussion of nineteenth-century industry along the Hudson River, see Maddox, 1983.

Cat. 29

1 For a brief biography of Francis A. Silva and a description of his war experience, see Mitchell, 2002, pp. 19–23.

2 See Mitchell, 2002, pp. 25–33.

3 Ibid., pp. 35–39

4 See the well researched catalogue entry by Sarah Cash for Francis A. Silva's *The Schooner 'Progress' Wrecked at Coney Island, July 4th, 1874* in Manoogian, 1989, p. 48.

5 See Mitchell, 2002, p. 37.

6 Francis A. Silva copied an article by an unnamed author called "Topics of the Time. Dandyism," *Scribner's Monthly Illustrated Magazine,* vol. 20, September 1880, pp. 788–89. See Mitchell, 2002, pp. 45–50, and 62, note 37. See also Francis A. Silva, "American vs. Foreign-American Art," *American Art-Union,* June–July 1884, pp. 130–31.

7 For the decline of the style of marine painting that has come to be known as Luminism, see Wilmerding, 1980, pp. 146–151.

8 For *Approaching Storm* (c. 1875; Location unknown), see Mitchell, 2002, p. 130.

9 See Manoogian, 1989, p. 48.

10 Sarah Cash suggested that Francis A. Silva based *The Schooner 'Progress' Wrecked at Coney Island, July 4th, 1874* on his drawing of 15 August 1874 (1874; Peabody Essex Museum, Salem, Mass.). See Manoogian, 1989, p. 48.

11 See Manoogian, 1989, p. 48.

Cat. 30

1 The literature on Frederic Church's travels in South America is abundant. See among many other sources, Manthorne, 1989, pp. 67–89. For Martin Johnson Heade's trip to Brazil in 1863, Nicaragua in 1866 and South America and Jamaica in 1869–1870, see Stebbins, 2000, pp. 61–105.

2 Theodore E. Stebbins Jr. suggests that Martin Johnson Heade benefited professionally in the late 1860s from his friendship with Frederic Church. Stebbins also notes that Church encouraged Heade's 1869–1870 return to South America. See Stebbins, 2000, p. 81.

3 See the letter from Frederic Church to Martin Johnson Heade, 7 March 1870, in which Church chides Heade for being a tepid traveler: "Bother your tigers and varmints

generally – why all the mountains of S.A. are full of them … I tell you – you have missed a big thing." Quoted in Stebbins, 2000, p.81.

4 For Martin Johnson Heade's complaints about Rome and Rio de Janeiro, see Stebbins, 2000, pp.61–62.

5 For Martin Johnson Heade's paintings of orchids, see Stebbins, 2000, pp.91–103. Many scholars, including Theodore E. Stebbins Jr., have discussed the influence of Charles Darwin's 1859 *The Origins of the Species* on the visual arts of the nineteenth century, as well as upon specific artists. More interesting and perhaps more relevant is the development of intellectual thought in the nineteenth century that led to work such as Darwin's. The impulse to classify, codify, and order reached a near fevered pitch in the mid-nineteenth century. See Henry Plotkin, *Darwin Machines and the Nature of Knowledge,* Cambridge, Mass.: Harvard University Press, 1994. See also Stephen Jay Gould, "Church, Humboldt and Darwin: The Tension and Harmony of Art and Science," in Kelly, 1989, pp.94–107. The quest for taxonomic order was nowhere more engagingly described than in Gustave Flaubert's late unfinished novel of 1881, *Bouvard et Pécuchet.* See Gustave Flaubert, *Bouvard et Pécuchet,* translated by T. W. Earp and G. W. Stonier, New York: New Directions Book, 1954.

6 See the letter from Frederic Church to Martin Johnson Heade, 26 May 1870, quoted in Stebbins, 2000, p.82. Heade not only painted orchids again and again, he painted the same orchid again and again. For the many variants on the orchid that appears in the Manoogian painting, see Stebbins, 2000, nos. 487–502, pp.321–25. For *Tropical Orchid* (c.1871–74; Olana State Historic Site, Taconic Region, New York), the painting by Heade in Church's collection, see Stebbins, 2000, no. 432, p.308.

Cat. 31

1 See Robert G. Workman, *The Eden of America: Rhode Island Landscapes, 1829–1920,* Providence, R.I.: Rhode Island School of Design, 1986, no. 31, p.57.

2 Fitz Hugh Lane died in 1865 and Frederick Kensett in 1872. William Bradford painted arctic seascapes, a fairly narrow specialty. By 1866, William Stanley Haseltine was spending most of his time in Italy. Francis A. Silva was a gifted painter and seemingly tried to adapt, but he was also a disagreeable crank who never attracted followers. Winslow Homer became America's leading marine painter in the 1870s, but it was his use of the human figure that made his seascapes so profound. James McNeill Whistler left the United States in the 1850s and never returned, but his marine paintings were very much admired in America. William Merritt Chase would not

emerge as a significant marine painter until his move to Shinnecock in the 1890s.

3 See S. G. W. Benjamin, *Art in America: A Critical and Historical Sketch,* New York: Garland Publishing, 1976. *Art in America* was first published in 1880. The passage is quoted in Brown and Lee, 1973, p.28.

4 See Clarence Cook, "Fine Arts – Music – The Drama. Fine Arts. Fifty-First Annual Exhibition of the National Academy of Design." *New York Daily Tribune,* 28 March 1876, p.4, quoted in Margaret C. Conrads, *Winslow Homer and the Critics: Forging a National Art in the 1870s,* Princeton, N.J.: Princeton University Press, 2001, p.94. Clarence Cook's "tide" metaphor would not have been wasted on Alfred T. Bricher. Two of his most successful canvases were entitled *Morning at Narragansett – The Turn of the Tide* (1871; Walter and Lucille Rubin Collection, Delray Beach, Fla.) and *Time and Tide* (c.1873; Dallas Museum of Art).

5 See the letter from Alfred T. Bricher to H. R. Latimer, 18 December 1879, quoted in Brown and Lee, 1973, p.65. By 1890, fashionable women and well dressed children no longer walked the shores of Bricher's seascapes. See Brown and Lee, 1973, p.29.

6 For a discussion of Alfred T. Bricher's 1871 drawings of Narragansett Bay and a detailed description of where they may have been made, see Robert G. Workman, *The Eden of America: Rhode Island Landscapes, 1829–1920,* Providence, R.I.: Rhode Island School of Design, 1986, no. 31, p.57. For an alternate theory of the site Bricher depicted, see the catalogue entry by Nicolai Cikovsky Jr. for *View on the Providence River* in Manoogian, 1989, p.42, note 1. For the painting, *Narragansett Bay* (1872; Location unknown), see Brown and Lee, 1973, no. 28A, p.54.

Cat. 32

1 In the 1860s, Clarence Cook, a young art critic for the *New York Daily Tribune,* held notoriously venomous views of the older landscape painters who then ruled the New York art world. He published some of his most caustic commentary in a short-lived periodical called *The New Path,* which was the official organ of the Association for the Advancement of Truth in Art – the American arm of the English Pre-Raphaelites. See Ferber and Gerdts, 1985, pp.11–14. For an early assault on both Albert Bierstadt and Frederic Church, see Jarves, 1864, pp.233–34. Henry Tuckerman noted the acquisition of *The Domes of Yosemite* (1867; Saint Johnsbury Athenaeum, Saint Johnsbury, Vt.) by Le Grand Lockwood in Tuckerman, 1867, p.393.

2 For the Le Grand Lockwood commission, see Anderson and Ferber, 1990, pp.183–84. For Black Friday, see Sarah

Burns, "Party Animals: Thomas Nast, Wiliam Holbrook Beard and the Bears of Wall Street," *American Art Journal,* vol. 30, nos. 1–2, 1999, p.21. See also Burrows and Wallace, 1999, pp.914–15. For Le Grand Lockwood's downfall, see Kugler, 2003, pp.22–24, 26, 28, and 30.

3 A. S. Hatch purchased *The Domes of Yosemite* on behalf of Horace Fairbanks for the St. Johnsbury Athenaeum in Vermont. See the St. Johnsbury Athenaeum website at stjathenaeum.org/bierstadt.

4 See *New York Herald,* 8 October 1877, p.6, quoted in Gerald L. Carr's catalogue entry for *The Shore of the Turquoise Sea* in Manoogian, 1989, p.52. All of the references in the present entry are derived from Carr's excellent research of *The Shore of the Turquoise Sea.*

5 See *New York Herald,* 13 January 1878, p.6, quoted in Manoogian, 1989, p.52. See the same source for the exhibition at the Brainerd Gallery in Boston and for the reviews of that presentation.

6 There was a good deal of controversy regarding the works of art chosen to represent the United States at the Exposition Universelle in 1878. The painter Elizabeth Gardner wrote to her sister Ria on 23 May 1878 that "The American picture gallery is small. The three men who managed it were persons 'unknown to fame.' … Bierstadt's picture they refused entirely." Quoted in Nancy Mowll Mathews, *Mary Cassatt: A Life,* New Haven, Conn.: Yale University Press, 1994, p.132. Many years later Mary Cassatt would describe to Ambroise Vollard her own rejection in 1878 by the selection committee: "the jury consisted of three people, of which one was a pharmacist!" See *Cassatt and Her Circle: Selected Letters,* edited by Nancy Mowll Mathews, New York: Abbeville Press, 1984, p.282. Albert Bierstadt was seemingly determined to get his large seascape into the 1878 Paris exhibition, and D. Maitland Armstrong was just as set on keeping it out. Armstrong wrote to Augustus Saint-Gaudens: "Bierstadt offered a picture here which was declined. He sent it to Paris & will try to get it in there. This Committee here to head him off passed a resolution that no picture offered here should be considered by the Committee in Paris – Look out for him. He shall not get it in but do not let it be known, as we do not wish to make a Martyr of Bierstadt." See Anderson and Ferber, 1990, p.59.

7 Jervis McEntee's lament is quoted in Blaugrund, 1997, p.90. McEntee was not the only artist in New York to rue the falling fortunes of American landscape painting. See Francis A. Silva, "American vs. Foreign-American Art," *American Art-Union,* June–July 1884, pp.130–31.

8 See Doreen Bolger Burke and Catherine Hoover Voorsanger, "The Hudson River School in Eclipse," in Howat, 1987, pp.71–90.

Cat. 33

1 For a summary of the Paris Exposition Universelle de 1878, see Paul Greenhalgh, *Ephemeral Vistas: The Expositions Universelles, Great Exhibitions and World Fairs, 1851–1939,* Manchester: Manchester University Press, 1988.

2 For the rejection of Albert Bierstadt's *The Shore of the Turquoise Sea,* see Anderson and Ferber, 1990, p.59. For Frederic Church's *The Parthenon* (1871; Metropolitan Museum of Art, New York) see Spassky, 1985, pp.275–79. For Church's *Morning in the Tropics* (1877; National Gallery of Art, Washington, D.C.), see Wilmerding, 1980A, pp.100–101. For Sanford Gifford's *Mount Rainier* and the submissions by Mary Cassatt, Walter Shirlaw, J. Alden Weir and Winslow Homer, see Paul Lefort, "Exposition Universelle: Les Écoles Étrangères de Peinture," *Gazette des Beaux-Arts,* vol. 18, 1878, pp.483–85.

3 For a short biography of James M. Hart, see Spassky, 1985, pp.305–306.

4 See "The Dollars and Cents of Art," *Cosmopolitan Art Journal,* vol. 4, March 1860, p.30.

5 See G. W. Sheldon, *American Painters: with Eighty-three Examples of Their Work Engraved on Wood,* New York: D. Appleton and Co., 1879, pp.47–48, quoted in Howat, 1987, p.87. Sheldon use of musical terminology alluded to James McNeill Whistler, whose work was very much the cutting edge of American painting in the late 1870s.

6 See *Massachusetts Charitable Mechanic Association, Thirteenth Exhibition,* Boson, September 1878, no. 161. For the announcement of medalists, see "The Art Awards," *Boston Daily Evening Transcript,* 13 November 1878, vol. 4, p.4.

Cat. 34

1 See Kugler, 2003, pp.7–8.

2 Ibid., p.9.

3 Ibid., p.10.

4 Ibid., p.11.

5 For William Bradford's first trip to Labrador, see Kugler, 2003, p.14. See Louis Legrand Noble, *After Icebergs with a Painter: A Summer Voyage to Labrador and around Newfoundland,* New York, 1861. For Frederic Church's *The Icebergs* (1861; Dallas Museum of Art), see Eleanor Jones Harvey, *The Voyage of the Icebergs,* New Haven, Conn.: Yale University Press, 2002. For Albert Bierstadt's 1859 journey to the American West, see Anderson and Ferber, 1990, pp.143–46.

6 See Kugler, 2003, pp.14–28.

7 William Bradford did not sign or date *Whalers Trapped in Arctic Ice,* which was not unusual for the artist. The uniformity of his themes makes it difficult to determine from the exhibition record what the original title of the painting may have been or precisely when it was made.

Franklin Kelly suggested that the present painting might have been the work Bradford exhibited in London in 1872 as *Crushed in Ice,* but that identification is far from secure. See Manoogian, 1989, p.50, note 5. For the expedition of Sir John Franklin, see Kugler, 2003, pp.29, 39, and 343. See also William Bradford, *The Arctic Regions, Illustrated with Photographs Taken on an Art Expedition in Greenland,* London: Sampson Low, Marston, Low and Searle, 1873. Interestingly, Bradford dedicated the publication to Le Grand Lockwood.

Cat. 35

1 For the decline of the landscape aesthetic that Thomas Cole invented, see Doreen Bolger Burke and Catherine Hoover Voorsanger, "The Hudson River School in Eclipse," in Howat, 1987, pp.71–90.

2 For the American embrace not just of Impressionism, but of the new more painterly international style, see Barbara Novak, "The Painterly Mode in America," in Novak, 1969, pp.235–261.

3 Among the more useful examinations of the life and work of George Inness remains Cikovsky and Quick, 1985. Inness and his wife officially joined the Swedenborgian Church in 1867. For a discussion of the influence of Swedenborg, see Sally M. Promey, "The Ribband of Faith: George Inness, Color Theory and the Swedenborgian Church," *American Art Journal,* vol. 26, nos. 1–2, 1994, p.49.

4 See George Inness, "A Painter on Painting," *Harper's New Monthly Magazine,* vol. 56, February 1878, p.461, quoted in Lauretta Dimmick's catalogue entry for Inness's *Clearing Up* in Howat, 1987, p.236.

5 For a short discussion of George Inness's extraordinary rise in popularity in the mid 1880s, see the catalogue entry by Nicolai Cikovsky Jr. for *A Breezy Autumn* in Manoogian, 1989, p.40.

Cat. 36

1 Theodore E. Stebbins Jr. was probably the first to suggest that *View from Fern-Tree Walk, Jamaica* was the painting Martin Johnson Heade exhibited as *Jamaica* in New York in 1870 and London in 1873. See Stebbins, 1975, pp.93–94. Diana J. Strazdes agreed with Stebbins's position in her catalogue entry for *View from Fern-Tree Walk, Jamaica* in Howat, 1987, pp.174–76. Similarly, Franklin Kelly did not question Stebbins's assigned date in Manoogian, 1989, p.58. Based on the recent recovery of Heade's letters from 1887, Stebbins now concedes that the date inscribed on the picture is indeed the year it was made. See Stebbins, 2000, p.272.

2 See Stebbins, 2000, pp.141–49.

3 For Henry Flagler's purchase of *The Great Florida Marsh,* see Stebbins, 2000, p.149. See the letters from Martin Johnson Heade to Eben J. Loomis, 11 April 1887 and 16 June 1887, quoted in Stebbins, 2000, p.150. For Flagler's placement of the two Heade paintings in the rotunda of the Ponce de Leon Hotel, see Stebbins, 2000, p.194, note 40.

4 For the price of the two paintings commissioned by Henry Flagler, see Stebbins, 2000, p.150. For Albert Bierstadt's *The Last of the Buffalo* (1888; Corcoran Gallery of Art, Washington, D.C.), see Anderson and Ferber, 1990, p.100.

5 I am grateful to Erin Riordan for her kind encouragement and her many contributions to this project.

BIBLIOGRAPHY *and*
SHORT TITLES FREQUENTLY CITED

Manoogian Collection

Manoogian, 1989

American Paintings from the Manoogian Collection,
Washington, D.C.: National Gallery of Art, 1989.

Manoogian, 1993

*A Private View: American Paintings from the Manoogian
Collection,* New Haven, Conn.: Yale University Art Gallery
and Detroit Institute of Arts, 1993.

Manoogian, 1996

*American Grandeur: Masterpieces from the Masco and
Manoogian Collections,* Knoxville, Tenn.: Knoxville
Museum of Art, 1996.

Manoogian, 1997

*From the Hudson River School to Impressionism:
American Paintings from the Manoogian Collection,*
Detroit: Detroit Institute of Arts and the Richard A.
Manoogian Collection, 1997.

Manoogian, 1999

*Celebrate America: Nineteenth-Century Paintings from the
Manoogian Collection,* edited by Nicolai Cikovsky Jr.,
Memphis, Tenn.: Dixon Gallery and Gardens, 1999.

Hudson River School
American Landscape Painting
Museum Collection Catalogues

Adamson, 1985

Jeremy Elwell Adamson, Elizabeth McKinsey, Alfred
Runte, and John F. Sears, *Niagara: Two Centuries of
Changing Attitudes (1697–1901),* Washington, D.C.:
Corcoran Gallery of Art, 1985.

Ayres, 1992

Linda Ayres, *The Spirit of Genius: Art at the Wadsworth
Atheneum,* Hartford, Conn.: Hudson Hills Press, 1992.

Barter, 1998

Judith A. Barter, Kimberly Rhodes, Seth A. Thayer, and
Andrew Walker, *American Arts at the Art Institute of
Chicago from Colonial Times to World War I,* New York:
Hudson Hills Press and the Art Institute of Chicago, 1998.

Blaugrund, 1997

Annette Blaugrund, *The Tenth Street Studio Building:
Artist-Entrepreneurs from the Hudson River School to the
American Impressionists,* Southampton, N.Y.: Parrish Art
Museum, 1997.

Boime, 1991

Albert Boime, *The Magisterial Gaze: Manifest Destiny and
American Landscape Painting, c. 1830–1865,* Washington,
D.C. and London: Smithsonian Institution Press, 1991.

Bryant, 1981

*William Cullen Bryant and the Hudson River School of
Landscape Painting,* Roslyn, N.Y.: Nassau County Museum
of Fine Art, 1981.

Burns, 1989

Sarah Burns, *Pastoral Inventions: Rural Life in
Nineteenth-Century American Art and Culture,*
Philadelphia: Temple University Press, 1989.

Burrows and Wallace, 1999

Edwin G. Burrows and Mike Wallace, *Gotham: A History of
New York City to 1898,* New York and Oxford: Oxford
University Press, 1999.

Clark, 1954

Eliot Clark, *History of the National Academy of Design,
1825–1953,* New York: Columbia University Press, 1954.

Cowdrey, 1953

Mary Bartlett Cowdrey, *American Academy of the Fine Arts
and American Art Union, 1816–1852,* 2 vols., New York:
New York Historical Society, 1953.

Driscoll, 1997

John P. Driscoll, *All that is Glorious around Us: Paintings
from the Hudson River School,* Ithaca, N.Y.: Cornell
University Press, 1997.

Falk, 1989

Peter Hastings Falk, *The Annual Exhibition Record of
the Pennsylvania Academy of the Fine Arts 1807–1870,*
including Anna Wells Rutledge, *Cumulative Record of
Exhibition Catalogues* (1955), 3 vols., Madison, Conn.:
Sound View Press, 1989.

Ferber and Gerdts, 1985

Linda S. Ferber and William H. Gerdts, *The New Path:
Ruskin and the American Pre-Raphaelites,* Brooklyn, N.Y.:
Brooklyn Museum, 1985.

Flexner, 1962

James Thomas Flexner, *That Wilder Image: The Painting of
America's Native School from Thomas Cole to Winslow
Homer,* Boston: Little, Brown and Co., 1962.

Foshay, 1990

Ella M. Foshay, *Mr. Luman Reed's Picture Gallery:
A Pioneer Collection of American Art,* New York:
Harry N. Abrams, Inc., 1990.

Foshay and Novak, 2000

Ella M. Foshay and Barbara Novak, *Intimate Friends:
Thomas Cole, Asher B. Durand and William Cullen Bryant,*
New York: New York Historical Society, 2000.

Graves, 1905

Algernon Graves, *The Royal Academy of Arts: A Complete
Dictionary of Contributors and Their Work from Its
Foundation in 1769 to 1904,* 8 vols., London: Henry Graves
and Co. and George Bell and Sons, 1905.

Harvey, 1998

Eleanor Jones Harvey, *The Painted Sketch: American
Impressions from Nature, 1830–1880,* Dallas, Tex.: Dallas
Museum of Art, 1998.

Hemingway and Vaughan, 1998

Andrew Hemingway and William Vaughan, *Art in
Bourgeois Society, 1790–1850,* New York and Cambridge:
Cambridge University Press, 1998.

Howat, 1987

John K. Howat, *American Paradise: The World of the Hudson
River School,* New York: Metropolitan Museum of Art, 1987.

Jackson, 1995

Kenneth T. Jackson, *The Encyclopedia of New York,* New
Haven, Conn. and London: Yale University Press, 1995.

Jarves, 1864

James Jackson Jarves, *The Art Idea,* New York: Hurd and
Houghton, 1864.

Kelly, 1996

Franklin Kelly, *American Paintings of the Nineteenth
Century,* Washington, D.C.: National Gallery of Art, 1996.

Kornhauser, 1996

Elizabeth Mankin Kornhauser, *American Paintings before
1945 in the Wadsworth Atheneum,* New Haven, Conn. and
London: Yale University Press, 1996.

Langer, 1974

Sandra L. Langer, *A Critical Study of American Landscape
Painting from 1817 to 1860,* New York University, Ph.D.
dissertation, 1974.

McCoubrey, 1965

John W. McCoubrey, *American Art, 1700–1960: Sources and
Documents,* Englewood Cliffs, N.J.: Prentice-Hall
Publications, 1965.

Maddox, 1983

Kenneth W. Maddox, *In Search of the Picturesque:
Nineteenth-Century Images of Industry along the Hudson
River Valley,* Annandale-on-Hudson, N.Y.: Bard College, 1983.

Manthorne, 1989

Katherine E. Manthorne, *Tropical Renaissance: North American Artists Exploring Latin America, 1839–1979,* Washington,
D.C. and London: Smithsonian Institution Press, 1989.

Meyers, 1998

Amy R. W. Meyers, *Art and Science in America: Issues of
Representation,* San Marino, Calif.: Huntington Library, 1998.

Miller, 1993

Angela Miller, *The Empire of the Eye: Landscape
Representations and American Cultural Politics,
1825–1875,* Ithaca, N.Y. and London: Cornell University
Press, 1993.

Miller, 1969

Jo Miller, *Drawings of the Hudson River School, 1825–1875,*
Brooklyn, N.Y.: Brooklyn Museum, 1969.

Myers, 1987

Kenneth Myers, *The Catskills: Painters, Writers and
Tourists in the Mountains 1820–1895,* Yonkers, N.Y.:
Hudson River Museum, 1987.

Naylor, 1973

Maria Naylor, *The National Academy of Design Exhibition
Record, 1861–1900,* New York: Kennedy Galleries, 1973.

Novak, 1969

Barbara Novak, *American Painting of the Nineteenth
Century: Realism, Idealism, and the American Experience,*
New York: Praeger Publishers, 1969.

Novak, 1995

Barbara Novak, *Nature and Culture: American Landscape*

and Painting, 1825–1875, New York: Oxford University
Press, 1995.

Novak and Blaugrund, 1980
Barbara Novak and Annette Blaugrund, Next to Nature:
Landscape Paintings from the National Academy of Design,
New York: Harper and Rowe Publishers, 1980

Nygren, 1986
Edward J. Nygren, Views and Visions: American Landscape
before 1830, Washington D.C.: Corcoran Gallery of Art, 1986.

Prown, 1992
Jules D. Prown, Discovered Lands, Invented Pasts:
Transforming Visions of the American West, New Haven,
Conn. and London: Yale University Press, 1992.

Richardson, 1965
E. P. Richardson, Painting in America from 1502 to the
Present, New York: Crowell, 1965.

Sanders, 1981
Richard Saunders, Daniel Wadsworth: Patron of the Arts,
Hartford, Conn.: Wadsworth Atheneum, 1981.

Sheldon, 1879
G. W. Sheldon, American Painters, New York: D. Appleton
and Co., 1879.

Spassky, 1985
Natalie Spassky, American Paintings in the Metropolitan
Museum of Art, vol. II, New York: Metropolitan Museum of
Art, in association with Princeton University Press, 1985.

Stebbins, 1992
Theodore E. Stebbins Jr., The Lure of Italy: American Artists
and The Italian Experience 1760–1914, Boston: Museum
of Fine Arts, in association with Harry N. Abrams, Inc.,
New York, 1992.

Stein, 1975
Roger B. Stein, Seascape and the American Imagination,
New York: Clarkson N. Potter, Inc., 1975.

Sullivan, 1991
Mark W. Sullivan, The Hudson River School: An
Annotated Bibliography, Metuchen, N.J.: Scarecrow
Press, 1991.

Truettner, 1991
William H. Truettner, The West as America: Reinterpreting
Images of the Frontier, 1820–1920, Washington, D.C.:
Smithsonian Institution Press, 1991.

Tuckerman, 1867
Henry T. Tuckerman, Book of the Artists, American Artist
Life, Comprising Biographical and Critical Sketches of
American Artists: Preceded by an Historical Account of the
Rise & Progress of Art in America, New York, 1867,
reprinted New York: James F. Carr, Publisher, 1967.

Veith, 2001
Gene Edward Veith, Painters of Faith: The Spiritual
Landscape in Nineteenth-Century America, Washington,
D.C.: Regnery Publishing, 2001.

Voorsanger and Howat, 2000
Catherine Hoover Voorsanger and John K. Howat, eds.,

Art and the Empire City: New York, 1825–1861, New York:
Metropolitan Museum of Art, 2000.

Wilmerding, 1980
John Wilmerding, American Light: The Luminist Movement,
1850–1875, Washington, D.C.: National Gallery of Art, 1980.

Wilmerding, 1980A
John Wilmerding, American Masterpieces from the
National Gallery of Art, New York: Hudson Hills Press, 1980.

Wilmerding, 1994
John Wilmerding, The Artist's Mount Desert: American
Painters on the Maine Coast, Princeton, N.J.: Princeton
University Press, 1994.

Wilton and Barringer, 2002
Andrew Wilton and Tim Barringer, American Sublime:
Landscape Painting in the United States, 1820–1880,
London: Tate Publishing, 2002.

Van Zandt, 1966
Roland Van Zandt, The Catskill Mountain House,
New Brunswick, N.J.: Rutgers University Press, 1966.

Selected Artist Monographs

Albert Bierstadt (1830–1902)

Anderson and Ferber, 1990
Nancy Anderson and Linda S. Ferber, Albert Bierstadt:
Art and Enterprise, Brooklyn, N.Y.: Brooklyn Museum,
in association with Hudson Hills Press, 1990.

Hendricks, 1974
Gordon Hendricks, Albert Bierstadt, Painter of the
American West, New York: Harry N. Abrams, Inc., 1974.

William Bradford (1823–1892)

Kugler, 2003
Richard C. Kugler, William Bradford: Sailing Ships and
Arctic Seas, Seattle: University of Washington Press, 2003.

Wilmerding, 1969
John Wilmerding, William Bradford, 1823–1892, Lincoln,
Mass.: De Cordova Museum, 1969.

Alfred Thompson Bricher (1837–1908)

Brown and Lee, 1973
Jeffrey R. Brown and Ellen W. Lee, Alfred Thompson
Bricher 1837–1908, Indianapolis, Ind.: Indianapolis
Museum of Art, 1973.

Frederic Edwin Church (1826–1900)

Adamson, 1981
Jeremy Elwell Adamson, Frederic Edwin Church's
'Niagara:' The Sublime as Transcendence, Ann Arbor,
Mich.: University of Michigan, Ph.D. dissertation, 1981.

Avery, 1993
Kevin J. Avery, Church's Great Picture: 'The Heart of the
Andes', New York: Metropolitan Museum of Art, 1993.

Carr, 1994

Gerald L. Carr, Frederic Edwin Church: Catalogue
Raisonné of Works of Art at the Olana State Historic Site,
2 vols., New York and Cambridge: Cambridge University
Press, 1994.

Carr, 1980
Gerald L. Carr, Frederic Edwin Church: The Icebergs,
Dallas, Tex.: Dallas Museum of Art, 1980.

Carr, 2000
Gerald L. Carr, In Search of the Promised Land: Paintings by
Frederic Edwin Church, New York: Berry-Hill Galleries, 2000.

Dee, 1992
Elaine Evans Dee, Frederic E. Church: Under Changing
Skies. Oil Sketches from the Collection of the Cooper-
Hewitt, National Museum of Design, Philadelphia: Arthur
Ross Gallery of the University of Pennsylvania, 1992.

Huntington, 1966
David Carew Huntington, The Landscapes of Frederic
Edwin Church: Vision of an American Era, New York:
Braziller, 1966.

Kelly, 1989
Franklin Kelly, Frederic Edwin Church, Washington, D.C.:
National Gallery of Art, 1989.

Kelly, 1988
Franklin Kelly, Frederic Edwin Church and the National
Landscape, Washington, D.C.: Smithsonian Institution
Press, 1988.

Kelly and Carr, 1987
Franklin Kelly and Gerald L. Carr, The Early Landscapes of
Frederic Edwin Church, 1845–1854, Fort Worth, Tex.: Amon
Carter Museum, 1987.

Manthorne, 1985
Katherine E. Manthorne, Creation and Renewal: Views of
Cotopaxi by Frederic Edwin Church, Washington, D.C.:
National Museum of American Art, 1985.

Stebbins, 1978
Theodore E. Stebbins Jr., Close Observation: Selected Oil
Sketches by Frederic E. Church from the Collection of the
Cooper-Hewitt Museum, Washington, D.C.: Smithsonian
Institution Press, 1978.

Thomas Cole (1801–1848)

Cole and Wadsworth, 1983
The Correspondence of Thomas Cole and Daniel
Wadsworth, edited by J. Bard McNulty, Hartford, Conn.:
Connecticut Historical Society, 1983.

Noble, 1853
Louis Legrand Noble, The Life and Works of Thomas Cole,
1853, edited by Elliot S. Vessell, Hensonville, N.Y.: Black
Dome Press, reprinted in 1997.

Parry, 1988
Ellwood C. Parry III, The Art of Thomas Cole: Ambition
and Imagination, Newark, Del.: University of Delaware
Press, 1988.

Powell, 1990

Earl A. Powell, *Thomas Cole*, New York: Harry N. Abrams, Inc., 1990.

Stilgoe, 1993

John R. Stilgoe, *Thomas Cole: Drawn to Nature*, Albany, N.Y.: Albany Institute of History and Art, 1993.

Truettner and Wallach, 1994

William H. Truettner and Alan P. Wallach, *Thomas Cole: Landscape into History*, New Haven, Conn.: Yale University Press, 1994.

Jasper Francis Cropsey (1823–1900)

Bermingham, 1968

Peter Bermingham, *Jasper F. Cropsey 1823–1900, A Retrospective View of America's Painter of Autumn*, College Park, Md.: University of Maryland Art Gallery, 1968.

Foshay and Finney, 1987

Ella M. Foshay and Barbara Finney, *Jasper F. Cropsey, Artist and Architect: Paintings, Drawings and Photographs from the Collection of the Newington-Cropsey Foundation and the New York Historical Society*, New York: The Society, 1987.

Talbot, 1970

William S. Talbot, *Jasper F. Cropsey 1823–1900*, Washington, D.C.: Smithsonian Institution Press, 1970.

Robert S. Duncanson (1821–1872)

Ketner, 1993

Joseph D. Ketner, *The Emergence of the African-American Artist, Robert S. Duncanson, 1821–1872*, Columbia, Mo. and London: University of Missouri Press, 1993.

Asher Brown Durand (1796–1886)

Durand, 1894

John Durand, *The Life and Times of A.B. Durand*, New York: C. Scribner's Sons, 1894.

Lawall, 1977

David B. Lawall, *Asher Brown Durand: His Art and Art Theory in Relation to His Times*, New York and London: Garland Publishing, 1977, Princeton University, Ph.D. dissertation, 1966.

George Henry Durrie (1820–1863)

Hutson, 1977

Martha Hutson, *George Henry Durrie (1820–1863), American Winter Landscapist: Renowned through Currier and Ives*, Santa Barbara, Calif.: Santa Barbara Museum of Art, 1977.

Sanford Robinson Gifford (1823–1880)

Cikovsky, 1970

Nicolai Cikovsky Jr., *Sanford Robinson Gifford (1823–1880)*, Austin, Tex.: University of Texas Art Museum, 1970.

Weiss, 1987

Ila Weiss, *Poetic Landscape: The Art and Experience of Sanford R. Gifford*, Newark, Del.: University of Delaware Press, 1987.

William Stanley Haseltine (1835–1900)

Plowden, 1947

Helen Haseltine Plowden, *William Stanley Haseltine, Sea and Landscape Painter (1835–1900), Notes and Recollections from His Daughter*, London: Frederick Muller, Ltd., 1947.

Simpson, 1992

Marc Simpson, Andrea Henderson and Sally Mills, *Expressions of Place: The Art of William Stanley Haseltine*, San Francisco: Fine Arts Museums of San Francisco, 1992.

Martin Johnson Heade (1819–1904)

Cash, 1994

Sarah Cash, *Ominous Hush: The Thunderstorm Paintings of Martin Johnson Heade*, Fort Worth, Tex.: Amon Carter Museum, 1994.

Eaton, 1992

Timothy A. Eaton, *Martin Johnson Heade: The Floral and Hummingbird Studies from the St. Augustine Historical Society*, Boca Raton, Fla.: Boca Raton Museum of Art, 1992.

Stebbins, 1975

Theodore E. Stebbins Jr., *The Life and Work of Martin Johnson Heade: A Critical Analysis and Catalogue Raisonné*, New Haven, Conn.: Yale University Press, 1975.

Stebbins, 2000

Theodore E. Stebbins Jr., *The Life and Work of Martin Johnson Heade: A Critical Analysis and Catalogue Raisonné*, New Haven, Conn.: Yale University Press, 2000.

Stebbins, 1999

Theodore E. Stebbins Jr., *Martin Johnson Heade*, Boston: Museum of Fine Arts, 1999.

George Inness (1825–1894)

Cikovsky, 1993

Nicolai Cikovsky Jr., *George Inness*, New York: Harry N. Abrams, Inc., 1993.

Cikovsky and Quick, 1985

Nicolai Cikovsky Jr. and Michael Quick, *George Inness*, Los Angeles: Los Angeles Country Museum of Art, 1985.

Inness, 1917

George Inness Jr., *The Life, Art and Letters of George Inness*, New York: The Century, 1917.

Ireland, 1965

LeRoy Ireland, *The Works of George Inness: An Illustrated Cata-logue Raisonné*, Austin, Tex.: University of Texas Press, 1965.

John Frederick Kensett (1816–1872)

Driscoll and Howat, 1985

John Paul Driscoll and John K. Howat, *John Frederick Kensett: An American Master*, New York and London: W.W. Norton & Co., in association with Worcester Art Museum, 1985.

Simon and Smith, 2001

Janice Simon and Ann Y. Smith, *Images of Contentment: John Frederick Kensett and the Connecticut Shore*, Waterbury, Conn.: The Mattatuck Museum, 2001.

Jervis McEntee (1828–1891)

Beacon Hill, 1997

McEntee and Company, New York: Beacon Hill Fine Art, 1997.

Homer Dodge Martin (1836–1897)

Carroll, 1913

Dana H. Carroll, *Fifty-eight Paintings by Homer D. Martin*, New York: Privately printed, 1913.

Martin, 1904

Elizabeth Gilbert Martin, *Homer Martin, A Reminiscence, 28 October 28th, 1836–February 12th, 1897*, New York: W. Macbeth, 1904.

Mather, 1912

Frank Jewett Mather, *Homer Martin, Poet in Landscape*, New York: Privately printed, 1912.

Louis Rémy Mignot (1831–1870)

Manthorne and Coffey, 1996

Katherine E. Manthorne and John W. Coffey, *The Landscapes of Louis Rémy Mignot: A Southern Painter Abroad*, Washington, D.C.: Smithsonian Institution Press, 1996.

Thomas Moran (1837–1926)

Anderson, 1987

Nancy K. Anderson, et al., *Thomas Moran*, Washington, D.C.: National Gallery of Art, 1997.

Kinsey, 1992

Joni Louise Kinsey, *Thomas Moran and the Surveying of the American West*, Washington, D.C. and London: Smithsonian Institution Press, 1992.

Francis Augustus Silva (1835–1886)

Mitchell, 2002

Mark D. Mitchell, *Francis A. Silva (1835–1886): In His Own Light*, New York: Berry-Hill Galleries, Inc., 2002.

Arthur Fitzwilliam Tait (1819–1905)

Adirondack Museum, 1974

A.F. Tait: Artist in the Adirondacks, Blue Mountain Lake, N.Y.: The Adirondack Museum, 1974.

Cadbury, 1986

Warder H. Cadbury, *Arthur Fitzwilliam Tait: Artist in the Adirondacks*, Newark, Del.: University of Delaware Press, 1986.

Thomas Worthington Whittredge (1820–1910)

Baur, 1969

The Autobiography of Worthington Whittredge, 1820–1910, edited by John I.H. Baur, New York: Arno Press, 1969.

Janson, 1989

Anthony F. Janson, *Worthington Whittredge*, Cambridge: Cambridge University Press, 1989.